Players of Shakespeare 4

This is the fourth volume of essays by actors with the Royal Shake-
speare Company. Twelve actors describe the Shakespearian roles
they played in productions between 1992 and 1997. The contributors are Christopher Luscombe, David Tennant, Michael Siberry,
Richard McCabe, David Troughton, Susan Brown, Paul Jesson,
Jane Lapotaire, Philip Voss, Julian Glover, John Nettles, and Derek
Jacobi. The plays covered include *The Merchant of Venice, Love's
Labour's Lost, The Taming of the Shrew, The Winter's Tale, Romeo and
Juliet,* and *Macbeth,* among others. The essays divide equally among
comedies, histories and tragedies, with emphasis among the comedies on those notoriously difficult 'clown' roles. A brief biographical
note is provided for each of the contributors and an introduction
places the essays in the context of the Stratford and London stages.

Players of Shakespeare 4

*Further essays in Shakespearian performance
by players with the
Royal Shakespeare Company*

Edited by
Robert Smallwood

CAMBRIDGE
UNIVERSITY PRESS

PUBLISHED BY THE PRESS SYNDICATE OF THE UNIVERSITY OF CAMBRIDGE
The Pitt Building, Trumpington Street, Cambridge CB2 1RP, United Kingdom

CAMBRIDGE UNIVERSITY PRESS
The Edinburgh Building, Cambridge CB2 2RU, United Kingdom
40 West 20th Street, New York, NY 10011–4211, USA
10 Stamford Road, Oakleigh, Melbourne 3166, Australia

First published 1998

Printed in the United Kingdom at the University Press, Cambridge

Typeset in 10.25/13pt Plantin Regular   GC

A catalogue record for this book is available from the British Library

Library of Congress cataloguing in publication data

Players of Shakespeare 4: further essays in Shakespearian performance
/ by players with the Royal Shakespeare Company; edited by Robert
Smallwood.
p.   cm.
ISBN 0 521 55420 9 (hardback)
1. Shakespeare, William, 1564–1616–Stage history–1950–
2. Shakespeare, William, 1564–1616–Characters.   3. Theatre–
England–History–20th century.   4. Royal Shakespeare Company.
5. Actors–England.   6. Acting.   1. Smallwood, R. L. (Robert Leo)
II. Royal Shakespeare Company.
PR3112.P556   1998
792.9′5′0941–dc21   98–16621   CIP

ISBN 0 521 55420 9

92.9
PL

Contents

Illustrations

With the exception of illustrations 16, 21, and 27, which are reproduced by permission of Ivan Kyncl, and illustration 18, which is reproduced by permission of the Folger Shakespeare Library, all illustrations are reproduced by permission of the Shakespeare Centre Library.

Preface

This collection, like its three predecessors, brings together a series of essays by members of the Royal Shakespeare Company. The essays discuss thirteen performances in eleven productions between 1992 and 1997 and the actors who write them had all talked about the roles with members of the programme of courses jointly run by the Shakespeare Birthplace Trust and the Shakespeare Institute of the University of Birmingham at the Shakespeare Centre in Stratford. All but one of the roles (as well as five of the plays) are new to the *Players of Shakespeare* series and the exception (the title role in *Richard III*) has not previously been considered in a production of the play independent of the *Henry VI* trilogy. The essays divide equally among comedies, histories and tragedies, with emphasis among the comedies on those notoriously difficult 'clown' roles which have figured little in earlier volumes in the series. The four essays on histories concentrate their focus on two plays, in each case contrasting the perspective of the titular character with that of his principal female antagonist. Among the essays on the tragedies are two on Roman plays which have not previously featured in *Players of Shakespeare* volumes. As in the preceding volume, references and quotations are from the New Penguin edition of the plays, the text normally issued to actors in RSC rehearsal rooms. A biographical note on the writer, with emphasis on work for the RSC and on Shakespearian roles elsewhere, appears at the beginning of each essay, and at the end of the volume there is a list of credits for the productions covered.

I am grateful to the editors of *Shakespeare Quarterly* and *Shakespeare Survey* for permission to repeat in the Introduction to this volume material that appeared first in the pages of their journals. I am grateful also to colleagues at the Shakespeare Centre and the Shakespeare Institute for their support, and particularly to Sylvia Morris of the Shakespeare Centre Library for generous assistance with the illustrations, to Margaret Walker for remarkable patience with some difficult manuscripts and to Paul Edmondson for help with one of the essays. Sonja Dosanjh, the RSC Company Manager, still finds time, among all her other responsibilities, to organize, with unfailing friendliness and efficiency, the elaborate programme of involvement of members of the RSC in university courses at the Shakespeare Centre from which the essays in this volume ultimately derive. To her, once again, my grateful thanks.

R.S.

The Shakespeare Centre
Stratford-upon-Avon

Introduction

ROBERT SMALLWOOD

'Do I have to play it in a flak jacket?' was, Jane Lapotaire tells us at the beginning of the essay she contributes to this volume, the first thing she asked when her director offered her the part of Queen Katherine in *Henry VIII*. The question goes to the heart of the whole issue of presenting Shakespeare's plays in the modern theatre: how should one approach the task, as director of *Henry VIII*, for example, of engaging an audience, sitting in a theatre in the last decade of the twentieth century, with events from the third decade of the sixteenth century as dramatized in a play written in the second decade of the seventeenth? A remarkable cross-section of the answers to that question on offer in current theatre practice is represented by the performances (and the productions of which they formed part) that the following essays describe. The range of Shakespearian work created by the Royal Shakespeare Company, from large-scale main-stage productions involving elaborate sets and costumes and big casts, to small-budget studio work of a far simpler kind, has justified the claim, in earlier volumes in this series, that it covered, in general terms, all the basic approaches and possibilities of modern Shakespeare production. With the opening of the new Globe Theatre in Southwark in the year in which this volume goes to press another possibility is now being explored: in a space intended to replicate, as precisely as knowledge permits, the original theatre building of 1599, and in costumes, so the programme note informed us, woven in the Elizabethan manner and using Elizabethan dyes, in natural light (or for evening performances in an imitation thereof), with even modern underwear banned, an all-male cast played *Henry V* in the summer of 1997 to audiences encouraged to eat and drink during the performance and to boo the French every time they came on stage in a way that was thought to replicate the patriotic behaviour of their sixteenth-century predecessors. Replication, or the attempt at replication, is a human activity with a long pedigree, and this was not its first appearance in the world of

Shakespeare production, though it may be one of its more determined. How, or if, the arrival of the Globe will affect the development of Shakespeare production by other companies and in other theatres remains to be seen. I mention it here only because there is now a more extreme opposite of the flak-jacket approach to Shakespeare production than anything represented in this volume or its predecessors.

What, apart from this desire to try to copy all the details of original performance, are the main choices of setting that face a director planning a production of a Shakespeare play? There is, obviously, modern dress (which may or may not involve flak jackets): the players wear the sorts of costumes that would make it possible for them to join the audience without appearing conspicuous. Though the evidence of the Peacham drawing of *Titus Andronicus* suggests some vague gestures towards the Roman, it is generally agreed that opulent examples of contemporary costume are likely to have been what the original audiences of Shakespeare's plays saw their actors wearing: no tenth-century Danish look for Burbage's Hamlet, or eleventh-century Scottish costume for his Macbeth. In a sense, therefore – though a distinctly paradoxical one – the modern director who costumes his actors in clothes that could have been worn by his audience might be said to be presenting the play 'traditionally'. Sir Barry Jackson's modern-dress Shakespeare productions at Birmingham Repertory Theatre before the Second World War ('Hamlet in plus-fours', as the most famous of them was dubbed) were the pioneers of a method that has become a significant part of the armoury of the modern Shakespeare director, exemplified most obviously among current directors in this country in the work of Michael Bogdanov, for whom modern-dress presentation of Shakespeare is more or less a creed. The one whole-hearted example of it in this volume is David Thacker's *The Merchant of Venice*.

Also represented by only one example among the productions in this volume is what used to be thought of as the standard and straightforward way of presenting Shakespeare – in Elizabethan costume. Steven Pimlott's production of *As You Like It* had a Rosalind who could genuinely wonder what she was to do with her doublet and hose when Orlando appeared and, as David Tennant tells us in his essay, Touchstone even wore a version of a motley coat. In no sense, however, did the stage setting attempt to match the temporally fairly specific costumes and in the final moments there was a departure from historicity as determined as could be.

The method which so dominated Shakespeare production in the nineteenth and early twentieth centuries, the re-creation, through design and costumes, of the period in which the play's story, fictional or historical, is set, is still with us as the end of this century approaches. Instead of a flak jacket Jane Lapotaire got costumes and head-dresses based on contemporary portraits of Katherine of Aragon, and Paul Jesson remarks in his essay on the need for actors in that production of *Henry VIII* to bring to their wearing of the authentic mid-Tudor costumes equally authentic mid-Tudor deportment. Much less precise in its care for authenticity of historical detail, but still overwhelmingly 'Roman' in the effect they created and thus placing the play firmly in the period of its subject-matter, were the designs for Sir Peter Hall's production of *Julius Caesar*.

Three of the productions discussed in this volume followed a route that has been much used by Shakespeare directors over the last two or three decades but was a comparative rarity earlier, the setting of the play in a specific historical period that is neither that of its story, nor of its composition, nor of its production. Paul Jesson writes in his essay of a putative production of *Henry VIII* that proposed to set the play in the early twentieth century, with Henry as Edward VII, Katherine as Queen Alexandra, and Anne Bullen as Lillie Langtree. Whether its failure to materialize represents a sad loss or a happy escape for playgoers we shall never know, but determinedly reaching their intended destinations along the same road were Ian Judge's *Love's Labour's Lost*, set very exactly in the twilight of the Edwardian era, just before the First World War; Adrian Noble's version of *Romeo and Juliet*, presented in a late nineteenth-century world; and David Thacker's production of *Coriolanus*, making broad and ample, if not altogether consistent, reference to the French Revolution.

The creation of coherent worlds in specific historical periods against which audiences can assess and measure the events of the play might thus be said, with varying degrees of vagueness and exactness, to have been the method of seven of the eleven productions represented in this volume – one 'modern', one 'Elizabethan', two 'historical' (setting the play in the period of its events), and three 'period' (setting the play in a specific period somewhere between its own and the audience's). The other four – and thus the largest single category – took the route which has become increasingly frequent in recent Shakespeare production, the 'eclectic', that is the deliberate evasion of the specific, the studied creation of a sense of temporal vagueness about the period in which the

3

1 'Modern-dress' Shakespeare: *The Merchant of Venice*, RST 1993, directed
by David Thacker, designed by Shelagh Keegan; Act I, Scene i. (Antonio
(Clifford Rose), Gratiano (Mark Lockyer), Lorenzo (Mark Lewis Jones),
Bassanio (Owen Teale).)

play's events are taking place. There are different levels and categories
of this technique: sometimes, as with Steven Pimlott's *Richard III*, the
production may seem mostly to belong in a single period – in this case
Elizabethan, certainly, rather than late fifteenth-century – which is
then dislocated by the intrusion of figures from another era. On other
occasions – Adrian Noble's *Macbeth* was an example, as was the same
director's *The Winter's Tale* – deliberately non-specific, or 'timeless',
costumes may be displaced for a scene, or a section of the play, by
visual evidence that seems much more dateable. And, thirdly, there is the
technique of straightforward eclecticism, using costumes or other visual
images from many different periods and simultaneously and anachron-
istically juxtaposing them, a method adopted most obviously, among
the productions represented here, by Gale Edwards's version of *The
Taming of the Shrew*, in which costumes from more or less every century
from Shakespeare's to our own were to be seen simultaneously on stage.
The photographs attached to individual essays provide a number of

examples of what I have been discussing; by a pleasing coincidence, however, it happens that the Folio order in which the essays are arranged means that the book opens with productions offering splendidly contrastive examples of four of the main categories – 'modern', 'period', 'Elizabethan' and 'eclectic' – and the illustrations to this Introduction (nos. 1–4) thus make their point most sharply by straying no further than *The Merchant of Venice*, *Love's Labour's Lost*, *As You Like It*, and *The Taming of the Shrew*.

Having offered those very broad, and inevitably over-simplified, categorizations of the productions upon which this collection is based, I turn now to each production in turn in the hope of providing a slightly fuller sense of the context within which the individual performances were created.

The Venice of David Thacker's 1993 production of *The Merchant of Venice* was the financial quarter of a modern city – its set might have been the Lloyds Building in London – with Antonio, in the opening scene, meeting his friends over a lunchtime drink at a smart restaurant (see Illustration 1) and Shylock's office fully equipped with the latest computer technology. Other parts of its multi-levelled playing area were peopled by bustling yuppies in sharp suits making enormous financial deals on mobile telephones or, when off duty, listening to appallingly loud rock music at parties where coloured lights dazzled and flashed. Through such a party, David Calder's Shylock, fresh from listening to Schubert on his gramophone, was pushed and jostled in his forlorn search for Jessica after her elopement with one of the denizens of this shallow, materialist, fast-track world. In the early stages, racial tensions were virtually invisible below the surface of this uniformly money-obsessed community (at a number of points the text was adjusted to replace the two syllables of 'the Jew' by the metrically equivalent 'Shylock'), and Shylock himself was indistinguishable from his fellow financial dealers; but as the loss of Jessica pushed him into isolation and the news of her elopement and extravagance drove him more fiercely in upon himself, he became increasingly racially self-conscious, adopting the outward evidences of his Jewishness with aggressive determination, and as all the reactions of his friend Tubal made clear, abusing his religion by enlisting it in support of his pursuit of vengeance. The trial scene thus became, in spite of the superficialities of modern dress, and particularly in the almost demented abusiveness of Mark Lockyer's Gratiano, a site of racial hatred at the most primitive level.

In spite of an elegant mirrored screen and a costume for Penny Downie's Portia that looked like a designer ball-gown chosen from an issue of *Vogue* a couple of decades earlier than those being consulted in Venice, there was enough of the Lloyds Building set left in Belmont – our imaginations were required, for example, to allow the stilts upon which it stood to double as the trees in the garden – to make one realize that all that 'old money' that Portia's father had bequeathed her in his peculiarly restrictive will had probably been augmented by dealings in the self-same markets where Antonio and Shylock traded. It was a coherent world that David Thacker had created and one in which the play's ancient story of money and marriage, racial pride and racial hatred, was perfectly at home. It was also one in which Christopher Luscombe's nervous and suburban Lancelot Gobbo, eating his Kit-Kat in his Debenham's blazer, could make rare sense of a notoriously difficult part.

In that same 1993 season Ian Judge created an equally fully realized world for *Love's Labour's Lost* by setting it in an Oxbridge men's college on the eve of the outbreak of the First World War, the vow with which the play begins, to study for three years, having an almost uncanny aptness in these academic circumstances – or, just as relevantly, perhaps, having no aptness at all, for these elegant, aristocratic undergraduates, in this idyllic *Charley's Aunt* world, were infinitely more likely to be seen in a punt on the river, or on the cricket field, than venturing into the unfamiliar territory of a library. At the end, after all the merry japes of the Pageant of the Worthies, played outdoors in the quad against a skyline of dreaming spires and watched by the Princess and her retinue from white wickerwork chairs, and after the ladies had postponed their decisions on the marriage proposals, the imminence of warfare in trenches left one painfully aware (perhaps a little *too* painfully aware for the play that Shakespeare wrote) that a year and a day was an excessively hopeful estimate of the length of the wait.

The production took the opportunity to present a virtual mannequin parade of Edwardian ladies' fashions, the scene in which Navarre met the ladies on their arrival at the railway station (see Illustration 2), complete with authentic steam-train sound-effects, providing a particularly elaborate example of its visual self-consciousness. It is no accident that this is the only production among those represented here that lists a choreographer among its credits. It also found niches for most of the characters – Holofernes was Professor of Latin, Armado a long-term (very long-term) Visiting Fellow from an Iberian sister institution,

2 'Period' Shakespeare: *Love's Labour's Lost*, RST 1993, directed by Ian
Judge, designed by John Gunter, costumes by Deirdre Clancy; Act II, Scene i.
(The King of Navarre (Owen Teale) greets the Princess of France (Jenny
Quayle); on the left Dumaine (Robert Portal), Berowne (Jeremy Northam),
and Longaville (Guy Henry); on the right Boyet (Paul Greenwood); in the
background Rosaline (Abigail McKern), Katharine (Virginia Grainger),
and Maria (Alexandra Gilbreath).)

Costard errand-boy and general hanger-on to the porters' lodge, and
Moth, a role that the recent stage history of *Love's Labour's Lost* has
often found so recalcitrant, became, as Christopher Luscombe's essay
describes, the senior chorister in the college chapel.

Steven Pimlott's 1996 production of *As You Like It* was played in a
determinedly non-realistic space – a shiny metal box of a set into which
were flown, in variable numbers and configurations, long metal poles to
represent the trees of Arden. Its costumes, on the other hand, were as
realistic-Elizabethan as the play has seen at Stratford for a long time,
Niamh Cusack's Rosalind appearing not only in doublet and hose for
the arrival in Arden but carrying a hefty spear that looked perfectly
adequate, to the non-expert eye, to deal with most boars. Its Arden was
a harsh and uninviting place in the first half, with howling wind and
swirling snow against which the exiled Duke's followers huddled in
blankets while he preached to them (unconvincingly, it appeared) on the

7

virtues of the life removed from public haunt. The climate, indeed, proved fatal to Adam, brought in a state of collapse to the ducal table and expiring in the arms of two of the Duke's followers in as solemn a way of marking the arrival of the interval of *As You Like It* as any production can have managed.

Sunlight and daffodils and an exhilaratingly energetic pace characterized the second half, observable not least in the lustful energy sparking between David Tennant's red-suited, cap-and-bells Touchstone, as traditional a version of an Elizabethan jester as one is likely to see, and Susannah Elliott-Knight's eagerly responsive Audrey. As David Tennant's essay mentions, the production ended in Stratford (he also describes the variation in London) with the arrival on a stage peopled by characters in flamboyantly Elizabethan costumes of a middle-aged, grey-haired woman in a black Marks and Spencers trouser suit, who entered by way of the front stalls and who must have seemed to many in the audience to be a member of the front-of-house staff accidentally strayed into the performance (see Illustration 3). It was, in fact, yet another attempt by a director of *As You Like It* to solve the problem of the appearance of Hymen, god of marriage, the idea seeming to be that if gods come from outside a play's everyday world, what better than to bring into this Elizabethan-costumed piece a figure from the twentieth century, and if a play in performance derives its power from the audience's willingness to believe, from where else should the figure of ultimate power come but from the auditorium. Not all intellectually interesting ideas work theatrically, however, and this was one of them. But if this aspect of the production is perhaps best forgotten, others are well worth remembering, among them David Tennant's demonstration that it is still possible to play an Elizabethan jester and get laughs on the lines.

Eleven productions figure in this book. Only one of them had a woman director. Whether the proportion is roughly in line with the ratio elsewhere in the profession or whether it is peculiar to Shakespeare productions or to Stratford, and why these things should be as they are anyway, is, unfortunately, no part of the purpose of this Introduction to enquire. What is worth observing, however, is that the Artistic Director of the RSC, planning to include a production of *The Taming of the Shrew* in the Company's 1995 repertoire, made sure that he had a woman to direct it. The play's presentation of the wooing and wedding of Petruccio and Kate, the methods of his 'taming' of her, and above all her

3 'Elizabethan' Shakespeare (with interloper): *As You Like It*, RST 1996, directed by Steven Pimlott, designed by Ashley Martin-Davis; Act v, Scene iv. (Orlando (Liam Cunningham), Hymen (Doreen Andrew), Rosalind (Niamh Cusack), Duke Senior (Robert Demeger), with Celia (Rachel Joyce), Audrey (Susannah Elliott-Knight), Oliver (Sebastian Harcombe), and Touchstone (David Tennant) in the background.)

final speech on relationships within marriage, have made it a contentious piece, one of the new 'problem plays'. Michael Siberry's essay offers a revealing insight into some of Gale Edwards's methods of coping with it. Significant among these was the invention of a new character, a wife for Christopher Sly, who was seen at the beginning of the play, in an episode roughly based on the Induction, quarrelling with him and throwing him out in a drunken stupor. Since Sly and his wife were played by Michael Siberry and Josie Lawrence, Petruccio and Kate in the main play, the whole piece thus became Sly's dream, his fantasy of sexual dominance, reversed again at the end as the dream unravelled and (as the essay describes) Sly awoke to return, submissive, to his wife. To some members of the audience the final image was of possible hope for the future, with a chastened Sly who might behave better in future; to others it was a deeply depressing signal of Mrs Sly's submission to the

4 'Eclectic' Shakespeare: *The Taming of the Shrew*, RST 1995, directed by
Gale Edwards, designed by Russell Craig, costumes by Marie-Jeanne Lecca;
Act II, Scene i. (Baptista (Clifford Rose) in nineteenth-century costume,
Tranio, disguised as Lucentio (Mark Lockyer) as modern pop star, and
Gremio (James Hayes) in Elizabethan dress.)

inevitability of more brutality. Our responses to theatrical images are
nothing if not subjective.

Because the events of the main play were all offered to the audience as
part of a dream, director and designer had *carte blanche* for eclecticism
and fantasy. The Lord and his followers only partly suggested hunts-
men; there was also something oddly sinister about them, figures in
black tailcoats who appeared intermittently through the piece silently
observing, perhaps even controlling, the action. For the wedding Petruccio
appeared in an outfit partly inspired by the plumage of some ornate
breed of cockerel (a product, no doubt, of Sly's fantasies of roosterly
dominance), and costumes throughout mixed the Elizabethan, the
modern and all points in between in an uninhibited gallimaufry – as
when Mark Lockyer's Tranio, pretending to be Lucentio, appeared in
all the glitter of a modern pop-star among characters whose sartorial
commitments were to distinctly earlier periods (see Illustration 4). A
dilapidated little red motor car conveyed the newlyweds from Padua, a
means of transport rather more uncertain than the dilapidated horse of

whose splendid description the production deprived us, and through this series of wild and disconcerting images one watched the development of the disconcerting (and sometimes wild) relationship of Kate and Petruccio described in Michael Siberry's essay.

Adrian Noble's 1992 production of *The Winter's Tale* also began with something of the suggestion of a dream. Outside a huge, floor-to-ceiling, centre-stage gauze box filled with dimly seen, motionless figures, sat a little boy playing with a glass snow-scene toy. When he set a spinning-top in motion its hum was gradually overtaken by the sounds of a party, bright lights illuminated coloured balloons, the gauze box flew out, the figures moved, and danced, and laughed, and the little boy, Mamillius, ran to join his father, Leontes. The court one was looking at belonged in some non-specific, vaguely early twentieth-century, aristocratic world, the men in high-necked jackets in dark purples and deep greens, the women in long, richly coloured, flowing dresses. The gauze box descended again on several occasions for the Sicilian scenes, marking the psychological isolation of Leontes in his soliloquies of sexual self-delusion, for example, or, highly effectively, separating Paulina and her visitors from the statue of Hermione in the final scene before it flew out for the last time as the play's wonderful concluding miracle began. But there was no gauze box in Bohemia, and its absence said much about the spiritual difference between the two worlds of the play.

The first half of the production had started with party balloons in colourful profusion; the second began with Camillo and Polixenes snoozing in deck chairs and the languorous descent of a single red balloon bearing what turned out, when Camillo read it aloud, to be the Chorus of Time. We were not yet done with balloons, however, for there then came something of a *coup de théâtre* with the splendid descent of Autolycus described in Richard McCabe's essay. Down he came against a glorious blue-sky cyclorama, dangling from the end of a huge bunch-of-grapes parachute of enormous green balloons, singing with massive enthusiasm and, as he himself describes, not quite complete tunefulness – as vivid a signal of the play's change of mood at this point as one could imagine. The sheep-shearing festival to which Autolycus brought his pedlar's suitcase of risqué undergarments and flashy trinkets was presented in the sharpest contrast to the temporal vagueness of the Sicilian scenes. Here we were quite specifically at an English village fête in the 1930s, everybody's kitchen chairs, in ill-assorted colours, brought out for the occasion, trestle tables, bunting, balloons (again), a touch of

Stanley Spencer's Cookham about it all. A chirpy little oompah-pah band (the vicar on drums) played foxtrots and quicksteps, and villagers danced in their Fair Isle pullovers and cotton-print summer frocks – and Autolycus accompanied his ballads on the accordion as he picked all their pockets.

The designs for the two history plays represented in this collection took quite different attitudes to the question of historical authenticity. The set for Steven Pimlott's 1995 production of *Richard III* divided the playing space vertically into three parts. The stage floor itself presented, for two thirds of its width, a wasteland of rocks and debris in a lurid sulphur colour, with a blasted sapling stage left. The remaining third (stage right) was stygian black, a limbo to which Richard's victims were banished one by one and to which (as David Troughton's essay describes) Richard himself finally, and purposefully, walked. The second level, an area at middle height intermittently thrust forth, was used for the presentation of interior (mainly court) scenes. It had a rear door that suggested a prison and the occupants of this level, among them Susan Brown's Queen Elizabeth in the extraordinary dress to which she refers in her essay, were presented in elaborate Elizabethan costumes, with a sense of self-conscious staginess about them that suggested figures in a costume drama strutting and fretting their hour on a little stage above the stage. The top level was a sort of bridge, set at a slight diagonal, on which Edward IV's court appeared simpering to Edward and giggling at David Troughton's Jester Richard below, and on which they all reappeared, in ghostly manifestation, at the end. On this upper level the play's citizens – the production used a large corps of volunteer extras – some in Elizabethan, some in vaguely Victorian, some in modern dress, appeared from time to time to watch the action below, the dupes and victims of these political events, and of countless more, too, down the centuries.

The production, then, invited us to be aware of the play's own self-conscious theatricality, an invitation repeated in David Troughton's performance of Richard. The point was made in the opening speech, its first half given, as entertaining performer, to the amused and trusting audience of courtiers behind him, its second half (from 'But I that am not shaped') addressed, also as entertaining performer, to the amused and trusting audience of playgoers in front of him. The performer's exploitation of those different trusts, and the development of those relationships, form the subject of David Troughton's essay. Among

Jester Richard's laughing court audience at the beginning, Susan Brown's vulgarly overdressed, bourgeois Elizabeth Woodville was setting out on a long journey of conflict with her terrifying brother-in-law, a journey starting in the superficial politenesses of court distrust, passing through the elemental grief and ritual lamentation for her dead babies, and ending in the grim struggle for political power that the marriage of her surviving daughter represents. That journey's stages are charted in her essay.

Gregory Doran's 1996 production of *Henry VIII* at the Swan Theatre provided the first opportunity to see the play at Stratford for thirteen years. Its simple design exploited the Swan's apron stage to excellent effect. Leaden double doors upstage, bearing the play's original title 'All is True' in large Roman capitals, swung open on occasions through the performance for scenes of ostentatious pageantry – a glimpse of the Field of Cloth of Gold at the beginning, Anne Bullen's coronation procession near the middle, the christening of Elizabeth at the end. The pomp, and the gold, and the music, were indeed, as Sir Henry Wotton wrote of an early performance, 'sufficient . . . to make greatness very familiar, if not ridiculous'. Our awareness thus alerted to the usefulness of sham patriotism and gaudy theatricality as means of sustaining political power, we watched, with the legend of its truth constantly before us, as the real power play of sordid political manoeuvring took over the playing space, the characters costumed like accurate reproductions of all the mid-Tudor court paintings one could remember. The juxtaposition of ostentatious power shows with the everyday world of intrigue and jostling for position around the king while the 'truth' that the play purports to be concerned with seemed to be just a malleable political commodity, were particularly effective in what Paul Jesson in his essay calls the 'debating chamber' space of the Swan, the audience challenged to assess where, if anywhere in all this, they might allow their trust to reside.

The political imperative that drives Henry VIII is the requirement that he maintain his dynasty's grip on power beyond his own death by begetting a male heir. His utter ruthlessness in response to that imperative lies behind all the actions that Paul Jesson discusses in his essay. Had Katherine of Aragon provided that male heir before reaching the age at which we meet her in the play, an age at which further childbearing is unlikely, there would be no divorce, and she would not, therefore, in her rejection by the man she loves, become the centre of the play's emotional sympathy. One of the curious things about *Henry VIII* is that, for all the closeness of the audience's relationship with Katherine that Jane Lapotaire analyses in her essay, we are never quite allowed the easy route to outright dislike of Henry, a fact which is very clear in Paul Jesson's discussion of the king's role, for Henry, too, is seen to be driven by the inexorable dictates of the power struggle from which there is no escape. At the end of this production, with Katherine dead and her last appeal to Henry ripped up by a Caputius who clearly perceives the futility of trying to deliver it, the king stood trying desperately to maintain the paternal beam that he had worn on his cheeks through the christening scene and with golden confetti falling from the roof, we were suddenly aware that Anne Bullen had silently appeared to Henry's left, her fingers tremblingly touching the neck that was soon to be severed by the executioner's axe – a victim, like so many others we had met, or heard about, of the dynastic power whose continuance we had just been invited to celebrate.

David Thacker's 1994 production of *Coriolanus*, also at the Swan, presented the play in a setting of the French Revolution, banners slung from the galleries proclaiming *liberté, égalité,* and *fraternité* and a version of Delacroix's painting of Liberty dominating the stage. Toby Stephens's Coriolanus and his fellow commanders wore the uniforms of French officers of the period and Philip Voss's Menenius, in velvet coat and turban and carrying a cane walking-stick, looked every inch the well-nourished eighteenth-century aristocrat as he told the parable of the belly to the starving, ragged plebeians (whose hands, stretched out for food, he had just shaken in a mockery of good will), or confronted the irascible tribunes in their shabby lawyers' gowns. The translocation of the play from the early Roman republic to the beginnings of the French worked well, on the whole, in focusing on the great political arguments about how a state is to be governed which lie at the centre of the piece, and the Senate scenes in which, as Philip Voss describes in his essay, Menenius's love for Coriolanus and his loyalty to Rome are so fiercely tested and juxtaposed, were immensely exciting. Less easy to assimilate, in this firmly established late eighteenth-century world, was the precise nature of the relationship between the state and its system of government that Menenius is so committed to protecting, and the long-running threat from the Volscians, for the struggle that Shakespeare presents between the nascent Roman republic and the traditional enmity of a neighbouring Italian tribe seemed to transfer less than satisfactorily to the international political situation in late eighteenth-century Europe. Within the city itself, however, the production was immensely powerful in its concentration on family relationships and emotions within the patrician class as they struggle to maintain their hold on political power; at the centre of that struggle is Menenius, and Philip Voss's essay analyses the personal and political loyalties that shape his journey through the play.

Also shifting its subject to a specific later time period was Adrian Noble's 1995 production of *Romeo and Juliet*, which presented the play in the restrictive world of small-town, late nineteenth-century Italy, Capulet a heavy father-figure in frock-coat and top hat, archetypally believable as he bellowed his rage at his daughter's disobedience over his choice of husband for her. The great gates which protected the entrance to his orchard may have been a pleasing example of the iron-worker's craft, but they were also a potent symbol of the system which entrapped his daughter in parental rule, while Capulet's choice of the tall, blond, conspicuously aristocratic Paris said much about the wealthy bourgeois's desire for social advancement, and ethnic purity, in his daughter's marriage. The production offered some splendid images of its period setting. In an elegant café the young men assembled in the evening before going on to the Capulets' masked ball, and there, too, at a pavement table, Julian Glover's Friar Lawrence paused in his early-morning botanical collecting to take a coffee, to be joined by Romeo with his confession of his new-found love for Juliet. Among those same pavement tables, to the terror of other customers, the brawl erupted that led to the death of Mercutio and to Romeo, in uncontrollable rage, stabbing Tybalt with a dinner knife grabbed from one of the place settings. The party where the lovers met was a grand coming-out reception for Juliet, with a hugely busy stage, the music of Verdi energizing the proceedings, the swirl of dancers, and the series of little private confrontations that the scene depicts – between Capulet and Tybalt or between Romeo and Juliet – taking place down stage in the privacy of communion with the audience. The procession of singing, flower-decked children carrying posies for Juliet's wedding morning and grinding to a halt, vocally as well as physically, at the sight of her corpse, was also highly effective.

Into this coherent and vivid world Julian Glover's Friar Lawrence fitted excellently. The choice of accent that he describes in his essay marked him off from the rest of his society and gave him a certain austerity, though with it, too, a sort of gritty dependability. One watched his confidence in his scheme develop, his determination unshaken by the apparently endless series of setbacks to which it is subjected. Tall and imposing in his Franciscan habit or his dark suit, he seemed in control of events, thinking fast as he bustled at his work-bench to mix the potion for Juliet until, in the final scene, his plans unravelled and his scheme crashed in ruin and despair. Julian Glover's discussion of his creation of this fine performance is notable also in one point of detail: his insistence on the significance for him of checking at many points on the Folio reading of his lines and on the usefulness of what he found.

Sir Peter Hall's production of *Julius Caesar* left the play visually more or less in the period of its events, though it may perhaps be doubted whether any Roman ever wore a jacket and trousers of such dazzling whiteness as those in which Mark Antony knelt over the corpse of Caesar, delaying for an unbelievably long time the inevitable moment when they became daubed with blood. The set, with many levels, its steps providing the means for elaborate spectacle as processions wound their way to the Lupercal or to the Senate and its near-central podium the site of the long-drawn-out and appallingly bloody assassination, was dominated by a huge white relief mask of Caesar. It hung on the back wall and began to ooze trickles of blood from its eyes and forehead as Caesar bled to death, and continued to do so through the disintegration of the state into civil war. The production used fifty or so volunteer extras who provided the crowd for the orations after the assassination, and the mob for the horrifically brutal killing of Cinna the Poet, literally torn apart as his blood swirled down the steps of the stage, and who were there again at the end to provide the rival armies at Philippi.

It seemed in some ways a rather old-fashioned production, but about its examination of the play's central relationship, that between Brutus and Cassius – a relationship that destroys them both and comes close to destroying Rome – there was an impressive clarity. John Nettles's essay discusses that relationship, Cassius driven by emotion and envy, Brutus by a myopic assurance of the unassailable rightness of his own principles, and in so doing offers a remarkable account of an actor's respect for the human qualities of the character he is portraying alongside an unalloyed contempt for the principles by which he steers his political course.

Adrian Noble's 1993 production of *Macbeth* opened at the Barbican rather than in Stratford, and played a solo run (as opposed to the RSC's usual repertoire system) there before coming to Stratford for a short season early in 1994. It was clearly conceived as a means of providing one of British theatre's major actors with a chance to tackle a Shakespearian role that had not previously come his way, though it was the director's second RSC version of the play. The dark and foreboding set was dominated by a high backstage door, the door behind which Duncan lies asleep until Macbeth at last finds the will to go through it, and so destroys his own life for ever; the same door behind which Duncan lies in gore and, as Derek Jacobi describes in his essay, through which Macbeth must force himself once more to join Macduff in discovery of the bloody killing. A black stairway and a black platform that carried the witches up to a black sky completed the basic design, the whole suggesting a dark and non-descript nightmare world in which dark-clad actors often appeared as disembodied faces in a great and frightening void. Costumes were deliberately timeless: there were kilts and armour for the warriors, and leather coats were much in evidence, but for the domestic scenes Macbeth and his household wore what seemed like modern pullovers and slacks, while Lady Macbeth's dresses might have come from any or none of the last two or three centuries and Duncan had a distinctly biblical appearance.

Such eclecticism of costume and spatial vagueness of setting provided an environment in which attention was focused on Macbeth's journey – that short journey through the door of Duncan's chamber which takes him on the immense spiritual journey from the world of emotional honesty and of professional, political, and personal success where, in this production at least, he began, to the lonely, dark, and destructive area on the edge of consciousness through which he blunders to damnation. Derek Jacobi was not, as he says himself at the start of his essay, an obvious choice for the role of Macbeth; his account of his confrontation with the part – and of his character's confrontation with evil and with despair – is evidence of how far the imagination and art of the actor can push back the boundaries of expectation. And that is a matter with which all the essays in this volume, and in earlier volumes in the *Players of Shakespeare* series, have been concerned.

Launcelot Gobbo in *The Merchant of Venice* and Moth in *Love's Labour's Lost*

CHRISTOPHER LUSCOMBE

CHRISTOPHER LUSCOMBE played Launcelot Gobbo in David Thacker's production of *The Merchant of Venice* and Moth in Ian Judge's production of *Love's Labour's Lost* in the same 1993 season. Both productions were at the Royal Shakespeare Theatre and were seen at the Barbican Theatre the following year. Earlier work for the RSC had included Francis the Drawer in 1 and 2 *Henry IV* and Dapper in Ben Jonson's *The Alchemist*. He returned to Stratford in 1996 to play Slender in *The Merry Wives of Windsor* and Dogberry in *Much Ado about Nothing*. In the mean time he had created and performed in *The Shakespeare Revue* at Stratford and the Barbican, in the West End, on national and overseas tours and on BBC radio. His one-man show *Half Time* has also been seen on British and overseas tours, as well as in London and Stratford.

Why are actors so reluctant to take on these particular roles? Whenever I told anyone that I was going to Stratford to play them I always seemed to be greeted with sympathy. It appears that Launcelot Gobbo has become an archetype of the impossible Shakespearian clown. Michael Green says that he had the part in mind when he wrote *The Art of Coarse Acting*:

FIRST CLOWN: Mass, 'twould make a neat's tongue turn French tailor and cry old sowter from here to Blackfriars, would it not?

In fact, Gobbo defies parody with his obscure references: 'My nose fell a-bleeding on Black-Monday last at six o'clock i' th' morning, falling out that year on Ash-Wednesday was four year in th' afternoon' (II.v.24–7), not to mention the archaic vocabulary: 'Do I look like a cudgel or a hovel-post?' (II.ii.62) and relentless wisecracks: 'Bid them prepare for dinner' – 'That is done, sir. They have all stomachs!' (III.v.43–4).

But why is Moth taken to be the short straw in *Love's Labour's Lost*? Well, he is fairly insufferable I suppose at first sight. Even Don Armado tires of his precocious wit: 'I love not to be crossed' (I.ii.32). The part has tended to become a breeches role taken by young actresses who would much rather be playing Rosaline (indeed Amanda Root has now played both parts for the RSC). The other obvious option is to cast a child. This inevitably leads to a good deal of cutting, because of the fiendishly complex prose and the treacherous acoustics of the Royal Shakespeare Theatre. And just when the young actor is beginning to find his feet (and his voice), the union rules demand that he is replaced by another newcomer – yet more rehearsals for the hapless Don Armado. So it's a relatively unexplored role, and that in itself is an incentive at Stratford.

I don't think I was aware at first that the RSC had offered me a poisoned chalice. I was just finishing my first season with the Company, and relished the idea of going back to Stratford with a couple of parts I could get my teeth into. In a vague way I felt that I had some sort of affinity with them, and throughout the months that followed I tried to keep faith with that initial instinct. A long rehearsal period can some-times muddy the waters. So much of a performance is governed by instinct. It's only afterwards that one can anatomize it and explain one's decisions. The best bits, I find, are based on a natural response to the text; other more conscious choices can seem calculating or knowing (a particular problem in comedy) and often get dropped in performance. So most of what I did in these plays was less rational than it may now appear, and it's only with the advantage of hindsight that I can find ways of justifying myself.

The Merchant of Venice and *Love's Labour's Lost* both had strong dir-ectorial concepts. The former was set in a modern city landscape, Venice becoming, to all intents and purposes, a yuppified City of London. The latter conjured up a late-Edwardian Oxbridge idyll, all dreaming spires and golden sunsets. So there were very clear parameters for our work, and when the actors gathered together on the first day of rehearsal a lot of decisions had been made for them. (Actually, whilst Ian Judge breezily kicked off with the completed designs and a play-through of the music, David Thacker would not be drawn on his steel-and-glass vision for a week or so, until I could bear the suspense no longer and asked him outright: 'OK, so when's it set?')

I have to say that all the actors were (I think) happy about these choices. Apart from the fact that the main house at Stratford demands bold design and strong direction, both concepts seemed to fit particu-larly well, giving the characters a recognizable context in which to oper-ate. *The Merchant of Venice* was clearly set in a world obsessed by money, where racism plausibly festered within a superficially polite, glamorous society. Navarre's 'little academe' (I.i.13) in *Love's Labour's Lost* fitted an Oxbridge quadrangle so well, with its 'three years' term', that you kicked yourself for not thinking of it first. And the pre-First World War period added a chilling poignancy to the lovers' separation at the end.

As for Launcelot Gobbo and Moth, they immediately fitted into these distinct worlds. The former was transformed from domestic drudge into office tea boy, a suburban lad ill at ease in his new hi-tech surroundings. Terrified of his martinet boss ('the very devil incarnation' (II.ii.24)), he'd rather work (who wouldn't?) for the complacent, likeable Bassanio 'who indeed gives rare new liveries' (II.ii.101) – clothes allowance too! The characters in *Love's Labour's Lost* found their places with similar ease. Holofernes had to be the Classics Professor, Sir Nathaniel the Chaplain, and Moth the Choirboy. I quickly promoted him to Head Chorister. This made him the big fish in a very small pond and accounted for his bumptiousness; it also allowed him to be a little older than I'd originally envisaged, maybe fourteen or fifteen. In 1914 the choristers often stayed on longer than they would today, taught the younger boys, were tutored by the dons and, if their voices had broken (mine had!), took a non-singing role in Chapel. I felt sure that Moth would have much preferred carrying the cross or turning pages in the organ loft to being one of the crowd in the choir stalls.

As I have said, everyone seemed worried on my behalf when I accepted this job, especially the offer to tackle Launcelot Gobbo. A friend who played it at Birmingham Rep some years ago told me that he had managed to 'work out a gag for every single line'. He offered a word of advice: 'don't work out a gag for every single line'. I took this to heart. It seemed much more important to create a believable character, and I was greatly helped in this by our eminently 'real' setting. I wasn't a stand-up comedian, but a character who happened to be funny. I'd just been working at the Barbican with Rob Edwards, who played the part in John Barton's 1981 RSC production. He told me that at the first preview, as he watched Old Gobbo exit, tapping his way with a white stick into the Venetian sunset, he found himself filling an awkward pause with an *ad libbed* 'mind the canals!' It brought the house down, but the next morning John reminded the company of Hamlet's advice to the players: 'Let those that play your clowns speak no more than is set down for them' (III.ii. 37).

In our production I was in fact able to speak *less* than was set down for me thanks to David Thacker's pragmatic approach to the text. He encouraged me to make my own cuts, feeling that the comic actor is probably the best judge of what he can make work. I was certainly ready with the blue pencil when even the Arden editor admitted defeat ('this passage has not been explained', he comments ominously in the footnotes):

'It is much that the Moor should be more than reason; but if she be less than an honest woman, she is indeed more than I took her for'. (III.v.37–9)

One is reminded of John Cleese's three laws of comedy: no puns, no puns and no puns.

Sometimes we made changes purely for the sake of clarity. In my first scene the Elizabethan use of the word 'father' meaning 'old man' complicated the gulling of Old Gobbo for a modern audience, so I simply said the latter. I also checked the first folio and the two quartos for textual alternatives. 'I'll take my leave . . . in the twinkling of an eye' (II.ii.155–6) seemed a preferable exit line to just 'in the twinkling'. Similarly I liked the idea of ironically referring to Jessica as 'Mistress Lorenzo' on my last entrance (v.i.47). The bonus of cutting and editing is that it forces you to grapple with the text. I did dither over the serviceability of certain lines, including them or omitting them at different performances in a sort of controlled experiment. But I am convinced that Shakespeare is better served by judicious cuts than a slavish attempt to breathe life into every last syllable. I was sure that, contrary to popular opinion, a lot of Gobbo's dialogue is very funny, and I didn't want the audience to miss the wood for the trees.

The real challenge of the part was to find a believable character who could accommodate a hint of stand-up comedy – even Shakespeare refers to him as the 'clown' in his stage directions (v.i.38). It's often suggested that Shakespeare's clowns rely on 'personality performances', where the perceived idiosyncrasies of the actor are more important than detailed characterization. Will Kemp, who created so many of these roles (including Gobbo), began his career as the Earl of Leicester's fool, and one can only assume that his solo work informed his acting style. Our own generation has seen comics such as Frankie Howerd as Bottom – or was it Bottom as Frankie Howerd? That blurring of edges seems to me to be part of an honourable tradition. A true comic spirit is hard to define, but it's obviously essential for the full realization of these parts. Meticulous psychological realism, unfortunately, is not enough, and indeed I suspect that it would be wrong to rationalize Gobbo's clowning

5 Christopher Luscombe as Launcelot Gobbo, *The Merchant of Venice*, Act II,
Scene ii: 'Launcelot, budge not . . .'

too much. Two minutes after sharing a profound dilemma with the
audience, he is idly 'trying confusions' with his father (II.ii.33); an
anxious examination of his palm reveals the ludicrous forecast of fifteen
wives. Such ambiguity is a familiar comic technique of course. In a recent
television interview, Norman Wisdom spoke movingly of his impover-
ished East End origins. With tears in his eyes he referred to his 'very sorry
childhood', adding, as if by reflex, 'both my parents were very sorry'.

Equally, I believe it would be wrong to dismiss Gobbo simply as
'comic relief'. Much of the part does depend on comic personality, but
there's more to it than that. As well as an effective piece of stand-up
comedy, the opening soliloquy is a dramatization of the moral confusion
at the heart of the play: should we be ruled by the devil or 'hard conscience' (II.ii.25)? The episode with his father is not only a front-cloth
sketch; it is also a comic version of the filial tensions in both Jessica
and Portia's stories. And although he enjoys a unique rapport with the
audience through the soliloquy and a number of asides, Gobbo does
become drawn into the plot as Jessica and Lorenzo's go-between; he
adds to the moral argument of the play (notably in the third act); and it is

possible to detect in his behaviour character-based motivation – fear of Shylock, love for Jessica and jealousy of Lorenzo, for example. The two scenes involving the Prince of Morocco were combined in our production, which meant that my soliloquy grew naturally out of Shylock's first scene, set in his sleek City office. In fact, I hope the audience assumed I was an extra, and were then taken aback to find me talking to them. I had appeared a few minutes earlier with a tray of coffee, so I was probably thought to be non-speaking. I mention this because I was anxious to be part of the Venetian world, not a 'turn' interrupting the play. The juxtaposition of scenes also meant that Shylock and I collided, set up our relationship (I dropped some files, he hit me with them) and I was given an impetus to embark on my speech. Since I'd made coffee for the others (literally – it was a great way to allay stage fright) I decided to treat my first scene as elevenses, an opportunity to take a break with a KitKat (again literally), and to chat to the audience. After the highly-charged verse of the previous scene, my prose did sound very like 'chat', and I tried to capitalise on that. It seemed that there was something inherently comic about an intimate coffee break in a Shakespeare play, especially sharing it with fifteen hundred people.

In looking at Gobbo's comic style, I was interested to see how much he anticipates the clowns of our own time. The neurosis of the soliloquy, with its conflicting voices (' "Budge," says the fiend. "Budge not," says my conscience' (II.ii.17–18)), is reminiscent of the angst-ridden Woody Allen. This helped me to plunge into a real dilemma, not just a comic routine. The maddening digressions ('being an honest man's son, or rather an honest woman's son . . .' (II.ii.13–14)) recall Ronnie Corbett's endless subordinate clauses, and this contributed to the homely style I was after, totally at odds with Shylock's hard-headed business world. The cruel duping of Old Gobbo that follows ('Master Launcelot . . . is indeed deceased, or as you would say in plain terms, gone to heaven' (II.ii.55–9)) came to mind when I saw Spike Milligan on a chat show recently. 'What's the funniest joke in the whole world?' asked the well-meaning host. 'You,' replied Milligan. In other words, the true comic is not concerned with pulling punches, and in this scene there's no denying the pain that Gobbo inflicts on his blind father ('I pray you tell me, is my boy, God rest his soul, alive or dead?' (II.ii.65–6)). It seemed important to face up to this unattractive trait in the character and not smooth it out to suit our 90s sensibilities. Nonetheless, I did undermine Gobbo's slick display. When he was really showing off to his audience I had him mime elaborate piano scales on his boss's computer keyboard. This went horribly wrong for him when the screen scrambled before his very eyes. One could only imagine Shylock's subsequent reaction. I quite liked the ambiguity of this moment – did it really take Gobbo by surprise or was it just another of his jokes?

Although not as overtly anti-semitic as many other characters in the play, Gobbo does derive comic mileage from the racial tensions in Venice. As we've just seen, he's not afraid to offend if he thinks there's a laugh to be had. I was at pains to show that his love for Jessica was sincere, but when he bids her farewell he displays a curious insensitivity, repeatedly labelling her 'most beautiful pagan, most sweet Jew' (II.iii.10–11). In the same speech, I played on the words 'adieu / a Jew' to suggest both a lapse of taste and an instinctive verbal dexterity. He knew he shouldn't have said it, but he just couldn't resist it. As Feste points out in *Twelfth Night*, 'a sentence is but a cheveril glove to a good wit; how quickly the wrong side may be turned outward' (III.i.11–13). But I couldn't help feeling that as an outsider himself in this ruthless, macho world, he is primarily commenting on contemporary mores rather than condoning them. His references to race often seem to be an attempt at satire – risky business though that may be. We played his later scene with Jessica as a heavily ironic Bible class, with Gobbo preaching palpable nonsense for comic effect: 'Yes truly, for look you [searching in the Bible for the reference], the sins of the father are to be laid upon the children. Therefore . . . I think you are damned' (III.v.1–5). Gobbo had been transformed by Belmont into a politically correct satirist.

The character's trip to Portia's estate did in fact seem to reflect a spiritual journey too – albeit less profound than that of his new master – and we were able to suggest this in the costuming. The production's modern dress was wonderfully helpful, because choices 'read' so clearly to the whole audience. So much could be signalled by the pattern of a tie or the cut of a jacket. I felt he should be uncomfortable in the Venice scenes – a fish out of water. While all the other office workers wore the *haute couture* of Armani and Versace, my costume was bought off the peg in Stratford High Street. Gobbo's Debenhams blazer was probably acquired (no doubt his mother, Margery, helped him choose it) when he landed his job with Shylock, or maybe he wore it at school. Either way, it reeked of suburbia in a world of urban sophistication. A pullover under the jacket ensured that he sweated whenever his boss was in the room.

When he left Shylock's house (we decided that he rented a room from him) he became even more buttoned up, with a voluminous anorak and a suitcase tightly strapped onto a trolley. I hope that this helped to suggest the constrained atmosphere of the household, where Gobbo can't seem to do right for doing wrong ('Who bids thee call? I do not bid thee call' (ii.v.7)). But Belmont proved his salvation. Not only was there time for leisured badinage with Jessica, but he was able to move into weekend 'casuals': polo shirt, checked chinos and sandals (with socks of course). I had planned to ride a bicycle in Act V as a modern equivalent of horse-riding (he is mimicking a hunting horn), but the steep rake of the stage and a number of steel columns presented me with a tricky slalom course. So at the eleventh hour I opted instead for jogging gear and a walkman: not only did it seem right that he should have adopted a fitness regime, but the headphones accounted for the fact that he couldn't hear Lorenzo (in the original it's his horn impressions that deafen him).

I first appeared in *The Merchant of Venice* while still at school, not as Gobbo, but as Lorenzo, sporting some unlikely headgear and a pair of wrinkly mauve tights. We performed in the grounds of a stately home, and I thought I should always associate the beautiful fifth act ('The moon shines bright . . .' (v.i.1)) with hay fever and the whiff of hot dogs from the hospitality tent. I was offered the part of Launcelot Gobbo a few years ago in another outdoor production (once bitten by midges, twice shy, I'm afraid), so I was very pleased to tackle it (indoors) for the RSC, particularly in such a stimulating reassessment of the play.

For Moth in *Love's Labour's Lost* I was not required to relate to the audience, or to draw on my own personality, as I was with Launcelot Gobbo. The challenge instead was to create a more conventional character performance. Somehow I had to think myself into the cloistered world of a teenage chorister. The obvious first step was a trip to Oxford, and I spent a day shadowing the choir of Christ Church Cathedral School. This confirmed my hunch that Ian Judge's Oxbridge setting was going to fit like a glove. The choirboys are bright, confident and inquisitive, and of course highly educated, musically and academically. In class they proved to be just as 'quick in answers' (i.ii.29) as Moth. They also mix on a daily basis with the undergraduates in chapel, so Moth's ease with the adult characters seemed entirely credible. I realized that laboured attempts to mimic the movement of a young child would be out of place. These were socially adept young men, and too much gaucherie in the performance would be patronizing. I did introduce one moment of crisis for the character, when he attempts to introduce the 'Russian' lords, and is overcome with the responsibility of it all ('they do not mark me, and that brings me out' (v.ii.173)), but this only seemed to emphasize how well he copes the rest of the time. He even manages to maintain an ironic detachment from his supposed superiors and their extraordinary conversation: 'They have been at a great feast of languages and stolen the scraps' (v.i.36–7).

Of course I did have to address the question of ageing down. For once I was grateful for the wide open spaces of the RST, and always relied on the fact that distance probably does lend enchantment. I think too that the costume helped with this. The cassock, the broad Eton collar, the breeches rather than trousers and the school uniform all served to create the right image, and having observed the boys at Oxford, I simply tried to reproduce their uncomplicated ebullience. First impressions are crucially important in the theatre, and in my initial scene with Daniel Massey as Don Armado, we sat on a slanting gravestone, he towering over me at the top end, while I squatted at the bottom, munching a packed lunch. In fact, Dan and I are about the same height, but it was an effective optical illusion. We had at first thought that Armado should be Professor of Modern Languages at the university, but playing on the word 'Don' was perhaps a bit too contrived, and he gradually became a more enigmatic figure – the sort of eccentric hanger-on that all such institutions seem to attract. It never seemed far-fetched that he and Moth should have developed such a cheerful rapport, sitting in graveyards after choir practice, musing on melancholia, love and literature.

I should perhaps mention that there has long been a battle between editors about the correct form of Moth's name. At the beginning of the season I blithely told a distinguished academic at Stratford's Shakespeare Institute that I was playing Moth, to which he retorted 'yes, I prefer Mote'. I then went on to mention that Jeremy Northam was joining the company to play Berowne and was corrected again: 'yes, I prefer Biron'. Even the *dramatis personae* of this play seemed to be a minefield. In fact there are very good reasons for opting for either spelling (see Appendix D of the Oxford Edition) but in production it felt like a slightly pretentious gesture to deviate from centuries of stage tradition. I also thought that the word 'Moth' was helpfully suggestive of something small, busy and irritating. And it sits happily with Costard's description of him as a 'most pathetical nit' (IV.i.149).

6 Christopher Luscombe as Moth, with Armado (Daniel Massey),
Love's Labour's Lost, Act I, Scene ii.

Initially the incessant wordplay between Moth and Armado seemed
wearing to the modern ear. But we began to realize that their brittle
dialogue disguise a delightfully symbiotic relationship. Moth manages
to talk Armado out of his melancholic state with the 'familiar demonstration' of logic (I.ii.9), and galvanizes him into a defiant declaration of
his love for Jaquenetta. This in turn creates an opportunity for Moth to
demonstrate his scholarship with a catalogue of the other 'great men
[who] have been in love' (I.ii.63). Thus they take it in turns to occupy
the psychiatrist's chair. Armado is of course a terrible snob ('I am ill at
reckoning. It fitteth the spirit of a tapster' (I.ii.40)); and Moth is quite
nauseatingly opinionated ('No, no; O Lord, sir, no' (I.ii.6)). But their
folies de grandeur are seen to be touchingly fragile. Moth's self-possession
evaporates when 'presence majestical' does indeed 'put him out' later in
the play (V.ii.102) and Armado may think of himself as a man of 'good
repute and carriage' (I.ii.67), but 'the naked truth of it is, I have no shirt'
(V.ii.706).

Our Oxbridge setting also helped to take the curse off some of this
elaborate verbal wit. In academia such conversational cut-and-thrust

27

seemed entirely natural. Friendships are forged in the delighted discovery of new vocabulary: 'The posterior of the day, most generous sir . . . the word is well culled, choice, sweet, and apt, I do assure you, sir, I do assure' (v.i.86–9). An afternoon could quite feasibly be whiled away inventing elaborate word games: 'Now will I begin your moral, and do you follow with my *l'envoi*' (iii.i.91–2). Not all the relationships were quite so cosy. While Costard takes to Moth immediately ('An I had but one penny in the world, thou shouldst have it to buy gingerbread' (v.i.66–7)), Holofernes seems almost threatened by his intellect: 'thou disputes like an infant. Go whip thy gig' (v.i.62–3). But Moth is equally dismissive: 'you hear his learning' (v.i.48). Anyone who has spent time in an academic institution would surely recognize such rivalry. I mentioned earlier the value of a suitable context for these plays, and in this case it was almost miraculous that a line such as 'is not *l'envoi* a *salve?*' (iii.i.78–9) could seem like a burning question.

I expect Ian Judge first thought of making Moth a choirboy because of Armado's instruction 'warble, child: make passionate my sense of hearing' (iii.i.i). Shakespeare doesn't in fact supply a lyric, but our composer, Nigel Hess, set an Elizabethan love poem to an enchanting pastiche parlour melody, and I had the nightly challenge of trying to do it justice. My other, easier set piece was the Nine Worthies pageant in Act Five, in which Moth impersonates the infant Hercules and his remarkable trick of snake-strangling. Deirdre Clancy designed an ingenious costume involving two padded snakes wrapped around my torso which I then spectacularly fought. This was always rewarded with a spontaneous round of applause, that is until the production visited Newcastle. The usually warm audiences there remained obstinately unmoved by my acrobatics, to the point where I advertised 'two snakes for sale, one careful owner' on the backstage notice board. No bidder came forward and I somehow recovered my round, and my composure, for the London run (much to the relief of my long-suffering colleagues).

For all the analysis that went into the rehearsal and performance of these plays, the most important ingredient was the instinct that the actors brought to bear. The relative success of the productions can mainly be attributed, I believe, to the fact that the directors gave us a structure which liberated our imaginations and allowed us to square up to such demanding texts. Casting is important too, of course, and there was one moment when this struck me very forcefully. It was during a costume fitting for *The Merchant of Venice*. When we had made the decision that

I should play the fifth act in jogging gear, I had impressed upon the designer that I didn't want a 'funny' outfit. It mustn't look as if I was playing for a laugh – it had to be real. She agreed with me, and so we went to Ray Fearon, erstwhile tennis player and awesomely fit actor who was playing the Prince of Morocco. We asked him what he wears when he goes jogging. He told us and we went out and bought it. I tried it on in the Wardrobe Department at Stratford, and everyone fell about laughing. It's good to know that, if nothing else, you're in the right part.

Touchstone in
As You Like It

DAVID TENNANT

DAVID TENNANT played Touchstone in Steven Pimlott's production
of *As You Like It* at the Royal Shakespeare Theatre in 1996 and at the
Barbican Theatre later that year and into 1997. It was his first season
with the RSC and his other roles were Hamilton in *The General from
America* and Jack Lane in *The Herbal Bed*. His earlier stage work had
included a wide range of classical and modern roles in seasons at the
Manchester Royal Exchange, the Royal Lyceum, Edinburgh, and elsewhere, as well as at the Royal National Theatre. He has also worked
extensively on radio and television.

'I hear Roy Kinnear was marvellous . . .'

I auditioned for Orlando. I knew *As You Like It* from seeing it at school
(but I didn't remember much about that) and, of course, I had read it at
drama school but it wasn't one of the plays that I was particularly familiar with. I knew it was broadly about some woman dressing up as a bloke
with some 'hey-nonny-no' type songs and a famous speech in the middle.

I was in the thick of rehearsals for *The Glass Menagerie* up in Dundee
when the call came to get to London for an RSC audition, giving me woe-
fully little time to prepare. I picked the brains of the people I was working
with to get a bit more of an idea what I was going up for. 'Basically',
the collective conclusion was, 'it's a play about a woman who dresses up
as a bloke with some "hey-nonny-no" type songs and a famous speech
in the middle . . . oh, and there's a clown called Touchstone in it, the
usual confusing Shakespearian jokes – thankless part.' I remembered
Touchstone from reading the play. It struck me as the sort of part I'd be
useless at, stuffed with endless 'routines' and thick with references
which had lost any contemporaneousness about three hundred years
ago. However, I didn't need to worry about that, they'd find some
brilliant comic to play that part and he'd fill it with plenty of hilarious
business that would bring it bang up to date. I had to concern myself

with Orlando – not an easy part in itself but at least I could approach it fairly conventionally. I could look at who the character was, what he wanted, what his through-line was and so on.

I flew down to London the next day, cribbing furiously. I'd skim-read the play the night before and now I was concentrating on each of Orlando's scenes in turn. It was a very tricky part, at once full of bullish machismo, then suddenly prancing through the trees in the depths of romantic gooey-ness, but by the time I arrived at the Barbican I had it all figured out (I thought) and I strolled in ready to thrill Steven Pimlott (the director) with my brilliant, intelligent and – dare I say – revelatory take on one of Shakespeare's trickiest lovers.

'I'd like you to have a read of a bit of Touchstone' was Mr Pimlott's opening statement. I was sure I'd misheard.

'Sorry?'

'Touchstone . . . I'd like you to read a bit of Touchstone.' Steven flashed me a large, open smile. If this was some audition tactic to disarm me, I was indeed duly disarmed.

'But . . . em . . .' – stay calm I told myself – 'I was to audition for Orlando.'

'Well, yes, but I'd like to hear a bit of Touchstone.'

'OK' I replied, trying (and failing) with all my Scottish Presbyterian stoicism to sound like I thought it was a great idea. 'Fine. What would you like to look at?'

We read a couple of scenes through. It was all I could do to pronounce some of it let alone fill it with charm or vivacity. I didn't understand most of it and as for being funny . . .

I was back on the plane that evening feeling very sorry for myself, nursing a bruised ego and smarting as the dream of an RSC season slipped away. So to say I was surprised two days later when my agent rang to say I'd been offered the part of Touchstone is the understatement of all time. Of course I accepted without thinking. It was a main part in a Shakespeare play at the Royal Shakespeare Theatre in Stratford-upon-Avon, not something I could consider turning down; but over the next two weeks before we started work on it I began seriously to doubt my own sanity.

To start with I re-read the play. It struck me how episodic it all is, how many different stories are going on at the same time and yet how little actually happens. It seemed different to any other Shakespeare play I had read with a pace and charm and quirkiness which I imagined would

7 David Tennant as Touchstone, with Corin (Arthur Cox), *As You Like It*,
Act III, Scene ii: 'Then thou art damned.'

be hard to get the measure of. It has one monster part (Rosalind the
heroine/hero) and a very full and varied supporting cast each of whom
seems to fulfil a very definite role. Orlando is the lover, Celia the friend,
Duke Frederick the bad guy, Jaques the contrast, Silvius and Phebe
the complimentary sub-plot, and Touchstone the comedian. Ay, there's
the rub. I could see that Touchstone was supposed to be funny in terms
of the structure of the play, the tone of his scenes, and the fact that
everyone keeps going on about how hilarious he is. Jaques in particular,
an otherwise miserable sod, when confronted with Touchstone, finds
his 'lungs began to crow like Chanticleer' (II.vii.30) and yet I could find
nothing in the part to make me even smile. Through the rest of the play
I found a lot of genuinely funny exchanges. Rosalind was very witty,
Celia sported a fine line in caustic sarcasm and Jaques's melancholy
cynicism gave him some wonderful put-downs, but all Touchstone seemed
to have was long speeches heavy with obscure double entendres and
long tracts of cool philosophy, but nothing obviously funny. I couldn't
imagine many Chanticleer-like lungs were going to be found in the Royal
Shakespeare Theatre in the coming summer.

The next morning I bought myself a copy of the Arden study notes on *As You Like It* (I liked the appropriateness of the publisher) as well as two more editions of the play and I began the slow process of finding a way into this character. It's not a huge part, just seven scenes of which three or four are little more than sketches which Shakespeare seems to use to puncture the action now and again with a breath of silliness. Unlike Feste in *Twelfth Night* or even the fool in *King Lear*, he does have his own bit of plot line in his relationship with Audrey, but quite what the nature of that is is far from clear. Does he love and want to marry her or does he just want to get his leg over? He seems uncertain himself and changes his mind from scene to scene, even from line to line – but more of that later.

All too soon it was our first day of rehearsal and . . . the read-through. Always a terrifying experience when you speak your lines out loud in front of people for the first time, a read-through at the Royal Shakespeare Company is particularly scary, not only because you are at the home of 'world class classical theatre' (as all the brochures tell you) with all the history and influence of hundreds of great, definitive productions hanging in the air, but also because it's one of the few theatre companies in the country that can afford to employ the numbers of actors required to stage a full scale Shakespearian production, so the room is full of people! I sat in my place in the huge circle of chairs with palms sweating and heart racing. Everybody else in the room seemed to attack their parts with intelligence and ability.

Niamh Cusack playing Rosalind was graceful and calm and the verse seemed to pour off her tongue; Rachel Joyce as Celia spoke the words like they were her own, not four hundred years old at all; Liam Cunningham gave Orlando a vigour and a believability (and I instantly understood why it shouldn't be my part). As my first cue approached I took a deep breath and hoped for the best. Feeling very small and hopeless I just gabbled Touchstone out as quickly as possible, fully expecting to be sacked at any moment and of course . . . nobody found any of it the least bit funny.

Before we began rehearsal proper Steven Pimlott and I talked through our initial thoughts and impressions of what Touchstone was all about. Court jesters or fools fall into two categories: the clowns and the naturals, the former being professional comedians employed to entertain by virtue of their comic talent and the latter being local simpletons or village idiots who would find themselves dressed up and kept around to be laughed at by the court.

We decided almost immediately that Touchstone was no natural. His wit was too logical, too satirical to be accidental. He was evidently very learned and he appears very much Rosalind and Celia's intellectual equal rather than some poor gormless idiot whom they take pity on. Although Celia calls him a 'natural' early on ('Nature . . . hath sent this natural for our whetstone' (I.ii.31–2)) that is almost certainly a term of gentle abuse rather than a statement of actuality. Therefore as a professional jester Touchstone is, quite literally, living on his wits. The life of a parodist or satirist in the retinue of a recently established usurping monarch cannot be an easy one.

Dictatorships are notoriously suspicious of entertainers, especially ones who comment on current affairs, however humorously, and yet that is one of the traditional roles that a court jester would fulfil. So at the start of the play Touchstone must be treading a fine line: he must make Duke Frederick laugh – and indeed he seems to do just that: 'the roynish clown at whom so oft/Your grace was wont to laugh' (II.ii.8–9) – but he must also prod at the bubble of this fragile new government without bursting it and being silenced forever by a paranoid new authority.

Bearing all that in mind makes Touchstone's escape to Arden with Rosalind and Celia both understandable and inevitable. But it is only later when Touchstone severs all his links with the court by (temporarily) leaving Rosalind and Celia that he can enjoy his own journey. As long as he's 'one of the girls' keeping the princesses company and making them laugh he can never really grow up, but once he's set free in the forest he experiences a sort of crude 'rite of passage' with Audrey as the catalyst. In Arden he can enjoy all the liberties of humanity denied him by his position at court. Of course he is drawn back to court life by the end of the play but he's grown up and he's in love . . . well lust at least! His horizons have expanded. But how should he be played? Steven and I talked through a few ideas. He should certainly be mercurial and chameleon-like; he'd need to be. To survive in Frederick's court he'd have to be all things to all men, responding to each situation appropriately to keep his head (quite literally). Perhaps he'd even have a collection of characters and voices that he could slip in and out of; and that could easily spill over into the way he relates to Corin or Audrey or William in the forest. There should certainly be some sort of play-acting going on in front of Corin and Audrey to whom he is telling, no doubt, all manner of lies about his pedigree. As Jaques notes at the end: 'he hath been a courtier, he swears' (V.iv.41).

There is also the problem about how to make sense of those long passages of text where Touchstone 'goes off on one' and strings long chains of thoughts and witticisms together out of thin air. We needed to create a character who liked the sound of his own voice and the buzz of his own brain. Even outside the court when presumably he wasn't being paid to be 'witty' any longer he persists in playing with words and twisting ideas around. His exchange with Corin in Act Three, Scene Two is full of convoluted lateral thinking and the encounter with William (v.i) is verbal diarrhoea on a grand scale. It struck me that he was like a manic depressive who suffered periods of melancholia – when Jaques reports his encounter with Touchstone (II.vii) the 'motley fool' sounds far from happy – before bouncing through periods of mild mania. The flights of ideas, the energy of thought and the inability to shut up are all traits of manic episodes in a bi-polar mental illness. It is perhaps an actor's affectation to think of Shakespearian characterization in this way, but it helped me to make sense of some of Touchstone's less easily motivated moments. A heightened libido can also be symptomatic of mania which certainly feeds into Touchstone's attachment to Audrey!

In terms of how the character would look, the decision had already been taken by Steven, who was keen that I should be dressed in a traditional fool's outfit. That was fine by me. There are so many references in the text to the 'motley fool' that it would be problematic and unhelpful not to wear the chequered coat and with that comes the three-pronged hat with bells on the end all in vibrant red, green and yellow. In a sense it would help to give the audience an immediate visual reference point as to what Touchstone was in this world and anyway I've always liked long coats so I'd feel very happy in it – whatever the colours. In the end our designer, Ashley Martin-Davis, came up with a very striking and stylish outfit which seemed perfect to me. If Touchstone had to wear the fool's uniform he's enough of a snob to make sure he cut a dash in it.

And so, with another deep breath, we began rehearsal proper. My first session was on Act One, Scene Two, my first scene (obviously enough). Steven's way of working begins with a good couple of hours just reading through the scene and discussing what is going on. Niamh Cusack, Rachel Joyce and I were keen that there should be a real 'girls' changing room' feeling to this scene between Touchstone and the princesses. Of course I felt immediately defeated by Touchstone's first exchange. All that stuff about pancakes and mustard – not exactly opening on a surefire laugh. Steven was keen that we should concentrate on the situation.

Touchstone is being sent to fetch Celia to her father – not his job. He's being used and abused by Duke Frederick, probably to the delight of the other courtiers, which will deeply disgruntle the proud Touchstone. Steven also encouraged me to think the 'certain knight' that swore 'by his honour they were good pancakes and swore by his honour the mustard was naught' (1.ii.61–3) was actually Duke Frederick himself, which added an extra dynamic to the scene as I was being rude about Celia's father. That way the scene began to take shape with the three chums having a bit of a falling out because Touchstone is so annoyed with the Duke. It also helped feed into the story of the play itself with Celia being forced to examine her loyalties – does she side with her increasingly disenfranchised friends or with her increasingly alienating father? – and it shows Touchstone's disenchantment and grumpiness about the state he finds himself in. Then the trio can be united again seconds later as they all take great delight in ridiculing Monsieur Le Beau.

My initial problem was that I felt a great presure to come on and be funny! I was the comic after all, but the whole pancakes/mustard section simply doesn't work as purely a comic turn: it isn't funny enough for a start and the language is so opaque so early on in the play that a modern audience is going to find it very hard to listen to such an odd argument. With something else to play it freed me up to concentrate on what I was saying and why I was saying it. This all sounds ludicrously obvious as I write it now. Of course actors need to be thinking of the situation and motivation for what they are saying, but these famous Shakespearian roles can come with a lot of baggage attached. A lot of people seemed very keen to tell me how hilarious Roy Kinnear had been as Touchstone; how memorable Patrick Wymark; how scene-stealing Kenneth Branagh; or Griff Rhys Jones in the movie version; how only a few years ago on the RST stage Mark Williams had received such glowing reviews in the part. I hadn't seen any of them (I'm sure they were all brilliant) but in my mind they hung like immoveable monuments to great comic acting and to a wee boy frae Paisley coming to the Royal Shakespeare Company for the first time they were spectres that proved hard to banish. Of course the only way to exorcize these ghosts is to do your own version of this new part as you would any other, to approach it as you would a new part in a new play, but I could feel the finger of history tapping on my inexperienced shoulder and the pressure was: 'be funny or sink!'

8 David Tennant as Touchstone, with William (Simeon Defoe), and,
in the background, Audrey (Susannah Elliott-Knight), *As You Like It*,
Act v, Scene i.

Meanwhile back in rehearsal Steven was hammering away at the text,
picking us up on each mixed emphasis and every ignored alliteration
point and slowly the ancient, often unwieldy language was beginning to
come to life and make sense.

It was very early on that we decided I should use my own accent in the
part. He's very much a 'one-off' character within the world of the play so
why shouldn't he have a 'one-off' accent? And besides, if we were going
to explore the idea of using different voices then I'd be in a much better
position if I started from my own. It seemed perfectly logical to me – I
never ceased to be amazed in the coming months how much attention
that particular decision received. I think people thought I was making
some great comment on the serfdom of a nation or something; it was
simply me giving myself one less thing to worry about!

By the time we came to rehearse Touchstone's next scene (II.iv), the
escape to Arden, Steven's vision of the play was beginning to come into
focus. He'd been keen to allow things to develop slowly. (The longer
rehearsal processes afforded at the RSC allow actors and directors a

little more freedom than elsewhere, where deadlines and design require-
ments mean a lot of fundamental decisions have to be made before
rehearsals even begin, sometimes before a full cast has been assembled.)
Steven had decided that we should be costumed fairly traditionally and
in a basically neutral set, but other ideas were evolving gradually as we all
reacted to the play day by day. As far as Arden was concerned, Steven
was coming round to the idea that it should be a far from welcoming
place, nothing like the Utopia that Rosalind and Celia think they're heading for. So we came onstage in the midst of a snowstorm. This allowed
me to play to the hilt Touchstone's self-righteous indignation at being
dragged along (even if underneath it all he's quite glad to be away from
the court). So a line like 'Ay, now am I in Arden, the more fool I. When
I was at home I was in a better place, but travellers must be content'
(II.iv.13–15) can positively drip with sarcasm. My biggest problem in this
scene, and it's one that I've never really come to terms with, is that if
Touchstone is genuinely miserable and disconsolate and unhelpful then
where does one find the springboard to launch into the whole 'Jane
Smile' routine on line 42? Steven suggested that Touchstone is taking it
upon himself to cheer the princesses up but that doesn't seem to be
in keeping with the grumpy complainer of only a few lines before. It
also lands you with the earlier problem of trying to do a 'turn' and very
little else. As a speech it is crammed full of double entendre: 'I broke my
sword upon a stone and bid him take that for *coming* a-night to Jane
Smile' (II.iv.43–4) and obscure references like 'batler' and 'peascod' so
there is a fairly technical exercise to be done in merely trying to help an
audience follow all the things one is trying to communicate as well as
trying to key in to the rest of what's going on. In the end I went for the
idea that Silvius's pining for Phebe has triggered a genuine memory in
Touchstone which he then relives as he retells it – fondly at first as he
remembers Jane, and even with a smile: 'I remember the kissing of her
batler and the cow's dugs that her pretty chopt hands had milked', then
bemusement 'I remember the wooing of a peascod instead of her', even
reliving the tearful frustration of saying ' "Wear these for my sake" '
before snapping out of his reverie to evaluate how ludicrous it all is: 'We
that are true lovers run into strange capers' (II.iv.44–50). And that, I
suppose, is the purpose of the speech – to illuminate the ludicrousness
of being in love so that the whole thing is also being used by Touchstone
as a message to the absent Silvius and, more particularly, to Rosalind,
warning them off all this romantic nonsense. I still don't feel entirely

happy with how it works. I'll probably be sitting in the bath in three years' time and I'll scream 'that's how I should have done that bit!', but for now I tinker away with it every night trying to make it fit its corners into a still round hole.

It's only really after this scene that Touchstone comes into his own as he begins to enjoy his country life. In our production the weather changes and Arden becomes a much more magical, welcoming place. The long exchange with Corin, the shepherd, in Act Three, Scene Two seemed impenetrable at first. Steven was keen to see a battle of wits between the two, like a pair of music hall turns trying to outdo each other. The old pro coming up against the young pretender, if you like, as the countryside meets the court. Of course Touchstone thinks he'll walk away with it, but Corin is much more of a match for him than he'd anticipated. I started work on the scene by trying to throw everything at it. Touchstone became a spinning top chucking off silly voices, silly walks, even acrobatics to try and inject some life into what appeared to me to be a long, wordy and dry argument. Of course what I was doing was running scared of the words and not trusting Shakespeare. I was taken in hand by Cicely Berry, the RSC's world famous voice expert and all round guru who has an almost supernatural gift for sniffing out what actors need to help them find a way into something. She took Arthur Cox (playing Corin) and myself and stripped all the fireworks away and just made us investigate the arguments. I just listened to the brilliantly lucid Arthur and responded to what he said, the arguments began to make sense and the sparring between the two characters became very real. Steven brought us right down stage and sat us with our feet hanging over the front of the thrust so the whole scene began as a very low key chat (as Steven put it, an after dinner stroll through the woods with two chaps content in each other's company) until Touchstone starts to show off: 'In respect of itself, it is a good life; but in respect that it is a shepherd's life, it is naught' (III.ii.14–15) and so on, then throws it over to Corin. 'Hast any philosophy in thee, shepherd?' (line 21) only to find that the simple countryman is more than a match for him. As we play the scene Arthur's Corin remains splendidly solid and unflappable, arching the occasional eyebrow at Touchstone's excesses. In our production, at least whilst Touchstone has the last word, it is Corin who wins the battle. The only silly voice that remains is a dash of Ian Paisley on 'Then thou art damned' (line 33). I'm afraid I couldn't resist it!

Following this exchange comes Touchstone's last scene with Rosalind. Early on in rehearsal Niamh and I cooked up all manner of elaborate ideas about their relationship; that the reason Touchstone ridicules Orlando's poems is due to his jealousy that Rosalind should be falling in love with someone else. Absolute rubbish of course: we tried it for a while but we were playing a subtext that simply didn't exist. The scene is more about Touchstone enjoying taking advantage of the fact that he can ridicule Rosalind and Orlando's affair whilst Rosalind is impotent to stop him, being dressed as the boy Ganymede in the presence of Corin. One nice touch that developed at the end of the scene was that I had a handful of poems torn off the trees and on the line 'You have said, but whether wisely or no, let the forest judge' (III.ii.117) I tossed them into the audience. Initially it was just a device to get them off the stage but it actually seems to ask the audience to act as jury on it all and to evaluate all these different versions of 'love' that are about to pass before them.

From there to the end of the play Touchstone is concerned with wooing the shepherdess Audrey. Susanna Elliott-Knight is a brilliant Audrey and we both toiled long and hard together trying to make sense of their relationship. Does Audrey love Touchstone or does she just like the idea of marrying a rich bloke? Does Touchstone love Audrey or does he just want to get his leg over at any cost? The fact is that Touchstone seems to have no clear idea of what he's after from one moment to the next. Certainly in their first scene together he tells Jaques that the vicar Oliver Martext: 'is not like to marry me well; and not being well married, it will be a good excuse for me hereafter to leave my wife' (III.iii.82–4), so this is not looking like someone ready to make a lifelong commitment, but then the very next time we see the 'happy' couple and Audrey is complaining that Martext would have done the job well enough, Touchstone calls him: 'A most wicked Sir Oliver, Audrey, a most vile Martext' (v.i.5–6) and proceeds to make a great deal of fuss at seeing off Audrey's previous boyfriend William when he comes to 'lay claim' to her.

I found the only way to deal with Touchstone's apparent contradictions through these last few scenes was to stop striving for the logical through-line and to play each moment as it arrives. After all, the evolution of any human relationship is far from linear and playing all the contradictions actually helps to make their courtship more believable in my opinion. I don't think Touchstone is ever convinced that he wants to get married until Hymen casts her spell in the final scene and his indecision is spirited away.

In the first half of Act Five Touchstone and Audrey have two short scenes, sketches really, that add virtually nothing to the (admittedly slender) plot. Act Five, Scene One is really just an elaborate set-up: Touchstone comes on and shows off in front of Audrey's boyfriend, Audrey's boyfriend is decidely unimpressed, Touchstone is crushed and Audrey sorts it all out; and Act Five, Scene Three is just an excuse for a song. In Shakespeare's day it would have given his comic a chance to do his turn and keep the groundlings happy, like a bit of music hall variety really. The cleverer we tried to be about it the harder it seemed to become. Act Five, Scene One is rather like a Monty Python sketch. I adopted a Terry Thomas-esque accent and the props department supplied me with a walking stick version of the traditional jester's stick so that Touchstone transforms himself into a medieval 'hooray Henry'. He is in his element throwing questions and witticisms at the simple William and as the scene goes on his fervour grows so that by the time he gets to: 'He, sir, that must marry this woman' (v.i.45) he is positively flying. We played the rest of the scene with William (Simeon Defoe) watching impassively as Touchstone's mania mounted so that by 'I will o'er-run thee with policy; I will kill thee a hundred and fifty ways' (line 54) I was dancing around him, shrieking and threatening him with my walking stick, and with 'therefore tremble and depart' I was screaming in his face. Simeon coolly grabbed me by the shoulder and floored me with a headbutt for a good bit of (hopefully) amusing bathos.

For most of rehearsal Act Five, Scene Three had been reworked and edited down so that we dispensed with the two singing pages and Touchstone and Audrey sang the song straight out front as a piece of pure music hall. I found it very useful to have that sort of up-front opportunity to develop a relationship with the audience but Steven decided after a few weeks that it clashed with the overall style of the production and put a spoke in the rhythm of the play, so with a week or so of rehearsal left we went back to the script and two of the actors playing foresters (Nathaniel Duncan and Simon Westwood) were roped into the scene as the two singing pages. Ultimately, it seemed the correct decision to play the scene as written and by keeping it within the world of the play it allows the relationship with Audrey to develop a bit further. As the pages sang Audrey started to dance around, embarrassing Touchstone in front of these courtier-singers, but then she came over and started flirting with him until he lost all self-control and as the song came to an end the couple were rolling around the stage together. The cynical Touchstone has been dragged kicking and screaming in to living in the moment as the pages sing: 'And therefore take the present time . . . For love is crowned with the prime.'

So the couple make their way into the final scene and the wedding. The whole sequence where Touchstone meets Duke Senior and goes through the seven degrees of an argument is a bit of a tricky section to be met with at the end of a long play. It isn't Shakespeare's finest comic writing, several commentators have noted how it looks as if it was written fairly hurriedly, probably at a dress rehearsal when the company realized that the two boys playing Rosalind and Celia would need some time to get out of their disguises and into their wedding finery. Again I felt this terrific pressure to 'be funny' – instant death to any comic invention. There is no plot to be moved on, it's simply a delay to the happy ending. I resisted the overwhelming temptation to panic and tried to find a simple way through the scene. It is, of course, an audition. Touchstone, with his new-found wife to support, will need a court to jest in, so the discovery of a benevolent Duke in the forest is an opportunity he can't miss out on. Jaques acts as his feed, introducing him and prompting him to go in to one of his routines. We played on this on the line 'I have had four quarrels, and like to have fought one' (V.iv.45) with Touchstone madly signalling to Jaques out of sight of the Duke until he tumbled what Touchstone was getting at and gave him his cue – 'and how was that ta'en up?' – allowing Touchstone to launch into his party piece on 'the Lie Direct' (whilst excusing his prospective bride as 'an ill-favoured thing, sir, but mine own'). I resisted the temptation to smother the 'Seven Degrees' speech with comic business or vocal gymnastics, firstly because I can't really do all that anyway and secondly because the speech is quite hard to listen to and I felt that if an audience were distracted by any gimmickry it would probably only help to make it sound like so much gibberish. So I concentrated, again with the invaluable help of Cicely Berry and Barbara Houseman of the RSC's voice department, on making it as intelligible as possible. I tried to give each of the seven degrees a different attitude and an increasing level of seriousness as the argument hots up. Jaques became the courtier in the story as I told it to the Duke advancing toward Jaques on each 'degree' then referring back to the Duke to explain what was happening: 'this is called the Reply Churlish' etc. By the time I reached the Lie Direct I was right by Jaques and it was very stern and full of portent; then with Jaques's next line 'and how oft did you say his beard was not well cut' I would let it all drop to a cowardly dismissal of the whole thing 'I durst go no further than the Lie Circumstantial, nor he durst not give me the Lie Direct. And so we measured swords and parted' (lines 82–4). The next speech is the final thing that Touchstone says in the whole play and it's a perfect example of his convoluted, lateral-thinking logic. After listing the seven degrees again he says: 'All these you may avoid but the Lie Direct; and you may avoid that too, with an "If". I knew when seven justices could not take up a quarrel, but when the parties were met themselves, one of them thought but of an "If": as, "If you said so, then I said so", and they shook hands and swore brothers. Your "If" is the only peace-maker; much virtue in "If" ' (v.iv.93–100). I always feel a great sense of achievement when the audience laughs at this bit because it means they've followed the circuitous arguments to the end and tuned in to Touchstone's bizarre way of thinking – and because they are genuinely responding to four-hundred-year-old jokes!

The play's ending is very difficult with Hymen appearing as a fairly crude *deus ex machina* to sellotape all these dodgy marriages together. It's hard to make something like that believable for a modern audience and in our production in Stratford Steven took the very bold step of having Hymen as an older woman entering the stage from the auditorium dressed as a member of the audience in modern-day clothes. It was certainly a disorientating moment for the audience and it proved a very controversial decision. With hindsight it probably didn't entirely work (indeed for the London run Hymen was transformed into an Elizabethan elemental figure who arrived through the back wall of the set) but Steven's intention was very valid: he wanted to emulate the shock of what it would actually be like for a god to appear to these characters and really to play with the frontiers of reality like that. It seems to me that Hymen *must* be a supernatural creature rather than Corin or another character in disguise as some directors have chosen to play it, because she does some fairly supernatural things to these couples: I can't believe Silvius and Phebe would ever get together otherwise and as for Celia and Oliver being 'heart to heart' – they've only just met and Oliver was a total bastard half an hour previously!

One of the last pieces of interpretation in our production comes when Touchstone presents Jaques with a skull just before he heads off to be rid of all the jollity at the new court. A lot of people have asked me why it happens and in truth I can't entirely enlighten them. Steven asked me to do it very early on in rehearsal: he had an idea about showing Jaques to be an elderly Hamlet figure – 'Alas poor Yorick', and so on – but to me it became about other things too. Touchstone is handing over cynicism and disillusionment to the only other character in the play who exhibits them, whilst he paddles off into the sunset for a bit of idealized wedded bliss with Audrey. It's also a way of saying: 'Sod off you grumpy old git!' One student that I spoke to had another opinion; she said: 'Well everyone else is getting married off and having fun – it gives Jaques someone to talk to.'

We've been playing the production now for about eight months and we've done around one hundred performances. As I write this we are about two months into our run in London with another four months ahead of us and around forty-five performances still to do. The production continues to develop and move on and I'm still discovering new ways of playing scenes or more effective ways of saying lines. The ghosts of RSC past still come to visit but they feel slightly more benevolent now; these parts have been being re-interpreted for four hundred years and will continue to be so for as long as there is theatre. I can't hope to do any of it definitively, just 'my' way, and when I realized that I was very liberated. I've never performed any part this many times and yet I'm nowhere near to getting bored yet – but that's usually a sign of good writing. I've tried to be as loyal to Shakespeare's words as possible rather than trying to embellish them with a lot of comic business – like I've said I can't do all that anyway – and I've been really delighted with how much audiences have actually laughed, not tittered knowingly at their own knowledge of what a 'peascod' is or how many Elizabethan double entendres they can count, but because the situations and the words are genuinely funny. I'm not an obvious choice to play the part and I was terrified at the prospect but I've gradually discovered that Shakespeare's clowns *are* funny . . . and I never thought I'd say that ten months ago.

Petruccio in
The Taming of the Shrew

MICHAEL SIBERRY

MICHAEL SIBERRY played Petruccio in Gale Edwards's production of *The Taming of the Shrew* at the Royal Shakespeare Theatre in 1995 and at the Barbican Theatre the following year. His other role that season was Clarence in *Richard III*. Earlier work for the RSC had included Laertes in *Hamlet*, Lorenzo in *The Merchant of Venice*, Jaques in *As You Like It*, Parolles in *All's Well that Ends Well*, Alsemero in Middleton's *The Changeling*, and Macduff in *Macbeth*, as well as the title-role in the revival of *Nicholas Nickleby*. He has worked also at the Chichester Festival Theatre and in Australia as well as in the West End and on television and his Shakespeare roles have included Gratiano, Posthumus, Prince Hal, and Hamlet.

Pleasure at being asked was mixed with apprehension when I was offered the role of Petruccio at Stratford. In my experience *The Taming of the Shrew* had always been a contentious play, the productions I had seen provoking divided responses; and within the play I had found the journey made by Kate and Petruccio an awkward one, not easy to believe in or to follow. I was apprehensive, therefore, about making something coherent out of a play that is traditionally difficult. I had not been in it before, but had seen it a couple of times and had enjoyed listening to Petruccio's language and his use of imagery. But what had always frustrated me, and what gave me pause before taking on the part, were the emotional transitions that Kate and Petruccio go through, the sudden jumps and leaps that it's hard to believe in. As an actor one likes to feel that the situations you are supposed to be in have been led up to in ways that make sense to you psychologically and emotionally.

As I worked on the play I became more aware, I think, that Petruccio is someone who never explains himself: he may tell you what he is doing, but he won't explain why. There are few indications of motivation, little to tell you whether to play it this way or that. The irony is that, as Petruccio, you have an awful lot to say, but sometimes you feel you're

45

not actually saying very much. At the first read-through, for example, I remember beginning with the eager intention of getting stuck into the event but finding myself very soon in one gear – which was pretty loud and fast and didn't stop; and just when one thought there was a pause, along would come another speech which would lead off at the same speed and in the same tone. It became a wearing experience for everyone, not least myself. I felt that I couldn't stop, that I was on a treadmill. The process of picking up the script and playing each speech at face value clearly wasn't going to fit within the context of an overall characterization – or at least that is how I felt on my initial meeting with the part.

Our production's doubling of Sly and Petruccio was there from the beginning. Gale Edwards explained when I first met her to discuss the part that her version of the play began with Sly having a row with a certain 'Mrs Sly'. Also there from the beginning was the idea of Sly's putting himself into his own fantasy as his own hero. There was also to be some kind of resolution at the end, though whether we played one of the existing endings or invented something new was to be explored and worked out in rehearsal. The whole piece, from the word go, was to be set in the context of Sly's dream, with the Slys' relationship paralleled by that of Kate and Petruccio. That relationship was to be rather wild, the world of the play was to be fairly surreal, and the style was to be quite large – broad, but also passionate and, we hoped, moving. I was content to go along with all this because, of the two productions I'd seen earlier, one rather darker and the other more irreverent, it was the irreverent one that seemed to work best and to provide the more endurable experience for its audience. I think a darker version switches off the audience, or at least makes them less responsive. We were determined, with this production, to be entertaining, to make people laugh, so long as, at the end of the play, it was clear that certain parts of the behaviour the audience had been watching were unacceptable. But we wanted to state this only at the end, not lay it on with a trowel from the start; the aim was to round the play off with a statement that would make the audience reassess the whole evening in the light of its final few minutes.

We were aware, as we set out on the rehearsal process, that there would be difficulties, for the play is not as well laid out as some and requires more invention from the actors – and perhaps invites you to take more liberties. Our principal intention was to make the central relationship credible, to make the audience believe that Kate and Petruccio belong together, that right up to the last scene it should work and is about to work. What happens after that is something you have to decide about, and in our case the decision came very much from Gale Edwards about how she saw the end of the play and how she wanted Kate's final speech to be presented. As Petruccio, having been ranting and raving all evening, I felt it was my turn to do some listening and that I had no right to offer an opinion on how it should be done. It was an interesting feeling as an actor that I had no rights here and that I had to take what came to me from that side of the play. So that big final speech was to be very much the work of Gale and of Josie Lawrence as Kate. I felt I had a say in how I responded to it, but the slant that was put onto it was, I felt, beyond my control as Petruccio – and I think it *should* be like that.

We began with the idea of performing the Induction in its entirety, not least because it was the intention of the production to offer Sly's world as the overall context within which the play was to be set. We read it in full at the first read-through and for some time in rehearsals worked on it uncut. And very satisfying it was to work on, very seductive – precisely what it is supposed to be, of course, a piece to 'induce' (the play) and to 'seduce' (Sly). It has an atmosphere and a mood that are delightful, reminding me of some of the scenes in the *Henry IV* plays, with their general feeling of warmth and of the good things of life. Its language and its poetry were all very powerful and compelling and to listen, as Sly, to what the Lord is saying to you is a delight: I could almost feel myself drifting off. The problem, as we discovered when we'd done all this, is that it goes on for about thirty minutes and the play that follows it, particularly in the style we wanted to do it, requires such a change of direction – in atmosphere, in playing style, and in energy level – that the clash seemed impossible. If one wanted to give full credit to the Sly pieces I'm sure one could make them wonderful, but their clash with the play was something we couldn't solve; so in the end they were drastically cut back, and then cut again, all this as we were getting quite close to opening. It was a problem we just couldn't solve, so we had to strip it down to the bare bones and make Sly's seduction by the Lord and his servants more or less instantaneous, which, if he's rather hung over, may make sense: they can say anything to him and he'll believe it. And, anyway, he's dreaming. The same thing happened again at the end of the play where we dispensed with everything and just let Sly embrace Mrs Sly.

Petruccio, in our production, was travelling the world when he arrived in Padua. The city is a step up from Verona, and Petruccio is free, after the death of his father and the inheritance of a certain amount of property, to take the world by storm. That, I thought, was what he had in mind and he's outrageous and transparently obvious to people. I think Petruccio comes into the play simply 'flying': he's happy to be in Padua, anticipates great times ahead, and is in search of wealth, power and adventure. And with him comes his servant Grumio, who sees through all his bluster and bragging and is there to pick holes in it and bring him down to earth. I wanted the audience to like Petruccio, but to see through him too. Nor do I think he himself wants to be taken too seriously to begin with. He knows he's a windbag and a boaster, but he's there to enjoy it, to have a laugh with it, to send himself up – and with the last, Grumio is certainly ready to help. All the talk of the battles he has fought, and the lions, is obviously hugely exaggerated, and when Grumio pulls the rug from under his feet he knows he's fair game; that is part, indeed, of the game they play together.

Playing games is something Petruccio does throughout the play, whether the games are funny or dark, and he sets the tone as soon as he arrives. He's not bothered about being mocked for it: it's water off a duck's back to him. He likes to be unpredictable, to startle people, to head off in unexpected directions; and he's not afraid of falling flat on his face, which he's no doubt done many times before. He simply picks himself up and carries on. He is unashamed, has no conscience to bother him, and he's up-front and totally honest. He's also quite sharp and when he becomes serious about something it concentrates his mind so that his genuine intelligence makes him play the game extremely well.

I assumed that this is the first time that the idea of marriage has ever crossed his mind. I took him to be in his early thirties – certainly not too young – and now travelling with marriage on his agenda. He sees it as something that it is about time to embark on and believes that it should be an advantageous, business-like arrangement: 'if wealthily, then happily', as he puts it (I.ii.75). His goal is a match that brings as much wealth, and power, as possible; feelings don't come into it. He thinks he is now going to play the game that everyone else has indulged in and win out with wealth. Padua, a wealthy town, is a good place to slip into this game of the arranged marriage and to do well at it. He is entirely confident that he can marry simply anyone so long as she is wealthy. The emotional side of it is of no consequence to him: he thinks he can deal with that. But on meeting Kate he realizes that she isn't anything that he has been led to expect.

9 Michael Siberry as Petruccio, with Katherina (Josie Lawrence), *The Taming of the Shrew*, Act IV, Scene iii: 'is the jay more precious than the lark/Because his feathers are more beautiful?'

Petruccio recognizes that Kate is not at all what he was expecting from the moment he sets eyes on her, before they even start speaking. In the course of that first conversation she sparks off him and he off her and instantly there is a rapport between two strangers that is intimate, witty, and erotic. It happens through a kind of mutual abuse, but it's a genuine spark, a real surge of adrenalin that goes through him when they meet. He has never experienced anything quite like this interchange and is obviously overjoyed that the wealthy woman he is to marry is also so extraordinary and so exciting to be with. I don't know that it is quite 'love at first sight'; there is an incredibly strong attraction, but love is perhaps something that comes a little later. But the instant response, and rapport, certainly change everything he has felt in his life up to that moment and there is something in the exchange that makes him more determined than ever that this *is* to be: the thought of marrying her now becomes an emotional commitment way beyond the question of marrying wealth. 'Will you, nill you, I will marry you', he says (II.i.264), and it is not so much a threat to her as a statement of intention for himself, almost an elated declaration. This is something he did not expect at all, but he knows that it is right for him. In spite of everything that has happened in the scene – the abuse, the slap in the face, the rolling around – he senses, he knows, that this is right, that this is the person he can marry.

In the course of meeting Kate's father and her family and household he has learned something of the situation in which she, and the persons in the subplot, find themselves. He is surprised, if not shocked, by the extent to which they are prepared to be rid of her under almost any circumstances. I think this explains something of his behaviour at the wedding: he is late, and dressed outrageously, partly to unsettle Kate, but also to humiliate the family, and in particular Baptista. He wants to see how far he can go, how unpredictable he can be, simply to shock. He enjoys being at liberty to do almost anything, knowing that they will put up with it to get rid of her.

He has also, of course, started to play his game with Kate, trying to wrong-foot her. It is an outrageous and even brutal game, but that is part of his nature, part of the way he is. In the wedding scene he shows something of this to her, seeming to say 'How about this? What do you think of this?' She had set out her stall very clearly at their first meeting and he now has a fair indication of the kind of woman she is. There is something in him that wants to lay down rules and conditions that say 'I'm in charge', but at the same time something in her response to him that pushes him further. In a way they wind each other up, provoking more outrageous behaviour. By the second half, of course, the game that Petruccio is playing has become very dark, and however one tries to perform it it remains dark. It's a tough game, the sort Petruccio plays when he plays games, and in playing it with the particular character of Kate it goes to new levels and into darker areas; there is something in the way they respond to each other that takes it into those places. Petruccio has probably always been a fairly wild and outrageous character, but he has never been as he now is with Kate.

The next stage of the game is played when the couple return to Petruccio's house. The idea in our production was that the servants are not always as extreme in their behaviour as this. It is obviously a fairly irreverent household – the relationship Petruccio has with Grumio is reflected to a lesser degree in that with his other servants – but the events that greet Kate's arrival have been set up. It is a sort of Gothic horror scene, a Breugelesque world, something out of a Hitchcock film

– amusing, in a way, but also quite extreme, and alarming. Kate is aware, I think, that something strange is going on, that it isn't quite serious or real, but there is still something frightening about it. She is also, of course, genuinely hungry, as well as uncomfortable, wet, and miserable, even if there is something about Petruccio's behaviour that makes it clear that he is playing with her. We decided that the bare bones of the situation had been decided in advance, the framework of the situation for the arrival of Kate and Petruccio laid out, but that beyond that the situation is to be extemporized as it goes along, with cousin Ferdinand and spaniel Troilus and the rest invented on the spur of the moment. Petruccio leads and the others take their cues from him. We tried, in rehearsal, the idea of making the situation a bit more obvious to the audience, with the servants being prompted and nudged into their roles, but we found that it all became rather heavy-handed. The audience quickly finds out that the servants aren't really like this and to allow them to share a little of Kate's side of the experience, a little of her bewilderment, may be useful. It is as if she has been set down in a foreign land; the idea is to faze her. We wanted the audience to be uncertain about it, to be asking the question 'Is Petruccio really serious in this?' – just as they might ask 'Is Hamlet really mad?'.

When one plays Petruccio there are, I think, roads that it is important not to go down. The text seems to say that you can be as cruel as you like, but if you really start putting on the pressure, being really cruel – for which you have the language and the structure of the speeches to support you – it becomes simply too dark and bleak. So much cruelty is implicit in what you say and do anyway, that to play it too strongly is to overstate the obvious, to lay it on crudely. If, on the other hand, you try to keep it light, if you look as if you are thinking 'this is wonderful and I'm more and more drawn to her by the way she deals with this experience or that' (and I think that *is* what is happening to him), if you look as if you are enjoying yourself and not simply putting pressure on Kate in a nasty, vindictive way, the result is much more interesting. In rehearsal, and in the early days of performance, I attempted to go altogether that way, trying not to allow the mood to darken at all. But that is a hopeless quest: no matter how much you try to jump around, no matter how good your comedy techniques are, the shadows are still there; you have to acknowledge them, but play against them too. Petruccio's speech at the end of the scene of their arrival at his house (IV.i.174ff.) is immensely helpful in this. It shows him, in its hawking images, absolutely full of admiration for Kate – and the images are splendidly powerful and striking. He may be talking about a falcon being under his control, but birds of prey are never truly tame: they come to you because you have something they want, something they need. The language, therefore, is all a wonderful compliment to her. Why he loves her, why he grows to love her more and more as the story goes on, is because he responds to her spirit. He tests that, and is testing it all the time, and this speech is a testament of his response.

The speech precedes the most difficult sequence of the play for Petruccio, the scenes of the so-called 'taming school' in which food is withheld from Kate and the clothes the tailor has brought are rejected. I always felt as if I were on the brink here with the audience, who are beginning to feel that this has all gone on long enough, and I wondered sometimes whether there might not be one or two scenes too many at this stage in the play: 'Here we go again – and again.' I have mentioned the feeling of growing darkness about the play and it is most apparent in this area. Petruccio's game-playing seems to have become less imaginative here, more repetitive, and in danger of becoming more brutal. It's difficult, too, because the tailor scene is followed by the 'sun and moon' scene where there is an important coming together between them; one wants to try to move the relationship towards that, to offer some kind of preparation for it, or audiences will find the fact that Kate has come round simply too hard to believe. Petruccio addresses her gently enough in the tailor scene – 'sweeting', 'sweet Kate', 'my honey love' (IV.iii.36, 41, 52) – but in the context of his actions while he says these things there are problems. During rehearsal I remember thinking, 'Take every chance that you get: just look at her, watch her, take every moment, because there is so little within the text that allows you to show any kind of sincere concern.' And it is important to try to do this with looks and gestures, because if you do it too much in your words you will find that your next line turns what you have just said completely on its head, and that undermines the sincerity that Petruccio should have in his feelings towards Kate and makes him seem sarcastic. I found little gaps in the action where I could just sit and watch her, perhaps while the tailor and Grumio were having their row, or I would try to get her interested in the fact that the tailor is flustered, perhaps nudging her to encourage her to find it amusing. It's not easy, however, and I found myself wishing the scenes were funnier. Certainly the audience is not terribly inclined to be amused at this point. I had the feeling that Petruccio was hoping against hope that she might have joined in more with the scene, might have found it less of an ordeal, might even have found that it made her laugh. I hoped that she might have joined in the game, have begun to ridicule the tailor herself, might just have got onto Petruccio's wavelength as he pokes fun at the clothes and at the man who made them. But it doesn't happen.

At the end of the tailor scene they are alone together for the first time since their initial meeting. Petruccio's speech here (IV.iii.165ff.) begins awkwardly; he really seems not to know how he is going to approach it. This is the one point in the play where he genuinely tries to explain himself, to articulate a theory he has about values (see figure 9):

> What, is the jay more precious than the lark
> Because his feathers are more beautiful? (IV.iii.171–2)

He tries to tell her that he doesn't care how she looks, or what people have said about her in the past; what she is, and what she is to him, is wonderful. Without fine clothes, without polished, acceptable behaviour, it is only what she *is* that he cares about: 'So honour peereth in the meanest habit' (line 170). He is trying to say something that matters very much to him and, as he sees it, to their relationship, but of course she isn't receptive because of what he's been doing for the last three scenes – and obviously he is insensitive to the effect that all that has had on her. He is not getting through because she has been driven somewhere else. Maybe he was hoping that in this moment of stillness she would say 'Well *that* was fun – what do we do now?', but of course she doesn't. I brushed a bit of hair off her face and tried to be as tender as I could in order to make some impression with what I was saying, in the hope that she might come on board; but she wouldn't, and I stormed off. It is an important moment in the development of their relationship, and an interesting clash. Petruccio has gone so far down the road he set off on that when he wants to call off the game and say 'Let's just talk', he finds that it's impossible to shift the direction. The game is no longer in his control; it is impossible to behave for so long in that way and then simply switch off.

His outburst at the end of the scene derives from precisely this. He says it's seven o'clock; clearly it isn't but his idea is simply 'All you have to do is to play my game'; she, of course, is thinking only 'I don't understand; obviously it's *not* seven o'clock.' He is deeply upset; the game has stopped when he says:

10 Michael Siberry as Petruccio, with Katherina (Josie Lawrence),
The Taming of the Shrew, Act v, Scene ii: 'And place your hands below
your husband's foot.'

> Look what I speak, or do, or think to do,
> You are still crossing it.   (iv.iii.188–9)

This is an emotional outburst; he wants the game to end now. He is
ready to move on, aware that what he is doing is becoming irrelevant;
and yet he is trapped within it because he doesn't quite know how to stop
the 'taming'. It is no longer about trying to break someone down; it
has become a battle of wills. But his desire to change the rules, to relate
as two people who, as he sees it, have become close and are, in spite of
everything, sharing an experience, is not as easy as he thinks it should
be. There is awful disappointment in Petruccio here, and confusion: he
has been showing off the methods of the 'taming school' to the people he
earlier tried to flout, so he can't just drop the game; but he also believes
that he and Kate have had what one might call a 'moment', and as far as
she is concerned, of course, they haven't. He wants to get off the hook,
and he can't.

The resolution to this comes in the 'sun and moon' scene – and in
our production it was Kate who got him off the hook. No one has won

or lost by the end of this scene, no one has been tamed or subdued or suppressed. Kate simply says to Petruccio, in perfectly clear language, 'Since what you say changes as rapidly as your mind, I'll say whatever you want me to say. But what does it mean if I do? What *does* it mean?' It's the end of one phase and the beginning of something new; the old, strange way of relating to each other is to move into something different. There is joy in this scene as there is in a lot of *The Taming of the Shrew*. People enjoy watching it no doubt because there are things about the central relationship that are absolutely real even in a contemporary setting – perhaps not in the basic premise of the play, but in the more general ways that people relate to each other. It's a fairly outrageous example, obviously, but there is the ring of truth about the way people invent a special language to talk to each other, whether it's mutual abuse, as here, or something else. And there is also the moment of realization that a relationship is working only on a superficial level, without addressing all the profound things for which a language has not been found, a language that allows you to be honest and open and vulnerable with each other. The sun and moon scene seemed to us to deal with this point in the development of a relationship. Kate's line 'Forward, I pray, since we have come so far' (IV.v.12) was, in our production, one of the most important things she says. We took it to mean, not simply that they have stopped on their journey and are now to continue, but that something with far more significant resonances is being recognized: 'We have come a long way together since our first meeting; we have been through the most outrageous experiences; and we have now come to an understanding in which we are just beginning to find out about each other; so let us go forward from here.'

It is at this point that she at last agrees to say what he wants her to say. It completely wrong-foots Petruccio; he doesn't quite know how to react. But by this point I think he loves this woman and when she says 'be it sun, or moon, or what you please . . . it changes even as your mind' (IV.v.13, 20) he is just charmed and overwhelmed by her energy of spirit. And I think she suddenly realizes that she can deal with him as well and for the first time we see happiness in her. He therefore carries on his game because she has also started to play it and in the encounter with Vincentio she really begins to enjoy it and plays it very well too. It thus becomes, for both of them, '*our* first merriment' (IV.v.76), the meaning of which, for Vincentio, is merely 'the joke we played on you at first', but for the two of *them* means, much more significantly, 'our first moment of mutual happiness'. The war of attrition between them has suddenly been called off, a war which has no doubt gone on for all the first part of the journey, with him insisting that she say that things are green that aren't green; and the dogged, tired, no longer funny (if it ever was) struggle between two weary people is suddenly over. There is immense release here, issuing into joyful fun at the expense of Vincentio, until he, too, is taken on board, for there is a great warmth that comes from these people and he responds to it. In a mood of enormous camaraderie they all set off to Padua – where, at last, Kate kisses Petruccio.

Our production certainly romanticized that kiss. It was a big, long 'screen' kiss, with a little of the dialogue cut to heighten the romance of it, to mark it as the moment when they are together as a couple. There is a bond between them now; they are on the same wavelength and at the beginning of a more conventional relationship. From here they can start to talk to each other, to respect each other, to begin to grow as two people who are together because they are right for each other. All this is marked in that kiss, a kiss that is participated in mutually. The kiss is the consummation of the ideal, recording the fact that these two wonderful people, these two larger-than-life, grand, heroic people, have come together. It's wild and it's powerful and it's fabulous and it's good – and, of course, it's all in Sly's dream. Whether or not it is real is the question that has to be faced in the next scene.

There are debts to be paid for the process of growing together that the audience has been watching. Kate may have agreed to play Petruccio's game, and to have a good time playing it, but there is a lot of residue left from the experience that she has been through. Sooner or later, as a couple, as two people who are now going to say that they are 'together' and that there is a bond between them, they will have to face the fact that there is ground that they must go back over, a past that must be revisited. In our production this happened sooner rather than later. The final scene was presented as a wedding reception, with everyone happy, everyone having had a bit to drink, and Kate and Petruccio coming in as a couple, happily together. In such an environment everyone starts to relax and to talk about things they would normally never dream of talking about; or they start to venture opinions that at other times they would keep to themselves, or to bring things out into the open that would otherwise be left unsaid; they feel at liberty to tease and indulge in a bit of leg-pulling at each others' expense. Inevitably in this situation the relationship between Kate and Petruccio becomes a source of needling and the challenge is thrown down: Baptista tells Petruccio that he thinks he's got 'the veriest shrew of all' (v.ii.64) and implies that his marriage is doomed.

Obviously this is something he should never say, but in the context of this slightly drunken situation it is a remark that everyone can relate to and understand. Petruccio emphatically denies it and is so confident in the wonderful relationship that he and Kate now have that he feels secure in making a wager on it. He sees it as yet another game, but his bet is not on the fact that she is now completely quiescent and under his thumb but on his belief that they have a relationship in which they understand each other: he genuinely believes that, if she understands the context in which this new game is being played, she will co-operate and they will score financially. Once more he is playing one of his games, and he does so without any thought of how Kate will feel or what it will mean to her. He simply imagines that, as a couple, they now function so well that she will understand. As it turns out she does understand perfectly well what is going on, but she also knows that the time has come to say that this is not acceptable: 'What you may have done in the past you don't do now'. The moment of reckoning has arrived.

Petruccio has pushed Kate too far; he has abused her trust. He would say to her, as they went home after the party: 'I'm sorry, but it was only a game. I'm sorry if it offended you, but I thought you understood. Because you co-operated we've made thousands and thousands of pounds. We've had a great success. Don't you understand?' What *he* doesn't understand is that he has abused her trust and used it to humiliate her. In her response to his demand that she tell Bianca and the Widow the duty that a woman owes to her husband she therefore humiliates him and the whole of the assembled company; she humiliates him by telling him what he expects to hear, over and over again, as if to say 'Is this what you want? Yes, this *is* what you want. And then, of course, it follows that *this* should happen.' And she does it over and over again, with increasing intensity, until it becomes obvious that by stating the ideal of marital relationships that Baptista, Petruccio and the rest of their world believe in, and that Kate is required to subscribe to, and by stating it with such power and passion, the very force and repetitiveness of the statement make it clear that something is wrong. The more Petruccio listens to it the more rapidly he is first sobered and then shamed by it. He realizes that what she is describing is not the relationship that he and Kate have, not the relationship that they ever wanted to have;

it is the beginning of his acknowledging that his behaviour has been unacceptable.

Petruccio's motive for risking his relationship with Kate on this wager seems to me to be largely financial. His initial motivation for marriage was money, not for itself but for the power it brings, and that has never quite gone away; it remains a powerful force for him and he acknowledges it from the beginning. It comes back here as the distraction that makes him abuse Kate's trust, and as the catalyst that makes him realize how wrongly he has behaved. He asks Kate to go through all these things in the final scene because he mistakenly thinks that she will understand his wish to win that great pile of money. When he sends for her initially she comes because he has asked her and because she is perfectly willing to do so. Then she realizes the game that is going on and sees that she is being used and it is at that point that the scene turns. He then goes even further because more money has been offered to him to fuel his ego. It would, however, be to oversimplify his journey to say that, at the beginning, his search for money leads him to a wife with whom he falls in love, while at the end his continuing search for money drives that wife from him. It is Petruccio himself, not the money, that destroys the relationship: he makes this final wager because he has failed to understand the nature of Kate's experience and the importance of the gesture of commitment she has made to him. He is certainly in love with her by this point, and overjoyed that they have come together; but he does not understand the journey she has made, even though he has been partly responsible for putting her through it. Here he shows how little he understands her, and what she has done; in the context of the dream it is therefore the end of the relationship. If it hadn't all been a dream perhaps they might have gone home together and Petruccio's education would have begun. It is curious, in a play in which money is so important (to Petruccio as he arrives in Padua, to Baptista, to everyone in the sub-plot, to the whole set of beliefs that they all subscribe to at the start), that money is not an issue addressed by Kate and Petruccio until this eleventh hour. And at the eleventh hour it precipitates the end of their relationship – for our production cut the dialogue that follows Kate's long speech. Petruccio now wakes up as Sly and returns to a marriage in which money plays no part, for the Slys haven't got any.

Kate, in our production, left Petruccio at the end of her speech. He understood and acknowledged that he had made a dreadful mistake and a permanent one – a mistake that cannot be undone. He fell to his knees, trying to make some sense of what had happened, understanding that he has made an awful mistake and trying to come to terms with it. But it is too late: Kate is receding, and the dream is fading. I dropped the bank-notes that had been wagered, and the cheque from Baptista, as I tried to move towards Kate, falling to my knees as she put out her hand on 'My hand is ready, may it do him ease' (v.ii.178). But he couldn't take her hand after what she has just said; he just put his head in his own hands, aware of his terrible mistake and of the abuse of her trust, but not knowing what to do. She begins to recede, and so do the characters around her, back into the dream; he reaches out to her, but she's disappeared, she's gone. The relationship of the couple in Sly's fantasy has vanished, has failed; the Lord comes back, puts a coat over him, tells him to wake up, and retreats. As Sly wakens his wife returns to find him on the ground; he is happy to see her, and they embrace. He is ready to return to the relationship he has always known, in the beginning and here again at the end.

And that was the end of our play. I simply don't know if what he has dreamed is going to affect him in the future. For me his final thought was something to the effect 'Well, this is our relationship, it's full of ups and downs and I expect it always will be, but I'm thankful for it.' For some people watching the production it was a final image of hope, for others of inevitable suffering for her. There is no saying who is right, for it was merely a gesture, she standing, he kneeling, she putting a hand on his back, like the father receiving the prodigal son in the Rembrandt painting. These two people mean something to each other; the meaning for those watching the play will always be subjective.

Autolycus in
The Winter's Tale

RICHARD MCCABE

RICHARD MCCABE is an Associate Actor of the Royal Shakespeare Company and played Autolycus in Adrian Noble's production of *The Winter's Tale* at the Royal Shakespeare Theatre in 1992 and at the Barbican Theatre the following year, after which the production toured nationally and internationally. His other roles that season were Tranio in *The Taming of the Shrew* and Christopher Marlowe in *The School of Night*. A wide range of earlier work for the RSC had included Chiron in Deborah Warner's production of *Titus Andronicus*, Lacy in *Hyde Park*, Sir Glorious Tiptoe in *The New Inn*, Wagner in *Dr Faustus*, Truewit in *The Silent Woman*, and Puck in *A Midsummer Night's Dream*. He returned to the RSC in 1996 to play Flamineo in *The White Devil*, Plotwell in *Three Hours after Marriage*, and Thersites in *Troilus and Cressida*. A wide range of roles, classical and modern, in the provincial and London theatre and on television, have recently included Caliban in *The Tempest* at Birmingham Repertory Theatre and Ford in *The Merry Wives of Windsor* at the Royal National Theatre.

If the casting of Autolycus depended on a pure singing voice I would never have been asked to play the part. An essential element of his character is an ability to express himself in song. Having always been embarrassed by my singing voice, the playing of Autolycus struck me as a potentially disastrous venture. However, it was not a challenge I could easily turn down although I knew it would be a painful process. I figured from past experience that if I met and overcame the challenge of the part I would feel a strong sense of achievement and exorcise some personal demons at the same time. If I failed I resolved to fail spectacularly; I believe there is a thin line between brilliantly good and thrillingly awful.

There is a honeymoon period between agreeing to play a part and the first day of rehearsal, and I often find this the most exciting time. Initial instincts are usually the best ones, and these I take into rehearsal to act as a foundation on which to build my character. It is not advisable to have too fixed an idea of a character though, as you invariably learn most about it by interaction with other actors in the process of rehearsals. Theatre is about compromise and once the director has given you her or his vision of the piece and the designer has shown you the model of the set and outlines for costume, there may be very few of your initial ideas that fit into this particular view of the world of the play.

My initial question when approaching a part is to ask what my character's function is in the play overall. This proved a surprisingly difficult question to answer. Autolycus doesn't appear until the fourth act. He has little to do with the plot. He is not a character who experiences an emotional journey, who is transformed, by the events of the play, into some one better or worse than before; he does not experience a Damascan moment of self-revelation. He appears and remains a self-contained entity, sure of his beliefs, unshakeable in his pursuit of them. On the surface he seems a light-hearted, likeable rogue, always ready with a song. On closer examination of the text he reveals himself as arrogant, selfish, self-centred and mean. Added to this that he is a thief, a liar, a pickpocket and all-round cheat, there was a danger he could in the playing come across as highly unpleasant. How could the audience possibly warm to this character (who disadvantages others at every turn), a man who 'beloved of no-one, cares for no-one'? I knew he should be charming and provoke laughter, but how?

I looked to his ancestry. In many ways he seemed unique. He was in the line of the all-licensed, prose-speaking fool but bore no resemblance that I could see (save for an ever-ready singing voice) to the Robert Armin line of fools that replaced the knockabout physical clown of Will Kemp. The advent of Armin heralded a darker, more intellectually complex character, with Touchstone probably the first of the Armin fools. This pedigree continues with Feste, Lavache, right through to the Fool in *King Lear*, whose wit is almost devoid of humour, a picture of grim desolation. Into this array of figures it is very difficult to place Autolycus, although he does share certain characteristics with his cousins; he talks directly to the audience, offers an alternative view to the action of the play, and is almost completely in prose.

The speaking of prose in Shakespeare can itself present problems. Verse gives actors a structure to work from. It is a support that usually gives us the rhythm of a speech. With prose there is no such obvious structure. One has to define one's own meter. I am constantly surprised that the RSC, who rightly place much emphasis on verse-speaking, do

11 Richard McCabe as Autolycus, *The Winter's Tale*, Act IV, Scene iii:
'When daffodils begin to peer'.

not lavish the same attention on prose, which is in many ways harder to speak.

Uncertain, then, of his function, his ancestry and even his essential sympathy as a character, I approached rehearsals with a feeling of excitement and dread.

Autolycus does not appear in the first half of the play. The audience, through Leontes, is treated to a display of the worst aspects of human nature. His obstinacy, and unwillingness to listen to reason, culminate in the death of his wife and child, and the rejection of a baby he believes, wrongly, to have been fathered by someone else. It is almost a complete three-act tragedy. With the fourth act time advances sixteen years and the action shifts from the ice-cold world of Sicilia to the warm shores of Bohemia. After so much guilt and remorse it is very daring of Shakespeare to introduce a character with no conscience or sense of morality, but Autolycus's entrance signals the beginning of spring and the regeneration of life.

Certain previous productions have made a stylistic connection between Sicilia and Bohemia to make the play a unified whole. Our director, Adrian Noble, felt very strongly that they should be as different as possible, as if moving from darkness into light. To this end, it was decided early in rehearsals to give Autolycus a fantastical, unnaturalistic entrance. I descended from above on a sort of tree whose multi-coloured branches sprouted balloons. It was a bold gesture that told the audience we were now entering a different world, and not to be influenced by what had gone before. I remember that when the screen lifted to reveal a sky-blue cyclorama and brightly coloured balloon tree, the feeling of release in the audience was almost palpable.

I flew down singing 'When daffodils begin to peer'. Shaun Davey wrote another version of the song which I felt did not possess the minor to major shift that the play here takes. Happily the second version was a triumph, and by selling the song in an Archie Rice end-of-the-pier manner it was not as traumatic as I had envisaged. After the song Autolycus gives us a summary of his character. He tells us that he has served Florizel in some capacity, worn fine clothes but is now out of a job. It was important to decide what sort of job he had and why he is no longer employed. I had recently seen a television programme on insider trading in the City of London, and how the so-called Thatcher boom years had created a type of high-flying, working-class financial dealer. It seemed possible that Autolycus may have been a minor court official attached to the privy purse, who succumbed to personal greed. Discovery of financial mismanagement would be good reason for ejection from the court. During rehearsals a photographic session was arranged in which we shot an image depicting two court henchman restraining a short-haired, Armani-suited Autolycus from striking a photographer. This photograph was enlarged above the legend 'SERVANT GUILTY', and both put on the cover of a large-print mocked-up newspaper named *The Bohemian Gazette*. By producing the newspaper on the line 'but now I am out of service' (IV.iii.14), I was able to give the audience a past history and a reason for my present situation.

Autolycus clearly enjoys his life. As a vagabond he is his own master and free to travel wherever his fancy takes him. All roads are the right road. 'And when I wander here and there [with a sexual implication] I then do most go right' (IV.iii.17). He tells us that his father named him Autolycus, betraying his classical ancestry. He was 'littered under Mercury' who was the god of all dishonest persons and noted for his cunning. There is a comparison with Florizel's character whose disguise as a swain associates him with Apollo. Shakespeare's source for this, as with so much else, was Ovid.

I was particularly struck by the admission that 'beating and hanging are terrors to me' (line 29). In such a declamatory opening speech, brimming with self-confidence, the uncertain tone of this one line gives us – albeit momentarily – a glimpse of vulnerability in his otherwise impervious, jocund outer shell. In performance I had my neck made up in an ugly, purple bruise which I revealed on the line, suggesting Autolycus had once narrowly escaped a lynching, the memory and scar of which will always haunt him. However, displaying great equanimity he delivers his personal doctrine and, I think, a key line to his character: 'For the life to come I sleep out the thought of it' (line 29).

The robbing of the Young Shepherd is the first opportunity we get to see Autolycus in action. Disguise and the ability to transform himself are chief constituents of Autolycus's character and I made a decision early on in rehearsals that accents should play a key role in this. This was not a decision I took lightly – accents being my other *bête noir*, occupying a twin peak of unattainability along with singing. However, I knew it had to be done to do full justice to the character so, along with my extra-curricular lessons to improve the tone and quality of my singing voice, I now added phonetic pronunciation lessons covering the three chief accents I intended to pursue. I say extracurricular: the truth is that the

whole job is extra-curricular, and once switched on to a part it is very difficult to turn off. It invades all your waking and sleeping hours like a bad
conscience and is only stilled by finding solutions that are acceptable to
both your character's inner life and one's own sense of personal truth.

I had Autolycus choose to adopt the Young Shepherd's accent having
overheard him in his monologue prior to our scene. This proved to be
somewhere between Warwickshire and Lancashire and gave ample
opportunity for highlighting words with rogue sounds. It led the Young
Shepherd to believe that I was truly a local man and to offer to help me.
The scene as a whole benefits greatly, as do all Autolycus's appearances,
from stage business. This has become something of a pejorative term
though I fail to understand why. I think gratuitous 'gagging' unsup-
ported by or unrelated to the text can be a bad thing, but audiences
can generally tell the difference between an actor massaging his own
ego, and a piece of well-executed, character-led stage business which
requires skill, invention and precision. All this may serve as an apology
for our playing of the scene which was full to overflowing with 'biz'.

Graham Turner and I thought to maximize the comic effect of the
scene by having me fleece him completely. Like so many others, the stage
direction 'picks his pocket' is editorial and not to be found in the first
Folio. This gave us the freedom to punctuate the dialogue throughout
with thefts beginning with Autolycus pocketing a handkerchief, and
culminating in him riding off on the Young Shepherd's bicycle. Autolycus can't resist the opportunity for self-publicity and spends nearly
half the scene talking about himself, delighting in the Young Shepherd's
acknowledgement of his fame. At the conclusion of the scene, buoyed
with the Young Shepherd's coffers, Autolycus sings his way off to the
sheep-shearing with, I think, another key character line:

> A merry heart goes all the day,
> Your sad tires in a mile-a.   (IV.iii.103–4)

The sheep-shearing is a monstrously difficult scene to pull off. Its
jollity can feel forced, its sweetness cloying, its dénouement savage. By
the time Autolycus enters (again with a song) the party is in full swing.
'Lawn as white as driven snow' (IV.iv.220) is a wonderful sales device. It
plays heavily on the ladies' vanity (every item in the song is for a woman)
as well as the mens' generosity to their loved ones, and with a chant that
speaks over four centuries to our own consumer-conscious society,
advises all to 'Come buy'. It also allows the actor a lot of freedom to

12 Richard McCabe as Autolycus at the sheep-shearing festival (*The Winter's Tale*, Act IV, Scene iv), with the Young Shepherd (Graham Turner), Dorcas and Mopsa (Jenna Russell and Stephanie Jacob), and villagers.

display his selling technique which is still to be found at any street market in the country. The audacity and complete confidence in his ability to deceive all is again evident. With a wonderful sense of self-irony, Autolycus's first line to the Young Shepherd is to be wary of cozeners.

A potential problem with the scene that follows was in taking Autolycus's sales pitch too literally. Talking of a usurer's wife giving birth to twenty money bags or a ballad-singing fish appears to stretch the villagers' credulity to the limit. But it is not necessary for their collective IQ to drop by seventy-five per cent whenever Autolycus appears. Street sellers in our own time use such techniques frequently. With tongue firmly in cheek any outlandish tale is permissible. Indeed the stranger the tale, the more delighted the audience, a harmless conspiracy at which the younger members of the community will gawp in wonder while the elders laugh and enjoy the tales; as innocent and commonplace as the selling of Santa Claus. The shepherds are no fools. Their world may not be as sophisticated as the court, but it is in every way as worldly. Autolycus's later dismissal of them is more a testament to his abilities as a trickster than to any overt naivety on their part. Indeed, Autolycus is taken by surprise at his own ability to dupe them.

During rehearsals Adrian had the inspired idea of setting up a full afternoon's improvisation in which the whole scene could be enacted in real time, in our own words. This took place in his Stratford house's back garden which looked onto fields and meadows: an ideal setting. The weather on the day was glorious. Food was prepared, drinks brought and people arranged into family groups. Florizel and Perdita billed and cooed, Mopsa and Dorcas fought for the attentions of the Young Shepherd, while Polixenes and Camillo, heavily disguised, skulked around convincingly. The great advantage of group improvisations is that it stops actors from being self-serving. It forces everybody truly to listen to each other and leave themselves open to the developing dramatic situation. Ideally, this should prevent people using the circumstances for their own ends. However, having said that, this is precisely what I went on to do.

Autolycus's nature obliges him to exist in a vacuum and to manipulate situations. A difficulty with Autolycus, as with other breakers of the fourth wall, is to define their boundaries. If one is given the licence to talk directly to the audience it puts your character in a privileged position. Knowing how far to take this 'special relationship' is the work of many years. Realizing the need to gain everybody's attention I placed myself some distance away and approached the assembly slowly, playing an accordion. This had the desired effect and I was able to launch into selling the assortment of impotency cures and anti-wrinkle creams I had prepared earlier. A large part of that afternoon's work was transferred straight into the production, although we all regretted the loss of the truly climactic rendition of the satyrs' dance which proved too wet to recreate on the Stratford stage.

In performance I used simple conjuring tricks to ingratiate myself with the villagers and, replete with a suitcase full of merchandise and a fresh costume, I was ready for business. To mislead the Young Shepherd I employed another accent. In selling the song 'Two maids wooing a man' Autolycus informs his audience 'there's scarce a maid westward but she sings it' (IV.iv.288) and earlier talks of a fish appearing on the coast. I used this to suggest that the pedlar was fresh from the West Country. Geographically, it is to be remembered that the sheep-shearing is no more set in Bohemia than is the wood where the mechanicals meet in *A Midsummer Night's Dream* in Athens. It is not something that has ever bothered audiences – nor should it. 'Two maids wooing a man' is a three-part song of sexual rivalry which corresponds with the dramatic situation between Mopsa, Dorcas and the Young Shepherd and allows Autolycus free rein within the convention of the entertainment to act out the Young Shepherd's role, in our case in a particularly lascivious way.

'Will you buy?' was an opportunity to show a more tender side to Autolycus, however contrived. In performance the start of the song was played to Perdita – something of a lost cause. On realizing this I shifted my focus to a stray lamb of a girl, saucer-eyed and highly impressionable. I reeled her in on the end of a silk stocking. The effect was to remind the audience of the amorality and danger of a character like Autolycus, whose name means 'All-wolf'. Had she not been rescued by an alerted mother, Autolycus might, to adapt Caliban 'Have peopled else this isle with Autolyci'.

This is the last of the songs. There are six songs in the play, five of which are sung by Autolycus solo, the sixth a trio which he leads. All are confined to Act Four, Scene Three and the first 324 lines of Act Four, Scene Four. The singing voice is a fundamental constituent in the natural vitality and freshness that the fourth act brings to the play. Had I been fully aware of this from the beginning I would probably have turned the part down!

We next see Autolycus having sold all his trumpery, mocking integrity and praising the rogue life. Shakespeare must have taken great delight in creating Autolycus. Being free from the shackles of convention he is allowed to undermine our belief in principles of virtue, honour, fidelity, and honesty, and despite the fact that he suffers no moral retribution, he paradoxically continues to appeal to us. It is hard not to have a sneeking admiration for people like him, outsiders who dare to challenge our comfortable certainties. Their unique quality can ostracize these true individuals from our society but their uncomfortable probing is as necessary as it is painful.

The exchange of clothes with Florizel puts more money in his purse. He resolves to conceal Florizel's escape with Perdita from Polixenes not out of any desire to help but just to be true to his dishonest nature. This is perfectly balanced by Camillo, the lovers' confederate, whose admission to the audience that he will tell Polixenes all, is born out of a complete desire to help the young lovers.

A similar deceit, although for different reasons, is practised by Autolycus on the Old Shepherd and his son. Autolycus leads them to believe he will plead their case to Polixenes when in reality he is going to bring them 'aboard' Florizel for his own selfish ends. The effect of the imagined punishments Autolycus describes is comical in performance but read off the page is startlingly brutal and violent. This section, along with many other such passages, provides an interesting angle on our perceived image of Shakespeare, the man. An imagination that could conceive of such savage, sadistic deaths must have belonged to a more complex personality than the mild-mannered man of tradition.

In performance I combed my hair through, drew on a pencil moustache with a child's crayon that had been left lying about, and used a bubble blower as an improvised monocle. This, coupled with a heavy Teutonic accent and newly acquired clothes changed my appearance sufficiently for the Old Shepherd and his son to accept me as a new character. At the end of the scene Autolycus seems to be at the height of his powers. He has made money from everyone he has come into contact with and more importantly, he has found a means of currying favour with Florizel. And yet why should he want to do this but to gain re-entry to the court? And why should he want that when he protests to be happy on the open road? He is not a fish out of water as Touchstone is in the Forest of Arden. This is an area that never made sense to me although it never seemed to trouble the audience.

It is interesting that after such domination of the fourth act, Autolycus becomes merely a cipher in the fifth. He is curiously mute in the scene with the three gentlemen (v.ii), indicating possibly that he is as moved as everyone else by Paulina's steward's story. This is followed immediately by a speech in which Autolycus almost appears sorry for himself, bemoaning the fact that he didn't get any credit for the royal reunion. But characteristically he corrects himself, confessing that this good action would not have sat easily amongst his misdeeds. At this point the newly-elevated Shepherd and son enter and Autolycus is forced into a false repentance, a parody of Leontes, in a bid to get the Shepherd pleading his case with Florizel. In performance I would steal the Young Shepherd's watch on the line 'Thou wilt amend thy life' (v.ii.150) and only at the very end of the scene take a decision to return it and follow them, indicating that Autolycus is dependent on their innate goodness for preferment, the same goodness ironically that allowed him to dupe them in the first place.

Towards the end of the rehearsal period I was asking myself why we forgive Autolycus his crimes. Could it be because ultimately his crimes

69

are venial, or maybe because he is such an entertaining thief, breaking through convention and conformity, and bringing to the play a fresh, natural vitality. Happily my attention was drawn to a Louis McNiece poem on this subject which concludes that we forgive Autolycus because we all recognize a bit of him in ourselves. I now fully understood Autolycus's function in the play. By excusing his sins we are more able to pardon the repentant Leontes, and accept the enchantment of the final scene. He acts as a bridge. Without Autolycus there could be no 'happy' ending. He allows us to forgive and move on and, as such, is central to the heart of the play.

Richard III

DAVID TROUGHTON

DAVID TROUGHTON is an Associate Actor of the Royal Shakespeare Company and played the title role in Steven Pimlott's production of *Richard III* at the Royal Shakespeare Theatre in 1995 and at the Barbican Theatre the following year. His other roles that season were Fitzdottrel in *The Devil is an Ass* and Lopakhin in *The Cherry Orchard*, a production which moved to the West End after its Barbican season. A long list of earlier roles for the RSC includes Cob in *Every Man in his Humour*, Sebastian in *The Roaring Girl*, Bottom in *A Midsummer Night's Dream*, Cloten in *Cymbeline*, Hector in *Troilus and Cressida*, Kent in *King Lear*, Holofernes in *Love's Labour's Lost*, and Caliban in *The Tempest*, as well as the twins Zanetto and Tonino in *The Venetian Twins*. He has appeared frequently on television and his wide range of work in the provincial and London theatre includes major roles with the Royal National Theatre.

THE BEGINNING

Like one lost in a thorny wood . . .

(*3 Henry VI*, III.ii.174)

The discovery of any character through rehearsals is always a combination of so many factors. A hotchpotch of ideas, thoughts, attempts (successful and unsuccessful), high days and low days, extreme elation and deep depression. It is both exhausting and energy giving, but rarely is it clear cut, neat and tidy. Rehearsals usually end up as a messy process of trial and error. Jumping into the freezing swimming pool of a role, thrashing about for a bit, jumping out, towelling yourself down and then jumping in again and never mind the cold. Hopefully and gradually, though, the water becomes warmer and swimming becomes easier. Failure turns into relative success and by the end you are covering whole lengths quite easily. But how to write all this down in a clear, logical sequence of events? I have, therefore, decided to categorize the many discoveries that I made when approaching the part of Richard III, under four main titles.

Having found it very difficult to remember the exact day-to-day developments in our rehearsals, these simple headings have helped me to explain in more detail the workings of my mind as I approached the task but, I hasten to add, not in any specific order of their occurrence. Inevitably, owing to the pressure of space, I have had to leave out many important themes – it would necessitate a whole book to encompass such an enormous part – so I regard the following pages as a snap-shot of my impressions as I embarked on the portrayal of this famous role.

It goes without saying that without Steven Pimlott and the rest of the cast, my Richard would not have been possible. Rehearsals are a co-production where every person, from the lowliest spear carrier to the leading actor should feel able to put forward his or her own thoughts and suggestions. Only in such a democratic atmosphere can true imagination flourish fearlessly and without bounds. It is no good simply acting a part in the vacuum of one's own mind. It may sound fantastic in the bathroom, but the real test comes when one is working together with other people and listening to what they have to offer. Whole new aspects of one's own character can be revealed because of what other people are finding in theirs. The director's job, apart from the initial casting, is to trust, encourage, cajole, criticize, inspire and focus this work; to mould all the separate performances into one coherent vision of the play. It is the stuff and essence of rehearsals.

While rehearsing *Richard III*, I encountered all these ideals and the atmosphere at all times was one of exciting discovery. Even when things were going badly, there was always a joke and a laugh to bring you back to earth. It made one realize that putting on a play is only pretend after all, and 'all that shouting in the evening', as my late father described working in the theatre, is certainly easier than mining.

A brief word as to how it all started. Me? David Troughton. Richard III? – an offer from the RSC that came as a great surprise. Having spent the last two years in Stratford and at the Barbican in London playing the two brothers in *The Venetian Twins* and Caliban in *The Tempest*, I was due to leave. Working for the RSC is an extremely rewarding but exhausting way of earning a living and both plays had been physically draining. The work load was such that I felt that I needed a break from the Company to recharge my batteries. Life as an actor, however, is not always that simple. It has a habit of throwing spanners in the works and there are always difficult choices to be made. My initial reaction to the proposal was that I could not possibly take on such a task, but I told Adrian Noble that I would think about it. When Simon Russell Beale, the most recent RSC Richard III, heard that I was 'thinking about it', he was apoplectic. 'Thinking about it? You don't *think* about doing Richard III, you just *do* it!' But there were other factors to consider.

The complete offer was made up of three plays. Fitzdottrel in Ben Jonson's *The Devil is an Ass*, Lopakhin in Chekhov's *The Cherry Orchard* and the name part in *Richard III*. Now, given the choice, I would always attempt something that would challenge and extend me. But this? Most actors would be extremely happy to play one of the parts that I had been offered, let alone all three in seven months. And would I be up to it? Three major roles in repertory for perhaps one and a half years. But then I thought, when would I ever have a chance like this again to play such a wonderful range of parts? So with all this in mind, and the mortgage to pay, I rejoined the Company to undertake the challenge of a lifetime.

Quite unusually, I think, I only met the director Steven Pimlott once before the first read-through of *Richard III*. Ever since he had cast me in the role in February, my work load and his prior commitments precluded any meeting before June. When we finally did get together with the designer, Tobias Hoheisel, we talked of the set and briefly about Steven's basic ideas for the production. I was shown early design sketches and most discussions centred largely on practical matters such as the health and safety aspects, which I hold to be of the utmost importance. It is no good having the most wonderful set on which to work if it is unpractical and dangerous. I remember the question of Richard's deformity came up, and we both agreed that firstly it should not be too much and secondly that there should be no complicated make-ups. Steven, even at this early stage, was adamant that the deformity, whatever it turned out to be, should somehow be able to change, matching Richard's mood swings. But that was all. The next time I saw him was on the first day of rehearsals, two days after I had opened in *The Cherry Orchard*.

THE DEFORMITY

Deformed, unfinished, sent before my time
Into this breathing world, scarce half made up . . .
(I.i.20–I)

Shakespeare tells us that Richard 'halts', has a 'crook-back' and a 'blasted sapling' of a withered arm. There is no getting away from this,

73

so addressing the problem early was of the utmost importance. There were two things to consider. What is the nature of the deformity and how to display it comfortably and with complete safety? The tales of pulled muscles and strained backs incurred by previous Richards are legion.

According to history, Richard had come into the world feet first, a breach birth – his mother speaks of a horrendous delivery. Having experimented for a few days with deformed feet and various limps, I decided to talk to Steve Young, an orthopaedic surgeon and friend of mine. I asked him how this difficult entry into the world might have affected the baby. He was very exact in his reply: hip dislocation. As Richard was dragged out by his feet, one of his hips might have been displaced causing extreme discomfort all his life. As he grew up, because of the pain of walking, a severe limp would develop, forcing his spine to grow crooked, giving the appearance of one shoulder being higher than the other. He would, in technical terms, walk with an antalgic gait. His arm could also have been deformed at birth or through an illness such as polio.

In pain all his life? What an insight into a character. Here was one very simple explanation for Richard's malevolence. I thought of the dull unending pain of toothache and how even that minor irritation can make one feel bad-tempered and at odds with the world. From then on, I tried to walk as if I needed a hip replacement. Every step was a painful one. I drew on memories of the hospital where I had had knee surgery in 1983. Men, ashen-faced with pain, with their hip-joints totally inflamed, struggling to limp the few yards across the ward. Care had to be taken not to strain my back, so I developed a rolling gait, and together with strengthening exercises for both my back and knees, this seemed quite comfortable.

The solution to Richard's withered arm came about by pure accident. During the regular morning movement sessions, I would let my arm hang limply by my side, as if paralysed. But I wanted to make it smaller. I had seen my children do a rather sick party piece, by tucking their arms into the opposite arm holes of their T-shirts. The effect was both comic and horrific. I tried the same, using my left arm only, but instead of crossing it over, I rested my elbow in the same arm hole. And there it was, a little withered arm nestling neatly by my side. This method worked so well that even in performance I still wear a simple T-shirt under my costume rather than any uncomfortable sling as support. Together with an exaggerated crooked stance aided by a bit of padding on my right shoulder, Richard's deformity was complete. An entire physical change with the minimum of external additions. This allowed me to use my body in extraordinary ways, 'adding colours to the chameleon' and changing 'shapes with Proteus'. Various degrees of deformity could be attained for different scenes to suit different moods. Ideas of completely discarding the deformity when speaking to the audience were tried. This had two benefits. It allowed me, purely technically, to have a rest because I could stand straight and have a good stretch. It also made the point that there were two perceived Richards in the play – the one he presents to the audience and the other to the Court. The idea that Richard could lose his deformity completely was eventually discarded until his death, but the fact that it could be minimized and exaggerated at will, creating various moods from that of aggression to the pretence of self-pity, still remained.

I found great uses for this, especially in the wooing of Lady Anne and in the attack on Hastings before he is beheaded. With Lady Anne, the idea of the tempting of Eve was uppermost: at first, the image of a devilish gargoyle, with a writhing snake-like gait of obsequiousness developing into the upright romantic hero professing undying love; with Hastings, the display of Richard's withered arm supposedly caused by the dastardly witchcraft of the Queen and Mistress Shore, a claim so bizarre as to defy belief.

This strong physical vision developed hand in hand with the text, never more so than in the final confrontation with the grieving Elizabeth. Here is a man struggling to survive as king by asking for her daughter's hand in marriage. But whereas before, when wooing Lady Anne, the deformity had proved weirdly beneficial, here it seemed to echo the 'cracked-mirror' image of that scene, placing Richard at a distinct disadvantage. Each of the former Queen's telling replies to his pleading arguments seem to stab the king to the very heart, and maintaining an upright posture becomes progressively more difficult and painful. As she exits the scene, Richard thinks he has gained another wife, but both the mental and physical effort in obtaining Elizabeth's supposed agreement to the alliance has taken its toll. From now until his final undoing, Richard's deformity becomes more and more crippling, making clear, logical thought impossible.

Having used the deformity in this way throughout the play, the image of Richard's death is portrayed quite simply. In our production, we discard the idea of grand battle scenes. There are no fights, no smoke, no soldiers, no sound effects and no final duel with Richmond. The battle is represented as a contest of words – Richmond atop the gantry, triumphantly urging his men to great feats in the name of God, and Richard below, desperately attempting to inspire his demoralized troops, pouring scorn upon the opposing army. The only hint of a tangible fight comes with the famous lines when calling for a horse. These are proclaimed while Richard flails the empty air with his sword as if surrounded by a host of soldiers bent on his demise. By now, the deformity is such agony that he even has to use his sword as a crutch, so difficult is it for him to stagger just a few steps. He painfully lays down his weapon and crown, gazes at the audience and pronounces, 'All the world to nothing.' He dies. But rather than falling to the ground, Richard stands upright, completely losing the deformity, his withered arm sliding comfortably down by his side, now recovering its full length. He turns and walks slowly but quite normally to the black corner of the stage where all his previous victims have appeared as ghosts and sits on a bench, silently listening to Richmond's promises of peace and forgiveness. In this one theatrical moment, we see Richard give up his life – a lost soul in hell has no manifestation of physical deformity.

I must point out here the work of two other people who have been so helpful to me in the creation of the physical side of Richard. Kate Slocombe, my masseuse, who gently persuaded my muscles to unknot themselves and Peter Overton, my osteopath, who made sure my spine did not seize up. Without their constant attention and advice, my deformed Richard would not have been possible.

THE JESTER

> . . . Nor more can you distinguish of a man
> Than of his outward show, which, God He knows,
> Seldom or never jumpeth with the heart . . .
> (III.i.9–11)

From my experience gained over the eleven years on and off that I have spent with the RSC, I have come to the conclusion that my job as an interpreter of Shakespeare is to incorporate any textual observations, such as why a speech is in verse or prose, the reasons for its basic rhythm and meter and the types of words used (especially with regard to their very sound and shape), into the basic foundations of the part one is portraying. Hopefully, then, a character first emerges from the *language*

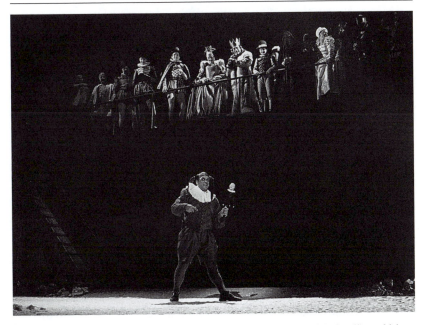

13 David Troughton as Richard, with Edward IV (Robin Nedwell) and his court, *Richard III*, Act I, Scene i: 'Now is the winter of our discontent . . .'

of the play, serving as the initial key to unlock its various traits. The actor's ultimate aim, then, is to take this technical appraisal into the practical everyday rehearsal situation and create a truly believable human being.

The idea of Richard as the metaphorical 'jester' evolved slowly but surely over our seven-week rehearsal period. The earliest thoughts I had about the Duke of Gloucester being able to 'perform', came directly from the text, which, allied with his unusual deformities, began to make me feel that here was not just an ambitious, embittered soldier but also an extraordinarily witty gargoyle of a man, who by his very immorality and shape seemed not human at all. In fact, a man possessed by evil which taken to its logical conclusion could reveal the fallen angel himself residing inside Richard's body.

(The following paragraphs consist of my assessments of the text. I have decided to write about them as fully as I can, and as such they might appear unnecessarily long-winded and simplistic. The discoveries made, however, were so important to my approach to playing the part of Richard that I hope the reader will bear with me.)

Having read the play simply as a story, I then went through every line, 'Humpty-Dumpty' fashion. This is my word to describe the reading of any Shakespeare text obeying the iambic rhythm at all times – Di *Dum*, di *Dum*, di *Dum*, di *Dum*, di *Dum* (Hum Di Dum Di). Like a detective, one is searching for clues, observing, probing and questioning, but in the most basic technical manner. At this early stage, however, there should be no definite answers. The main purpose is to start one's imagination working and if there are any choices to be made and questions to be resolved, then the rehearsal room, with the director and cast, is where they are put to the test.

How I read and appreciated the famous opening soliloquy is a good example of what I mean:

> Now *is* the *wi*nter *of* our *dis*con*tent*
> Made *glor*ious *summ*er *by* this *son* of *York*,
> And *all* the *clouds* that *loured* up*on* our *house*,
> In *the* deep *bos*om *of* the *oc*ean *bur*ied.   (I.i.1–4)

Of course, lines cannot be acted like this, but one can immediately perceive that the word 'buried' has an importance in the fourth line, because it leaps out at you – it is unrhythmical. Also, the language in this introductory speech has two very distinct styles. The first, up to 'But I, that am not shaped for sportive tricks' is one of lyrical antithesis. Words such as 'winter' and 'summer', 'victorious wreaths', 'bruisèd arms' and 'monuments', 'Grim-visaged war' and 'wrinkled front', 'barbèd steeds' and 'fearful adversaries' point to a concise poetic statement on events past and present. The second is much more personal, colloquial and direct. 'Rudely stamped', 'deformed', 'unfinished', 'weak, piping time of peace' seeming, even by their very plosive sounds, to display the forceful nature of the man and the anger that lurks within. The issue then becomes not why does *Shakespeare* break the rhythm with a word like 'buried', but rather, why does *Richard*? Why is the language of the first part of the speech different to the second, from *Richard's* point of view? So immediately we notice two styles of delivery – one, the public, for the world in general, and the other, the more colloquial and confidential, when addressing the audience. Further investigations led to many more discoveries of this kind.

In Act Two, Scene One, in which Richard befriends his dying brother, King Edward, and seemingly desires reconciliation with the Woodvilles, he talks of patching up old quarrels: ' 'Tis *death* to *me* to *be* at *enmity*' (II.i.61). What struck me about this simple line was not only its very strong iambic beat, which is mirrored throughout the inexorable sweep of the play itself, but more interestingly, the internal rhyme therein – 'Me' rhyming with the 'ty' of 'enmity'. Why was it there? Maybe it was an accident of Shakespeare? Or, maybe, Richard himself meant to exhibit the rhyme as a conceit. Why? Could it be the way Richard 'performs' to mask his real intentions, a device by which he amuses people and thereby throws them off the scent as to his true depth of purpose. A comic, after all, could not possibly be deemed a threat. I looked for more of these 'conceits' and found the text to be littered with them.

The simplest of these I found at the end of his early soliloquies, in the form of rhyming couplets:

> Clarence still breathes; Edward still lives and *reigns*;
> When they are gone, then I must count my *gains*.   (I.i.161–2)

and similarly:

> Shine out, fair sun, 'till I have bought a *glass*,
> That I may see my shadow as I *pass*.   (I.ii.262–3)

These couplets seemed to endow Richard with a malevolence above and beyond his stated treacherous intentions. He appeared to enjoy not only the logistics of his evil intent but also the manner in which he expressed them.

This is further refined by the fact that at the end of two later soliloquies, he leads the audience to believe that another rhyme is in the offing, and then surprises them by choosing a non-rhyming word, making it even more poignant. He seems to be playing verbal tricks, thereby enhancing the devilish delight of his machinations:

> And thus I clothe my naked villainy
> With odd old ends stolen forth of Holy *Writ*,
> And seem a saint, when most I play the *devil*.   (I.iii.335–7)

and:

> And by that knot looks proudly on the *crown*,
> To her go I, a jolly thriving *wooer*.   (IV.iii.42–3)

In the initial quotation, three points arise. Firstly, 'devil' unusually does not rhyme with 'writ'; secondly, the word completes an eleven syllable line making it unrhythmical and, therefore, giving it emphasis; and thirdly, it is antithetical – a religious opposite to 'holy writ – a device which he uses throughout the play. The whole idea of Richard being possessed by the devil can also be introduced in performance, as I whisper the word with an evil grimace and take up an extremely deformed body posture. It is as if Satan himself rises out of his body for a brief instant and then slips silently back into his host – a nightmare vision which helps to establish the religious metaphors in the play, leading to its rather unusual ending.

In the second instance, we see the non-rhyming word, 'wooer' (which ironically enough could very easily have been the extremely apt word, 'clown'); a feminine ending for emphasis; and the opportunity to increase the ugliness of the proposed marriage in the relish I portray when grotesquely mouthing each syllable, investing the romantic notion of courtship with one of devilish lust. Ratcliffe then rushes in, an interruption which causes Richard to blast him with: 'Good or bad news, that thou com'st in so bluntly?' (IV.iii.45). The king's extreme reaction could derive from the schizophrenic fear that he might have been discovered talking to himself in this deranged fashion. Again, one tiny word throwing up so many possibilities.

In the same way as the rhymes appeared to give Richard a childish relish of his horrific schemes, his proverbs lent a humorous normality to his murderous plans. When revelling in the idea of his elder brother's murder, he admonishes himself because it is yet to be achieved: 'But yet I run before my horse to market' (I.i.160). Similarly, while feigning adoration for his nephews but in reality knowing that they have to die, I turn to the audience with an evil smile for 'So wise, so young they say do never live long' (III.i.79) and 'Short summers lightly have a forward spring' (III.i.94).

Indeed, the last two examples rhyme wonderfully with the naive proclamations of the Prince of Wales – the word 'say' rhyming with his 'general all-ending day' and 'spring' with 'as I liv'd a king'. Richard not only makes up his own rhymes, he wittily completes them for others.

These, then, are just a few examples of the textual basis for Richard's 'outward show' – the brilliant wit of the wordsmith protecting the true inner nature of the man. The development of this notion into the actual persona of 'Jester' had a very unusual beginning.

The first week of rehearsals was spent sitting down at a huge table with the whole cast, reading the play several times. Everyone took part in the many resulting discussions concerning the history, situations and characters involved. I had beside me one of the books I was reading at that time – it makes you look as if you are working! – and for a book mark, I had used a single playing card that I had found lying about at home. Steven, for some unknown reason, was curious as to what card it was, and not knowing myself, I looked and discovered it to be the Joker. There he was, a man with a funny three-cornered hat and a little joker's stick. Out of little tricorns, great oak trees grow!

This image from a pack of cards certainly made an impression. I started rehearsing with a similar stick carrying it everywhere and at all times. You might say that I had been taken over by it but Steven was very patient and trusting and allowed me to embrace the idea whole-heartedly – it is one of his many talents to allow such freedom in rehearsals. I spoke to it, hit people with it, in fact I did everything with it, even using the stick as my alter ego when playing the conscience speech. Thoughts of the famous film in which a ventriloquist is taken over by his dummy pervaded my mind. I was the typical actor relying on and enjoying using a 'prop' to the full.

Eventually, having tried it in every possible situation, Steven wisely (and very tactfully) suggested areas where it did not work and I reluctantly complied, for I was loathe to have my 'dummy' taken away. He was right, of course, and eventually I learned to be selective. In actual performance, I use it only twice – once in the opening oration, to establish the idea of the court jester, and once with the Princes on their arrival in London, to enhance the idea of the funny, jokey uncle. Most importantly, however, the jester in Richard, the concept of a man performing in order to disguise his true intentions, still remained uppermost in my thoughts.

During this time, Tobias Hoheisel, the designer, showed me some sketches for Richard's costume. He had taken the jester scenario and incorporated it into his designs. At first, I was fairly taken aback. His extreme ideas completely dispelled the conventional Richard look, the one of a plain, fighting man, dressed from top to toe in black. An Elizabethan-looking doublet together with very odd short culottes, both coloured a bright red, gave Richard a mischievous 'Mr. Punch' feel which, in actual fact, was just what I had in mind. I realized that the real significance of this 'jester' idea only truly came to fruition when married to the 'devil' in Richard, so bizarrely displayed in the scarlet costuming. Not only was he a joker, he was an evil joker, bent on mass destruction for his own ends, which made him very dangerous indeed – the funny man in red whom no-one suspects, sitting quietly in a corner with only his shadow for company, smiling as he stabs his victims in the back.

THE MAN

Seeking a way and straying from the way,
Not knowing how to find the open air,
But toiling desperately to find it out . . .
(*3 Henry VI*, III.ii.176–8)

Richard, the man: a scheming villain with one aim in life – to become king no matter how much havoc he causes; or a victim of the troubled times in which he lived, emotionally bereft due to the lack of motherly love?

Of all Shakespeare's characters, apart from perhaps the fictional Shylock, the Duke of Gloucester's posthumous reputation seems to engender the staunchest of defences. 'Tudor propaganda!' goes up the cry. Countless 'Richard III Societies', on hearing of a new production, make themselves known and challenge the actor playing the part to justify the truth of the king's supposed evil machinations. Even before I had started rehearsals for *The Cherry Orchard*, I had had numerous invitations to speak at their meetings to justify Shakespeare's 'misrepresentation' of the Duke.

I knew that the important discovery of the metaphorical jester could in no way be the only facet of what was, after all, a well-drawn, complicated, and many-sided character. I set about some historical research which I hoped would yield useful insights into the man himself.

Having perused all three parts of *Henry VI*, which proved extremely productive, I then read three books. The first, *The Daughter of Time*, by Josephine Tey, is an excellent fictional account of a detective discovering incontrovertible proof of Richard's innocence of the young Princes' murder – a good read but not much help as it ran contrary to Shakespeare's play. The second, a history of *Richard III* in performance called simply *King Richard III*, by Hugh M. Richmond, deals in detail with the critical appraisal of the play on the stage from Burbage to Sher – interesting, but again not much help. The third book, however, entitled *Richard III: England's Black Legend* by Desmond Seward became an endless source of assistance, as it compellingly argued the case that Shakespeare's Richard was much closer to reality than the 'betrayed hero of his modern defenders'. I had struck gold and during rehearsals I was for ever delving into its pages for inspiration. Above all it was the marvellous quotations heading the chapters, ranging from Sir Thomas More's *History of King Richard III* (the work upon which Shakespeare himself based his play), to Machiavelli's *Il Principe*, which proved most useful. Two extracts, above all, stood out. The first from Machiavelli and the second from More:

In seizing a state the usurper should carefully examine what injuries he must do, and then do them all at one blow so that he does not have to repeat them day after day; and by taking care not to unsettle men he can reassure them and win them over with gifts. Anyone who fails to do this, either from cowardice or bad advice, has to keep a knife in his hand all the time.

and:

Where he went abroad, his eyes whirled about, his body secretly armoured, his hand ever on his dagger.

I employed many small but significant character points that arose from these statements. Richard was terrified of being assassinated, protecting himself by wearing a chain mail vest and carrying a knife wherever he went. From day one of rehearsals, I carried a knife at my belt. And because wearing a sword all the time would have hampered my very specific movement (I kept tripping up on it), I wanted the dagger to be extremely obvious, a fearful stiletto of a weapon. After all, stabbing people in the back was Richard's way, not running them through with a sword.

The idea of a metal 'vest' fascinated me. I experimented with one in rehearsals, specifically for the wooing of Lady Anne. I had the notion that Richard could reveal this protection to the audience after the scene in which he had offered up his life for her. If she had indeed attempted to run him through then no harm would have been done. This idea, as with countless others, was eventually discarded as I felt it diminished the scene's innate danger, thus lowering the stakes for which Richard was playing.

Richard does, indeed, 'take care not to unsettle men' by making himself the man 'least likely to', the metaphorical jester being the perfect disguise. The bestowing of gifts as favours can be seen not only in the support offered to his brother in the past, as in, '. . . a weeder out of his proud adversaries/ A liberal rewarder of his friends' but also in his own ascent to the throne, liberally scattering his largesse to both murderers and dukes alike.

Desmond Seward's book was also a great source for the realities of the historical events in the play. To take one example – the demise of Hastings. More's wonderfully evocative description of that frightful day might apply to any contemporary dictatorship; one could imagine these same events taking place in the vast offices of the Kremlin or the Reichstag. An extremely dangerous and tense scene is, therefore, played with no regard to Shakespeare's iambic pentameter. Long pauses serve to heighten the pressure on the 'unsuspecting' Hastings, culminating in the horrific desecration of the Last Supper imagery, with Richard leaping onto the table in his frenzied damnation of his former ally. Richard's suppressed violence is given its full rein; he has finally shown his true intent.

These are just a few examples of the marrying of historical research with theatrical reality, a very necessary part of the rehearsal process. However, as I have stated before, I believe language to be the key, and so I returned to my old friend 'Humpty-Dumpty', looking for further clues.

I noticed that certain words, owing to the iambic nature of the line, were lengthened and made to sound odd and old-fashioned. These fell into two categories – one, which I call the 'èd' words such as 'provokèd' and 'banishèd', and two, the 'ion' words such as 'factiòn', 'recreatiòn', and 'executiòn'. All, of course, could be said normally without any stress. But what would happen if I found a character motive for obeying the rigid meter?

> When have I injured thee? When done thee wrong?
> Or thee? Or thee? Or any of your factiòn? (I.iii.56–7)

In lines such as these, Richard could heighten the stress on the end of the word 'faction', endowing it with an angry displeasure at the Woodvilles. He could *purposefully* use the word in this manner, and, as a 'double gain of happiness', almost make it rhyme with 'wrong'. I found this extremely exciting and looked for more examples.

With the word 'recreation' as spoken to the young Prince of Wales, on his arrival in London, Richard, as royal counsellor, suggests that the boy 'repose' in the Tower of London:

> Then where you please, and shall be thought most fit
> For your best health and recreatiòn. (III.i.66–7)

By obeying the rhythm here, the word is stressed playfully and indeed, in performance, I tickle the Prince at the same time, which forces the boy to shy away. The child's next question, therefore, as to who built the Tower, is not addressed to Richard, whom he fears, but logically to the apparently friendly Buckingham. The reason for *his* answering the Prince, and not Richard, sometimes a textual problem, is solved because the question had not been asked of his wicked uncle in the first place.

Another example: in our production, during the mock siege of London, Hastings's severed head, albeit covered in a white, blooded cloth, is brought on by Ratcliffe, invariably causing a laugh of revulsion from the audience as it is hurled into the air, landing on stage with a heavy thud. This is perfectly in keeping with the humorous charade that Richard is perpetrating, and indeed, I heighten the moment by stabbing my knife through it, then presenting the skewered head to the Mayor of London. More laughter follows. The blade, however, gets stuck and only comes free with a struggle, as I deliver:

> But that the extreme peril of the case,
> The peace of England, and our persons' safety
> Enforced us to this executiòn. (III.v.43–5)

In stressing the five separate syllables in the word, 'ex-ec-ut-i-on', the difficulty of withdrawing the knife and the horror that that entails, can be increased as action and speech match each other perfectly. It is, therefore, the abnormal sound of the word, and not necessarily its meaning, which heightens the audience's gleeful horror.

As for the 'èd' words, similar choices can be made. In the Lady Anne scene, I noticed that Richard uses the word 'provoked' twice, and in both cases an iambic stress on 'èd' was required. However, in the line, 'I was provokèd by her sland'rous tongue' I decided to drop the stress, but still make up the ten beats with a slight pause after 'provoked': 'I was provoked, [beat] by her slanderous tongue' (I.ii.97). The first half of the line is the reply, the second half, after the tiny pause, is the desperate qualification of that reply.

In the second instance, I make use of the stress, hopefully conveying the lyricism of his supposed romantic love for Anne: 'But t'was thy beauty that provokèd me' (I.ii.180).

In Act One, Scene Three, the stress on the tri-syllabic word 'banishèd' when accusing the hated Margaret with 'Wert thou not banishèd, on pain of death' (I.iii.166) allows a biting sarcasm, making quite clear Richard's opinion of this old crone of a former queen.

And finally in the following lines:

> . . . Bid him levy straight,
> The greatest strength and power that he can make,
> And meet me suddenly at Salisbury. (IV.iv.449–51)

two further points emerged: firstly, my purposeful rhyming of 'suddenly' and 'Salisbury', almost sing-song in its delivery, to display Richard's growing insanity as he loses his ability to command; and secondly, the actual word 'Salisbury'. In order to complete the iambic pentameter, the word could be pronounced with three stresses – 'Sal-is-bry.' To fulfil the meter, however, I decided to leave a slight beat after 'suddenly', as if Richard himself, with a wry smile, is well aware of the rhyme to come – a pathetic reminiscence of a time when his rhyming couplets denoted confidence and success.

Further important reasons for Richard's behaviour were also discovered by studying the nature of the verse. The play itself, being one of Shakespeare's early works, has a very regular beat to it. This enhances the inexorability of the catastrophic events and also suggests, in Richard's case especially, the down-to-earth soldier, the 'plain man' of which he himself speaks. Rare metaphors employed by him are simple and commonplace, mostly alluding to metal and the law, such as, 'with lies well steeled with weighty arguments' (I.i.148), '. . . now do I play the touch,/ To try if thou be current gold indeed' (IV.ii.8–9), and, 'Be the attorney of my love to her:/ Plead what I will be, not what I have been' (IV.iv.413–4).

When speaking of his late father, however, Richard becomes comparatively lyrical. In addressing Lady Anne, he tells of the sad reaction to the news of the former Duke of York's death:

> Nor when thy warlike father, like a child,
> Told the sad story of my father's death
> And twenty times made pause to sob and weep,
> That all the standers-by had wet their cheeks
> Like trees bedashed with rain . . . (I.ii.159–63)

And he painfully recalls his father's tortured death, when confronting Margaret with:

> The curse my noble father laid on thee
> When thou didst crown his warlike brows with paper
> And with thy scorns drew'st rivers from his eyes,
> And then, to dry them, gav'st the Duke a clout
> Steeped in the faultless blood of pretty Rutland . . . (I.iii.173–7)

Both these passages are unusual, displaying a truly poetic side to Richard. The former, full of onomatopoeic imagery, enhancing the true depth of feeling; the latter, beautifully lyrical, throwing up many finer points. The stress on the unrhythmical and very ordinary sounding, 'paper' and 'clout' lends an angry counterpoint, and in playing is hurled accusingly at Margaret. (I actually changed the word 'clout' to 'cloth', as I did not want the audience to think that Margaret had hit the Duke!). Richard's memory of his father is obviously very dear to him, and whenever the 'noble Duke' is mentioned, I try to make that clear. Here is a man still mourning his father's death, a man who, I think, would have had a very different future had he still been alive.

In dealing with Richard's attitude to women in the play, especially towards his mother, one tiny clue enlightened me as to his undoubted misogynistic nature. Whenever Richard swore, he invoked not God, but Saint Paul, a man renowned for his anti-female attitudes. I decided that Richard either hated women or, at least, felt uncomfortable in their company. He certainly did not understand them, as the revelations in the famous speech after the wooing of Lady Anne make amply clear:

> And will she yet abase her eyes on me,
> That cropped the golden prime if this sweet prince
> And made her widow to a woeful bed. . .
> All the world to nothing! (1.ii.246–8, 237)

This last line I chose to scream out in anger rather than surprise, a violent release of Richard's pent up 'enmity' and frustration.

But from where had this hatred derived? Obviously, as Richard goes on to say later in the speech, his own body causes revulsion not only to himself but to other people, especially women. He admits he wants 'love's majesty/To strut before a wanton ambling nymph' (1.i.16–17). With the hindsight of modern psychological thinking (of which Shakespeare, of course, had no knowledge) I turned to Richard's relationship with his mother. With his father dead, she would be the only one who could have helped him, nurturing him through all the angst of puberty until he reached manhood. The Duchess of York, however, despises and loathes him, calling him the very devil, and taking every opportunity to tell him so. Here was the perfect psychological reason for his twisted outlook on life, for his difficulty in forming any meaningful, loving relationships: a man, indeed, 'rent with thorns' – the complete absence of any motherly love.

The problem was to make this clear as there are only two short scenes in the whole play where she and Richard meet. The first, in his brother's throne-room, is, therefore, made comic, as the Duchess discovers him trying out the crown for size, introducing to the audience the deep rift between them. The second, in the interruption of his 'expedition' to quell Buckingham's revolt, I try to show the inherent tragedy of this situation as Richard desperately cries out, 'You speak too bitterly' (IV.iv.182).

Having placed the crown carefully on the ground, I lie in her lap, curled up in a foetal position anticipating the soothing comfort that only a mother can bring. But as Richard listens to the ghastly dying curse that ensues (one of the few instances in English literature where a mother damns her son to his face) he realises that there never was nor can be any love between them – no reconciliation is possible. As she leaves the stage, Richard despairingly replaces the crown on his head, now certain in the knowledge that the ultimate power he has craved all his life is merely the substitute for the love he has never known, and the 'torment' spoken of in the past was and is his only means of fulfilment. The fact that when he reaches this goal he finds no such satisfaction only serves to heighten the tragedy of Richard's existence.

THE AUDIENCE

My conscience hath a thousand several tongues,
And every tongue brings in a several tale,
And every tale condemns me for a villain . . .
(v.iii.194–6)

Shakespeare's soliloquies are, in the main, true expressions of a character's emotions, hopes and dilemmas. Addressing the audience directly, looking them straight in the eye and speaking to each person individually, allows the actor a wonderful theatrical freedom, and rather than just generalized thoughts spoken to the air, the soliloquy can become an informal dialogue involving the audience completely in the play. No longer are they passive observers, but, rather, active participants.

In approaching *Richard III*, I wanted to take this one stage further. I was struck by the number of times that Richard speaks directly to the audience using wit and comedy to form a particularly intimate relationship with them. One passage in Antony Sher's book, *The Year of the King*, struck me as extremely informative. He writes that during the previews of his *Richard III*, he was surprised that the audience laughed so much and that this had quite an effect on the way that he approached the rehearsals during these early performances. Many reconsiderations took place because the audience had shown him new insights into the way of playing the character. I was determined to address this element from the very start by wholeheartedly embracing the innate black humour in the play, and hopefully using it to my advantage. Not only did I want this special involvement, I also needed the audience itself to become an actual character; a character which had the power to influence and affect the direction that Richard takes during his murderous assault on the English crown and, more especially, throughout the nightmare that follows his coronation, ending with the final confrontation of his Conscience speech.

In the beginning, we see a man at odds with the world, complaining bitterly about the new order that peace has brought. A disaffected person hiding behind the disguise of the jester. He immediately dispels this pretence, informing the audience of his secret plans to cause havoc with his machinations. The overriding need at this stage is to get the audience on Richard's side and by so doing introduce the idea that they themselves are part of Richard's psyche – his confident alter ego. While engaging them directly, he is talking to himself and can revel in the hideous enjoyment that he feels, encouraging laughter to increase the sense that the audience and Richard are one and the same person.

His brother, Clarence, is locked away in the Tower and all is going well. The next step is to get a wife – Lady Anne. There follows the most extraordinary scene in which we see Richard wooing his intended over the dead body of her father-in-law, the successful outcome of which leads into, 'Was ever woman in this humour woo'd?' (i.iii.227).

The whole scenario is bizarre to say the least – how can a deformed misogynist win the heart of a beautiful young lady despite his admittance that he has killed 'her husband and his father' and why does Lady Anne agree to marry him at all? Both these questions posed monumental challenges for Jennifer Ehle and me, and during rehearsals various options were discussed and tried out. This one short scene comprises all the elements of a tempestuous courtship which in real time would have lasted perhaps a year. However, while exploring all its naturalistic intricacies and differing poetic styles (from Sophoclean irony to the rhetoric of stichomithia), one overriding objective became clear: the absolute necessity to demonstrate the ever-present danger that Richard might not succeed in his task. He has to work hard and must play the scene with utter sincerity, both for the sake of Lady Anne and the audience, displaying a true virtuosity when encountering his future wife's grief and intellect. In my loving kiss that follows, 'Vouchsafe to wear this ring' (i.ii.201) must be seen the culmination of Richard's awe-inspiring powers of persuasion and both must succumb to his bravura.

We see, therefore, a man verbally adept at winning all the initial arguments, then brilliantly playing for sympathy, and finally heroically offering his life as an appeasement for her revenge. All these are calculated risks, fraught with danger, and at no stage should the audience be sure of the outcome. They must be hoodwinked into believing that perhaps Richard does truly love her after all and it is only afterwards, when he reveals that he 'will not keep her long' (i.ii.229), that the deception is unveiled. The resulting speech, having bidden her farewell, encapsulates two elements – elation at what he has achieved and a self-discovery that, despite all life's cards being stacked against him, he is now capable of anything. Any previous doubts in Richard's mind, and likewise the audience's, are completely dispelled and as he exits the stage he can even command the sun to shine, such is his new found confidence. He and the audience are truly one, and together they have forged a seemingly immutable partnership which, for the time being, drives Richard forward to even greater feats.

On he goes to the first political scene, in which Richard berates the Queen, accusing the Woodvilles of plotting against his family. Once again, at the end of the outburst, Richard divulges his true intentions and that there is worse to come. It is still of the utmost importance that Richard and the audience should be delighting in all this together, and any laughter that occurs at this early stage should be of wicked enjoyment. The clever turning of Margaret's curse upon herself, together with the sparkling wit and intellect displayed in this scene serves this purpose well.

There follows the murder of Clarence. For the first time in the play a scene arrives without the main protagonist, and members of the audience are on their own. This is the first opportunity for them to witness the results of Richard's infamy, but whereas before they had been cushioned by his gleeful and sometimes comic narration, here there is no escape and the awful realities of his machiavellian ambitions are suddenly laid out before them in a most horrifying manner – that of a violent and messy death. They are also introduced to the idea of 'conscience', as one of the murderers has second thoughts. Hopefully, then, the first seeds of doubt are sown: should they be as enamoured of Richard as they first thought?

The main character then returns, up to his old tricks, this time feigning declarations of peace and utter dismay at Clarence's death. The King goes off to his death-bed and the Duchess of York interrupts him trying out the throne for size – a schoolboy caught with his hand in the sweetie jar. The concept of Richard's awful relationship with his mother is shared with the audience as I turn directly to them with the comic but undoubtedly painful utterance of, 'My mother'.

Buckingham becomes an ally and the Princes arrive in London. Richard appears again as the evil jester, this time in the guise of the jokey uncle, but by now there should be a sense of trepidation amongst the audience. Their laughter is tinged with revulsion at the historically well known fact of the Princes' impending demise. The murders of Rivers, Vaughan and Grey at Pomfret and the arrest of Hastings, so graphically displayed in our production, only serve to heighten their doubts. As yet, Richard should be totally unaware of this shift in allegiance. His other self, the audience, has not yet found a voice inside its own mind and things seem to be proceeding quite smoothly.

The mock siege of London is where Richard first has a fleeting glimpse of this growing antipathy and a realization that his alter ego is starting to have doubts. Having forced the Mayor to agree to Richard's succession, Buckingham tells of his failed efforts to gain the approval of the citizens of London:

BUCKINGHAM: And when my oratory drew to an end, I bid them that did love
      their country's good cry, 'God save Richard, England's royal King!
RICHARD: And did they so?
BUCKINGHAM: No, so God help me, they spake not a word.   (III.vii.20–4)

For Richard, this is the most serious obstacle that he has had to face. Without the people's approval the crown will still remain a distant dream. Shakespeare, however, sets up a wonderful laugh on the reply, 'No, so God help me' by leaving a six beat pause immediately before it. The audience seems to find Richard's dilemma extremely funny – not the right reaction at all. For the first time they are laughing *at* Richard and not *with* him. This moment is enhanced by my look of disbelief, for the audience must be made to realize what effect they have had. A tiny seed of doubt has been sown, a fatal chink in Richard's armour has been exposed, and although for now it can be shrugged off quite easily, the devastating dénouement of the play has had its small beginnings.

And so to the fulfilment of Richard's purpose in life, 'the open air' he speaks of in *Henry VI, Part Three*, the day for which he has 'toiled' so desperately – his coronation. From the start, however, things go very wrong. In our production there is complete silence as he steps forward for what he believes should be a rapturous reception. (This idea stemmed from seeing pictures of the Rumanian dictator Ceaucescu walking on to a balcony to jeers instead of applause.) Problems such as Buckingham's allegiance and the worrying threat of Richmond cloud Richard's mind. But this is nothing compared to the dangerous schism that is developing between the audience and himself. As Queen Anne is led off the stage to her death by the ghosts of Richard's previous victims, a silent questioning voice of disapproval enters his soul in answer to his explanation of why all this is necessary:

> Uncertain way of gain! But I am in
> So far in blood that sin will pluck on sin. (IV.ii.62–3)

This is played not with fiendish exuberance, almost self-congratulatory in tone, but rather as a sudden terrifying thought of sad realization. The next line, 'Tear-falling pity dwells not in this eye' is a fervent denial both to the audience and to himself. Richard must not allow any sentiment to enter his being and the panic displayed when this 'pin-prick' of conscience stings him is a direct consequence of the shattering of the audience/Richard relationship. Their silence now threatens much worse to come. He is now of two separate minds – the one, still greedily growing in evil designs and the other, the audience, questioning and disapproving, threatening Richard's very sanity.

Alone once more, Richard desperately tries to regain the audience's confidence with news of the removal of all possible young contenders to his crown and of his plans for thwarting Richmond by marrying his late brother's daughter, Elizabeth. But the old magic has gone and the glee with which he regales them falls on deaf ears. The sense of revulsion at his triumphantly mocking statement, 'To her go I, a jolly thriving wooer' (IV.iii.43), is palpable and the murder of his wife and both Princes, although politically necessary, has finally turned the audience against him for ever.

14 David Troughton as Richard, with his mother, the Duchess of York (Diana Coupland), *Richard III*, Act IV, Scene iv: 'I will be mild and gentle in my words.'

The meetings with the Duchess of York and the Dowager Queen also have a profound effect in hastening his path to destruction. Already by this time approaching madness because of his self doubts, he readily accepts a chance of reconciliation with his mother and slowly curls up in her lap, relishing a love that he never experienced. But instead of words of comfort, he receives a vicious condemnation of his life ending with a damning curse of death. Once more the dream has turned into a nightmare, with the audience displaying no sympathy at all for his silent scream of agony (the inspiration for this coming from Munch's 'The Scream'). The ironic echo of the mock scream Richard let out when Margaret damned him in Act One, Scene Three haunts him further.

During the highly charged political persuasion scene that follows, the audience rears its ugly head once more. Elizabeth maintains that a marriage with her daughter is impossible

> Unless thou couldst put on some other shape,
> And not be Richard that hath done all this. (IV.iv.286–7)

93

Richard retorts:

> Men shall deal unadvisedly sometimes,
> Which after-hours gives leisure to repent.   (IV.iv.292–3)

His first line is explanatory; I insert a long pause before 'unadvisedly' as he wildly searches for this much less damning word, inducing laughter from the audience. What a facile adjective to describe all the foul deeds he has committed – 'economical with the truth' one might say. But again, this is not the usual Richard laugh, the one of evil appreciation. This is one of disbelief which visibly shakes Richard and the second line, therefore, becomes another 'pin-prick' of conscience which stops him in his tracks. The word 'repent' hits home. He carries on with the scene, now burdened with the certainty that all is not well, manifesting itself not only in the urgency of his delivery but also through the increased pain experienced from his deformity. The audience is now affecting both body and soul and is beginning to win the battle.

This then is the Richard who attempts to defeat Richmond on the field of Bosworth, the man who started the play in complete control, with the audience fascinated by the sheer genius of his 'performance', willing to be 'woo'd' by his devilish delight, but now in complete disarray, the audience acting as his 'conscience' which has slowly invaded his mind like a pernicious tumour. The slide from confident protagonist to crazed victim is almost complete.

At the opening of Act Five, Richard is on the verge of breakdown, crazily barking out orders to his demoralized henchmen. The audience has by now taken a firm hold as Richard answers their imaginary questions:

> Here pitch our tent, even here in Bosworth field . . .
> Here will I lie tonight.
> But where tomorrow? Well, all's one for that.   (V.iii.1, 7–8)

In the four-syllable pause of the second line, I gaze out at the audience as if someone has inquired of me, 'where will you lie tomorrow?', the two other meanings of the word 'lie', as 'deceive' and 'die', being horrifically obvious. Richard repeats the inquiry out loud and then dismisses it with the curt, 'Well, all's one for that'. He declines the proffered food, a piece of bread, but asks for wine which he pathetically explains he needs as Dutch-courage.

Alone at last, Richard attempts a final reconciliation with the audience and God. I take both the bread and wine and set up a simple altar on the rubble-strewn stage, using my cross-handled dagger as a primitive crucifix. But instead of finding a restored friendship and possible redemption in this act of the Last Sacrament, on drinking the blood of Christ I conjure up a manifestation of the audience's hatred; the ghosts of all Richard's past victims who sit beside him at a large oblong table, surrounding the beatific Richmond, praying for Richard's defeat and the future King Henry's success. The image of Jesus and his disciples looms large but this time it is Richard, the devil, and not Richmond, the son of God, who has certainly had his Last Supper.

This episode is the catalyst for the Conscience speech, a stumbling block for any actor playing Richard III. There are two main problems to be solved. How can a totally evil character suddenly have a conscience and to whom is he talking? In our production, however, these difficulties never seemed part of the equation. Richard had already displayed an awareness of a 'conscience' and had made quite clear that the audience was a theatrical extension of his own self, with whom he could converse at any point in the play. The whole speech, therefore, becomes the logical conclusion to all that has gone before, and not the sudden unlikely occurrence that seemed traditional. It can be seen in its true light as pure debate, without the need for any 'frightened acting' – a direct confrontation with the audience, with Richard seated at the front of the stage, daring them to criticize the life that he has led. He starts by explaining: 'Richard loves Richard; that is, I and I' (v.iii.184). (The reading of the first Quarto, not the more familiar 'I am I' was important to me here.) My pointing gestures indicate that the first 'Richard' in the sentence is the audience and the second is himself, the man. Two separate identities forming one complete person creating 'I and I'. The voices inside his head, however, are not to be placated and the accusations start coming thick and fast. Through a series of their imaginary questions and his spoken replies, he realizes for the first time that the widening gulf between him and his 'conscience' might well be his undoing.

And then the most important lines in the speech, the ones upon which I had based the entire premise that the audience should be the active protagonist that they had finally become:

> My conscience hath a thousand several tongues,
> And every tongue brings in a several tale,
> And every tale condemns me for a villain.   (v.iii.194–6)

And there they sit, these 'thousand several tongues', right in front of him – fifteen hundred on a good night! They have laughed with him, gone along with him, been amazed by him and finally have separated from him, forming two halves of the same character – good and evil, devil and God. I play the last line with stress on the word 'me' making quite clear that Richard alone, and not the audience, is the 'villain'. Technically, I break the iambic rhythm, but in doing so cause the line to falter, echoing the gravity of his realization. The small seed of conscience which had been planted initially as a mere 'pin-prick' all those scenes ago, has been carefully nurtured throughout the play, and finally the flower of morality has attained its full, glorious blossom.

Richard panics and threatens the audience with 'I shall despair . . .' (v.iii.201). That small word 'despair': it had occurred before in the scene with Lady Anne:

ANNE: Fouler than heart can think thee, thou canst make
           No excuse current but to hang thyself.
RICHARD: By such despair I should accuse myself.   (I.ii.83–5)

What does it actually mean? A brief word of explanation: according to the Arden editor, it is 'the state in which one loses all hope of being worthy of divine forgiveness, a state so degraded that its automatic concomitant was suicide.' To any Roman Catholic it was, and indeed still is, a cardinal sin. Judas Iscariot had experienced this state after he had betrayed Christ, and had hanged himself, which neatly explains the ironic reference in the above. In the Conscience speech, however, the word assumes a much darker meaning. From Richard's point of view, it is perhaps the most important word in the play so far because it reveals not only the depths to which he has descended but, more especially, the certainty of his imminent death. Even the iambic stress emphasizes this fact, falling as it does on the word 'shall' – not just that Richard shall *die*, but that he *shall* die. 'There is no creature loves' him. He continues:

> Nay, wherefore should they, since that I myself
> Find in myself no pity to myself?   (v.iii.203–4)

Once again I make perfectly clear with gestures that the first 'myself' is the audience, and the other two, himself. There is nothing he can do, no redemption to be found. While his other self remains implacable, Richard will, indeed, march 'hand in hand to hell' (v.iii.314).

This terrible perception is of paramount importance to what follows. Upon being awoken the next morning, I point in panic at the audience when exclaiming:

> Ratcliffe, I fear, I fear! . . .
> By the apostle Paul, shadows tonight
> Have struck more terror to the soul of Richard
> Than can the substance of ten thousand soldiers
> Armèd in proof and led by shallow Richmond.
>
> (v.iii.215, 217–20)

Richard conjures up the terrifying vision of his impending death not via Richmond but through the ominous 'shadows' that are the audience. This culminates in the harrowing discovery that he himself is finally capable of tears, a physical emotion never experienced before. On noticing that his favourite 'sun will not be seen today' all the horrors of the previous night cause him to break down completely; he touches the tears that come to his eyes and holds one up to examine it; and the sad realization of what life could and should have meant for him is present in 'I would these dewy tears were from the ground' (v.iii.284). (In actual fact, Shakespeare was probably indicating that it was raining and that Richard would have preferred the 'tears' to be dew, foretelling of fine weather for the battle. In changes of interpretation such as this one, which I feel is completely justified, can be seen the limitless discoveries that can be made when performing Shakespeare, and why, over four hundred years later, in the phrase of Terry Hands, his plays are still so 'actor-friendly'.)

The need for any specific battle scenes, therefore, becomes superfluous. Unable to live with the two separate identities within himself, Richard dies at the hands of his conscience rather than on the point of a sword. Of course, historically, it is thought that Richard met his end in a suicidal charge of two hundred cavalry against the ranks of ten thousand soldiers, in a desperate bid to reach Richmond before the wavering Stanley could lend his weight to the opposition forces. He failed and was viciously killed, having had his mount fall under him. Richmond then had him dragged through the streets of Leicester attached by the hair to a horse's tail, and buried with a minimum of ceremony in a monastery garden. Years later, during Henry VIII's break with the Roman Church, Richard's grave was dug up, his bones were thrown into a river and his coffin was used as a pig-trough. Such was the end of the aspiring Duke of Gloucester.

97

In trying to capture the flavour of this inauspicious demise, rather than having a full-blown battle on stage with the devilish Richard receiving the victorious final coup de grace from the God-like Richmond, our play ends on a dying fall. With several cuts and the addition of lines, both from the beginning of the play and *Henry VI, Part Three*, the severance of the relationship with the audience can be completed, his death can be portrayed more theatrically and the overall 'devil versus God' metaphor can be realized.

Richard's famous, 'A horse! a horse! my kingdom for a horse!' (v.iv.7) is first screamed out as if in the midst of battle. Its repetition, however, is aimed sotto voce at the audience, a last dying plea for help from those who have had the greatest hand in his downfall. In performance, each separate phrase is purposefully directed to the whole theatre from the stalls to the upper circle – no-one must be ignored – but there can be no final reprieve, his state of 'despair' is complete and the audience remain silent. The spotlight that has illuminated me throughout the play begins to fade as I turn to watch the ghosts' eerie pavane above. Richard's spirit is slowly ebbing away, his past life flashing before him, back to the opening lines of the play to a time of the jester when anything seemed possible. But now there is no laughter or cheering, just accusing stares. I turn once more to the audience hoping to recapture Richard's malevolent glee – 'But I, that am not shap'd for sportive tricks . . .' – but this too gets no reaction. He is then transported further back in time, remembering a vow that he had once made:

> And I – like one lost in a thorny wood,
> That rents the thorns and is rent with the thorns,
> Seeking a way and straying from the way,
> Not knowing how to find the open air,
> But toiling desperately to find it out –
> Torment myself to catch the English crown;
> And from that torment I will free myself,
> Or hew my way out with a bloody axe.   (*3 Henry VI*, III.ii.174–81)

This one speech marvellously encapsulates his whole reason for existence. It describes the psychological workings of an emotionally confused human being and his reckless craving for power and it ends with a definitive statement about the consequences should he fail. The innate poetic imagery is savagely 'cut off' with the tiny but telling word 'axe', which I venomously spit out to the audience. He is about to die, and reluctantly lays his sword and crown to the ground. With a gesture of incomprehension, his final words, 'All the world to nothing' settle quietly on the hushed auditorium. Richard ceases to be. He sits at the edge of the stage listening to Richmond's victory speech, reproachfully eyeing each member of the audience, thinking of what might have been. His 'conscience' has triumphed and Richard resides in hell – but is that the end?

In the four slow hand claps which make up the cynical acclamation of the newly crowned king, Richard's soul, in the guise of the very devil, rises once more and with a wicked grimace seems to say, 'You ain't seen nothing yet! You people may have won this time, but what of Cromwell, Hitler, Stalin, Hussein et al?' Here, there is the dreadful promise of worse to come – you may destroy the purveyors of foul deeds but you will never rid the world of evil itself. *Richard* is dead but the *devil* is still very much alive.

Admittedly, the conclusion of our play bears little resemblance to what Shakespeare actually wrote. To the purist, the cuts and added text would seem sacrilegious – what a way to treat the Bard! – and I understand entirely the criticisms that could be levelled against this rather unusual dénouement. I would, however, stoutly defend this alternative outcome.

Firstly, it derives from the very essence of what had been plotted before and has not been added for its own theatrical sake. All the above events slowly evolved throughout rehearsals, many different ideas being tried out and discarded in favour of this foreboding finale. And whether one likes it or not, the fact that people might go out of the theatre pondering the issues proposed and the whole premise of good versus evil, rather than wondering what shopping they need to buy at Safeways tomorrow, is, I think, a good objective to have in mind. The experience of theatre must be enjoyable, uplifting and thought-provoking. Without that, we may as well vegetate at home, slumped in our armchairs, mindlessly watching, 'Home and Away'.

And secondly, and most importantly, I feel that, from Shakespeare's point of view, this ending serves his play extremely well. The many quarto editions are entitled, *The History of Richard the Third* while the Folio bears our title *The Tragedy of Richard the Third*. If we are to believe modern academic thinking, Shakespeare himself made this amendment in what I feel to be an attempt at recognizing the wider aspects that abound in the play. It is not solely a historical drama, the final part of the tetralogy to which it is the conclusion, 'The Wars of the Roses', but rather an insight into the development of good inside a seemingly impenetrably evil man, the 'tragedy' of the piece being his self-inflicted downfall, which in our production is brought about by the audience itself.

Indeed, the simple change of the word 'History' to 'Tragedy' allows the play to be performed without the strictures of supposed historical accuracy and the usual argument that a knowledge of past events is essential in appreciating *Richard III* becomes superfluous. It is a play about the struggles of human experience in its most universal sense; a true tragedy, and as such, having rehearsed and performed it over the past few months, I deem it to be a much richer piece of theatre than it is ever given credit for, when allowed the freedom to be produced in its near entirety and as a separate drama in its own right.

Queen Elizabeth in
Richard III

SUSAN BROWN

SUSAN BROWN played Queen Elizabeth in Steven Pimlott's production of *Richard III* at the Royal Shakespeare Theatre in 1995 and in
the following year at the Barbican Theatre. It was her first season in
Stratford, though earlier that year she had appeared as Mrs Heyst
in Strindberg's *Easter* for the RSC in the Pit theatre at the Barbican. Her
other role at Stratford in 1995 was the Nurse in *Romeo and Juliet*. Earlier
Shakespeare roles had been Titania in *A Midsummer Night's Dream*,
Nerissa in *The Merchant of Venice*, Regan in *King Lear* at Birmingham
Repertory Theatre, and Gertrude in *Hamlet* at the Royal Lyceum
Theatre, Edinburgh. A wide range of modern and classical work in
London and provincial theatre, and on television, includes Mrs Sullen
in *The Beaux' Stratagem*, Mrs Arbuthnot in *A Woman of No Importance*,
Poncia in *The House of Bernarda Alba*, Millamant in *The Way of the World*
and Helen in the original production of *Road*.

There are many ways to make the journey to the discovery of the heart
and soul of a character, and my memory of Elizabeth Woodville from
doing the Plantagenets at school sent me first to the history books.
What emerged was a subtle but fascinating difference between the real
woman and Shakespeare's Elizabeth. Over and over again the same
adjectives are used by historians to describe her: greedy, ambitious,
arrogant, unscrupulous, wily, ruthless. Shakespeare's words for her are
bold, quick, ingenious, forward, capable. In other words he cleaned her
up and in the process, I think, simplified her. I knew I wanted to reclaim
her complexity. For that reason I decided that my Elizabeth should lean
as much towards the real woman as the text and the director would
allow. With that thought in my mind I put the history books away and
came back to the play.

    Richard III is the longest play in the canon after *Hamlet* and *King Lear*.
Steven Pimlott's inevitably cut script arrived some time before rehearsals began. Retyped on A4 paper and split into acts but not scenes,

it looked like a new play – not a published text with swathes of crossings out. Initially, along with most of the cast, I was disoriented by this and spent much time scrabbling through my Penguin copy to see what exactly had been cut and where scenes began and ended. But I grew to love its continuity on the page and the fact that there was so much room for notes opposite the text. The women in *Richard III* are often savagely cut, but not in this production: Steven, on the first day of rehearsal, talked of them as the emotional and intuitive heart of the play – the antithesis of the conspiring men. An almost exclusively male world of politics operates alongside the darker world of pain and retribution that Margaret brings with her. Elizabeth has a foot in both camps, and is radically changed by events, which makes her journey especially exciting to play.

At the start she is a woman in a man's world, playing a male game with some success, desperate to survive in the power struggle. For a commoner, albeit of the upper middle class, she has attained an extraordinary position in the English court. But her meal ticket, Edward IV, is on his last legs. She is surrounded by power-hungry nobles: she has a dying, syphilitic husband. She and her young son, the heir to the throne, are more and more precariously placed.

The court is full of Elizabeth's over-promoted relatives – historically dozens of them. Small wonder that she had a legendary talent for making enemies. Shakespeare presents her three most important relatives: her brother Lord Rivers and her two sons by her first husband, Lord Grey and the Marquess of Dorset. In the first court scene (i.iii) there is a short exchange between the four of them before the heavyweights come in. 'If he were dead, what would betide on me?' (i.iii.6) is Elizabeth's first line. By putting a particularly heavy emphasis on the personal pronoun, I can start as I mean to go on. Me, me, me is the motif for Elizabeth's early scenes. Whatever her political influence over her husband, she hasn't been able to stop him from offering Richard the lord-protectorship of the young prince. But even when she gives the others this information she adds, of Richard, 'A man that loves not me, nor none of you' (line 13). Her days as queen may be numbered, but she sure as hell wants to be the comfortably positioned queen mother.

She is in the last throes of being a real political force. When Buckingham and Stanley (the Earl of Derby) enter she is still trying, in status terms, to play a ten, although her actual status is dwindling fast. With an arrogant and patronizing tone of voice I can use her speech to Stanley to show how much she must have needled the court over her years as queen:

> The Countess Richmond, good my Lord of Derby,
> To your good prayer will scarcely say amen.
> Yet, Derby, notwithstanding she's your wife
> And loves not me, be you, good lord, assured
> I hate not you for her proud arrogance.   (I.iii.20–4)

How they all must have loathed this parvenue.

It's important for me to say that I don't loathe her at all. I can see and understand her effect on other people, but she is a survivor, and I have a lot of regard for her sharpness, her wit and her single-mindedness. At the start of any rehearsal period I always feel as if there are two of us, the character and I, walking beside each other, then overlapping, and then if possible fusing, like a double image coming into focus. As Elizabeth, for much of the play I feel an overriding sense of loneliness surrounded by machismo. She is hanging on so tightly that when real grief comes to her and all her artifice is stripped away, the emotion that rises in her is truly cathartic.

At court Buckingham and Stanley keep up a frosty politeness, but not Richard. The exchange between him and Elizabeth bars no holds. Her position may be weakening, but she won't give up trying to match him in verbal dexterity. David Troughton (who plays Richard) and I agreed that, however allergic they may be to one another, there is a relish in their adversarial clashes. He knows her – indeed, it is from him that 'bold, quick, ingenious, forward, capable' comes – and she thinks she knows him. This exchange is particularly revealing:

RIVERS: My lord of Gloucester, in those busy days
             Which here you urge to prove us enemies,
             We followed then our lord, our sovereign king;
             So should we you, if you should be our king.
RICHARD: If I should be? I had rather be a pedlar.
             Far be it from my heart, the thought thereof!
ELIZABETH: As little joy, my lord, as you suppose
             You should enjoy, were you this country's king,
             As little joy you may suppose in me
             That I enjoy, being the Queen thereof.   (I.iii.144–53)

Rivers puts Richard on the spot, and Richard parries deftly, but Elizabeth strongly suspects his ambitions, although at this point she has no idea of the lengths he will go to to achieve them. So rather than imbuing her speech with self-pity – 'I'm having a terrible time and feeling so joyless' – I use a heavily ironic tone. In other words, 'I know exactly how much you would enjoy being king, and that is exactly how much I enjoy being queen; and what's more, you're not and I am.'

When the king is present (II. i) Elizabeth is more circumspect. Edward is trying to unite the factions before he dies. Hypocritical professions of love abound. When Edward asks Elizabeth to be reconciled with Lord Hastings he adds, 'And what you do, do it unfeignedly' (II.i.22). Some hope. But she allows Hastings to kiss her hand with reasonable grace. Richard is particularly fulsome in his protestations of reconciliation. He ends by saying 'I thank my God for my humility' (line 74). Elizabeth doesn't believe a word of it. Her response, 'A holy day shall this be kept hereafter', is delivered with barely concealed acidity.

In this scene Richard gives the news of Clarence's death. Historically there is little doubt that, at least indirectly, Elizabeth and her relatives bore the responsibility for his murder. Clarence was the king's brother: he could have stood in the way of the young prince's accession. This is probably the strongest example of Shakespeare whitewashing Elizabeth's character. In the play Elizabeth is deeply shocked by Clarence's death. She doesn't know that Richard is responsible, but strongly suspects it. The screws are tightening.

What was she going to look like, this Elizabeth? It is a recurrent problem that, with only an eight-week rehearsal period, the set and costume designs are necessarily presented as a *fait accompli* before the actors have taken hold of the play. There is no time for decisions to be arrived at organically and room for manoeuvre is limited. It was therefore a delight to me that Tobias Hoheisel's costume for Elizabeth as queen accorded so well with my feelings about her. I wanted her to look flashy and a bit overdressed, as if her clothes budget had made a pretty big hole in the royal coffers – not vulgar, but bordering on the tasteless – and that is exactly how it is. The style is loosely Elizabethan with, in Tobias's words, a flavour of the 1950s. Students I talked to during the Stratford season often asked why there was a rabbit sewn on the hem of my dress. Tobias knew that rabbits were symbols of good luck in Elizabethan England and had spoken of introducing one somewhere in the costumes. When the costume department were putting the trim round the hem of my dress they turned one of the triangles into a small rabbit, intending to remove

15 Susan Brown as Queen Elizabeth, with Dorset and Rivers (Simon Chadwick and Robert Arnold), Edward IV (Robin Nedwell), and Richard (David Troughton), *Richard III*, Act II, Scene i: 'Who knows not that the gentle Duke is dead?'

it when it had been noticed and the joke enjoyed. Tobias fell in love with it, so it stayed. I love it too, first because I like the idea of Elizabeth as a superstitious woman, second because I like the ostentatious display of that superstition, and third because I think she needs all the luck she can get. In the same vein I decided to take Margaret's 'painted queen' taunt (which in fact means counterfeit) at face value and wear, at the start, a heavy and elaborate make-up; the detail of it can't be seen in such a large theatre, but I hope the effect of it carries. It is a cover-up, part of her armour in the men's world, and the hour spent putting it on is a helpful preparation. As Elizabeth's world falls apart, and the selfishness and posturing give way to genuine emotion, she becomes exposed. During the play I spend much of my offstage time removing more and more make-up until, by the end, she has a bare face.

The way she changes, and her growing humanity, follow in great part from the development of her relationships with the other women in the play. Elizabeth's mother-in-law is the Duchess of York: blue blood from top to toe. Dominic Mancini (a fifteenth-century monk-diplomat in

London at the time of Richard's accession) says that following her son's marriage to Elizabeth the Duchess 'fell into such a frenzy that she offered to submit to a public inquiry and assert that Edward was not the offspring of her husband but was conceived in adultery, and therefore in no wise worthy of the honour of kingship'. In the play Elizabeth's first meeting with the Duchess (ii.ii) is just after Edward's death. Diana Coupland (who plays the Duchess) and I decided to make the animosity between the two women explicit (something that I admit would be more difficult if Clarence's children were present; they have been cut from the scene). The stage direction says that Elizabeth enters 'with her hair about her ears' – Shakespearian, presumably, for grief. Following my chosen line I decided to ignore this direction and play the scene in a state of selfish anger and of worry for my own future. It seems to me to make perfect sense. Elizabeth's marriage to Edward, however sexually and emotionally successful at its outset, had become for her little more than a way of securing her position; and Edward's illness (as Robin Nedwell's performance shows) had ravaged him grotesquely. The decision means that Elizabeth's line 'Edward, my lord, thy son, our king, is dead' (ii.ii.40) is delivered to the Duchess with scant regard for her feelings at having just lost another son, and the speech continues in the same vein. The Duchess's reply ends:

> Thou art a widow; yet thou art a mother,
> And hast the comfort of thy children left;
> But death hath snatched my husband from mine arms
> And plucked two crutches from my feeble hands,
> Clarence and Edward. O, what cause have I . . .
> To overgo thy woes and drown thy cries!   (ii.ii.55–61)

It becomes an accusatory acknowledgement of Elizabeth's insensitivity. (The dots in the quotation are mine. Where they appear they indicate a cut in the text as we performed it.)

In rehearsal Steven, who was completely in support of the road my Elizabeth was travelling, became concerned that this scene was being pushed too hard to accommodate my personal brief; he thought the shape of the play perhaps needed an outpouring of grief at this point. I had worked with Steven before and I have great trust in him, so I gave it my best shot. For several days he coaxed more and more genuine grief from me. It felt wrong, but I kept my counsel and an open mind. After one run-through he suddenly said 'Go back to what you were doing – it

106

works.' I was glad, but it had been important to explore the more traditional way of playing the scene, and when I did go back I felt much braver and more confident about the choice we had made.

The Duchess, much to Elizabeth's surprise, offers (II.iv) to go with her to sanctuary when the news comes that Rivers and Grey have been arrested. In the face of Elizabeth's impending tragedy the older, wiser woman offers support. But it is not until I hear her curse Richard, her own son, as he lies in her lap (IV.iv) that I realize the depth of her pain and fortitude. The Duchess, as much as Margaret, gives Elizabeth the strength to deal with Richard in their final gladiatorial scene together.

Anne also contributes to that for me. Elizabeth and Anne appear in only one scene together – the women at the Tower (IV.i) – and when they meet, Elizabeth is on the defensive. Anne is now married to Richard, Elizabeth's most dangerous enemy, and defensiveness anyway is built into Elizabeth: she has had to deal with disapproval and barely concealed scorn from the blue-bloods for many years. To paranoid ears even a greeting as straightforward as Anne's 'God give your graces both / A happy and a joyful time of day' (IV.i.5–6) can sound double-edged. Things move quickly during this scene. Elizabeth discovers that she is forbidden to visit her sons, that Richard is about to become king, and that Anne is to be crowned queen. There is a way of saying, as Elizabeth does to Anne, 'Go, go, poor soul! I envy not thy glory. / To feed my humour wish thyself no harm' (IV.i.63–4) that says 'Well, if you have to be crowned, you'd better get on with it, and please don't even *think* of killing yourself on *my* account.' Anne replies simply, with none of my archness. She confesses her weakness, her regret and her misery. In an instant it cuts through all my recalcitrance, all my attempts to cling to royal status. When Elizabeth says 'Poor heart, adieu. I pity thy complaining', it is deeply, truly meant. Anne replies 'No more than with my soul I mourn for yours' (lines 87–8), and on Elizabeth's initiative they hold on to each other tightly and for a long time. This mutual support brings a new, very different kind of strength to me. Elizabeth is a man's woman. I can't imagine her having embraced, with real empathy, any other woman in her life.

When Brackenbury bars her (earlier in the same scene) from seeing her young sons she is combative; when she urges her eldest son Dorset to flee to Richmond it is politically sensible, but she still can't help bringing up her own loss of position as 'England's counted queen'. After the

16 Susan Brown as Queen Elizabeth with Queen Margaret (Cherry Morris),
   Richard III, Act IV, Scene iv: 'Teach me how to curse mine enemies.'

exchange with Anne a wholly new tone comes to her. Her final speech is more lyrical than anything that has gone before:

> Stay, yet look back with me unto the Tower.
> Pity, you ancient stones, those tender babes
> Whom envy hath immured within your walls –
> Rough cradle for such little pretty ones!
> Rude ragged nurse, old sullen playfellow
> For tender princes – use my babies well!
> So foolish sorrow bids your stones farewell.   (IV.i.97–103)

She is reaching out; the emotion is of love and deep motherly anxiety. For once there is no mention of self-interest.

The next time Elizabeth is seen (IV.iv) is after the murder of the princes. The timescale is unstated: she could have known of their deaths for some hours before her appearance; but it seems to me to be much more theatrically interesting to let the audience in on the moment of her most terrible discovery – that her young sons are dead. 'Ah, my poor princes! Ah, my tender babes' (IV.iv.9), are the words she enters with. The first 'Ah' becomes a prolonged cry that starts offstage at the moment she is given the news and develops into an outpouring of agony and grief. Margaret and the Duchess are there too, but the three of us start off very separated from each other. We talked a lot in rehearsal of the great differences between them. They are so often lumped together as the weeping queens, and we wanted to avoid a miasma of interchangeable emotion. The Duchess's sorrow is generations old and she relates it with a quiet stoicism; Margaret's sorrow is alive with long-felt rage and with triumph at the fulfilment of her vengeance; Elizabeth's sorrow is shockingly fresh, and it pours out of her like a river bursting its banks. This is, as I see her, a woman who has never previously felt – or perhaps allowed herself to feel – real emotional pain. (Sustaining, over many performances, this high level of emotional intensity can play havoc with the voice. Without the RSC voice department I could never have developed the vocal reserves necessary.)

When in the early court scene (I.iii) Margaret burst in with her voice of nemesis, Elizabeth was able to face her out, to bury her own worst fears, to let herself be a part of the men's mockery and disrespect towards Margaret; to dissociate herself. But now the chips are down. This is her initiation into Margaret's world, and Margaret doesn't let her off the hook for a moment. When Cherry Morris (who plays Margaret) starts the speech 'I called thee then vain flourish of my fortune' (line 82) she puts her arms round me, to bait me, to rub salt into the wound, and I find myself desperately needing that physical contact, holding on to her and trying to draw strength and comfort from her, not wanting to let her go even as her handling of me becomes increasingly harsh, both verbally and physically (see figure 16).

Throughout rehearsals Steven, together with Liz Rankin in charge of movement, constantly encouraged an expansive and full-blown phys-icality of the kind that English actors are so often accused of lacking (a charge which I think is anyway a myth). This scene, which we all felt had strong resonances of Greek tragedy, particularly benefited from that encouragement. It is full of grand gesture which I hope we inhabit with real emotional truth.

Interestingly, Elizabeth is the only one of the four women who never directly curses anybody – not even Richard. She believes in the power of the curse, as they all do: she talks about cursing, and as Margaret leaves she begs for instruction in how to curse; but I think she has spent so much of her life trying to operate on the political level that this incantat-ory, black-magic world of sorcery does not come easily to her. This is a woman with a rabbit on her dress rather than a curse on her lips.

When Richard enters, my instinct is to attack him physically, to draw blood, and when the words come they are not a curse but a cry of rage and loss:

> Hid'st thou that forehead with a golden crown
> Where should be branded, if that right were right,
> The slaughter of the prince that owed that crown
> And the dire death of my poor sons and brothers?
> Tell me, thou villain-slave, where are my children? (IV.iv.140–4)

It is a long time before Elizabeth speaks again. I lie on the ground feeling completely empty and emotionally spent. Then comes the moment of the Duchess's curse. I can never quite believe what I have heard. In rehearsal we realized that we could think of no other example in literature of a mother cursing her own son, wishing him dead. In performance that moment is always shocking and extraordinary to listen to.

The Duchess leaves. Elizabeth has nothing to stay for. When she says, 'Though far more cause, yet much less spirit to curse / Abides in me, I say amen to her' (lines 197–8), she means it. She is drained, utterly exhausted. Then she hears Richard say:

You have a daughter called Elizabeth
Virtuous and fair, royal and gracious.   (IV.iv.204–5)

Now a remarkable gear-change happens. The political side of her nature snaps back into place. But this is not the old Elizabeth. It is an altogether wiser, more humane, less posturing creature. Through her genuine grief she has gained in genuine stature. She doesn't have to try to play a ten any more: she is a ten.

When she replies to Richard about her daughter, she immediately comes up with a piece of political strategy:

> And must she die for this? O, let her live,
> And I'll corrupt her manners, stain her beauty,
> Slander myself as false to Edward's bed . . .
> I will confess she was not Edward's daughter.   (IV.iv.206–11)

In other words, 'Spare her life and I'll make sure she has no claim to the throne.' Soon after, the bombshell comes:

> I mean that with my soul I love thy daughter
> And do intend to make her Queen of England.   (lines 263–4)

It takes me several seconds to respond to this, and it is hard to describe the mixture of thoughts that flood through my mind. When I ask him 'Well then, who dost thou mean shall be her king?' (line 265) I already know the answer, but I need to hear Richard actually say it: 'Even he that makes her queen. Who else should be?' (line 266). In rehearsal, at this point, my instinct was to burst into laughter, partly with relief – he's not going to kill her – and partly in sheer amazement at the gall of the man: 'You can't be serious.' The laughter was useful – I do still have a moment of inward hysteria – but wrong. The stakes are too high. This is no joke. I have to think fast and think clearly. Elizabeth knows that Richmond has shown an interest in marrying her daughter, but I don't believe that at this stage she has consented to that marriage. I also don't believe that she has any intention at any point during this scene of letting Richard near the young Elizabeth. But there is a life-or-death political game to be played to keep her daughter, and probably herself, alive. It is a game I think Elizabeth plays brilliantly. Undoubtedly Richard's powers are declining; he is not the man he was, but neither is she the woman she was. Now she has found a truly effective voice and can counter every argument he advances.

This is not to say that she has lost every shred of her own ambition; David Troughton's Richard knows that this is the Achilles heel of my Elizabeth. The throne is on the stage; Richard arrived being carried on it, and during his speech beginning 'Look what is done cannot be now amended' (line 291) he leads me to it and puts my hand on the back of it. At the end of his speech I sit down, and it feels pretty powerful – sitting on the throne with the king standing beside me. But my own ambition is very much under control now, and besides, if my daughter marries Richmond, and he defeats Richard, I become queen mother anyway.

I make a supreme effort to stay in my head during this scene, but the anguish of Elizabeth's bereavement is only just beneath the surface, and in one speech I find it impossible to stop her heart from breaking through:

> God's wrong is most of all . . .
> If thou hadst feared to break an oath by Him,
> Th'imperial metal, circling now thy head,
> Had graced the tender temples of my child,
> And both the princes had been breathing here,
> Which now, two tender bedfellows for dust,
> Thy broken faith hath made the prey for worms.
> What canst thou swear by now? (IV.iv.377–87)

But this battle is going to be won with words, not with tears, and by the last line I can get myself back to an intellectual attack. It is towards the end of Richard's long speech beginning 'As I intend to prosper and repent' (line 397) that I absolutely decide that my daughter shall marry Richmond. I know the danger. I have to let Richard believe that he has won me over, but I want the audience to know that he hasn't – and yet if I make it too obvious, then they won't believe that Richard believes me. It's a delicious problem to play.

ELIZABETH: Shall I be tempted of the devil thus?
RICHARD: Ay, if the devil tempt you to do good . . .
ELIZABETH: Yet thou didst kill my children.
RICHARD: But in your daughter's womb I bury them,
Where, in that nest of spicery, they will breed
Selves of themselves, to your recomforture.
ELIZABETH: Shall I go win my daughter to thy will?
RICHARD: And be a happy mother by the deed.
ELIZABETH: I go. Write to me very shortly,
And you shall understand from me her mind. (IV.iv.398–429)

Telling Richard to write is a play for time. She has to get a message to Richmond – which, as the audience learns in the next scene, she manages to do. It is clever that she calls Richard 'you' in the last line, rather than 'thou', which is the form she uses for the whole of the rest of the scene. 'You' has a respectfulness designed to make him sure of his success. 'Bear her my true love's kiss', he says (line 430), as I am leaving, and I know it has to be done. With a flourish I put out my hand to be kissed. David takes my hand, and then wrenches me towards him and kisses me on the mouth with ferocity. At every performance I remember how deeply shocked I was when this first happened in rehearsal. It has nothing to do with sex and everything to do with power. But I know that it means I have succeeded in deceiving him. I can face him out, smile, and turn to leave. Further reassurance comes before I am out of earshot: 'Relenting fool, and shallow, changing woman!' (line 431) he tells the audience. But if he chose to look behind him he would see what they see. I wipe the taste of his kiss off my mouth with contempt. No fool, not shallow, and changing only for the better.

Henry VIII

PAUL JESSON

PAUL JESSON played the title role in Gregory Doran's production of *Henry VIII* at the Swan Theatre in 1996–97 and the following year at the Young Vic Theatre in London and on a tour to the United States. In the same season he played the Gravedigger in *Hamlet*. Earlier work for the RSC had included Ulysses in *Troilus and Cressida*, Northumberland in *Richard II*, Polixenes in *The Winter's Tale*, Enobarbus in *Antony and Cleopatra*, and Prospero in *The Tempest*, as well as Shakespeare in Bond's *Bingo*. His wide range of television work includes major roles in several Shakespeare productions among a variety of other parts, classical and modern. His extensive work in theatre, both in the provinces and in London, including seasons at the Royal Court and the Royal National Theatre, has added to his list of Shakespeare roles those of Gloucester in *Richard III* and Horatio in *Hamlet*.

'Politics is about emotion'
(Tony Benn)

In the friend's house where I am finally piecing together this essay, very mindful that one of the few characteristics I share with Henry VIII is a problem with putting pen to paper, I have come across an empty sweet tin and there on the lid is the portrait that has become so familiar to me. He stands four-square, alone, viewed a little from below to emphasize his height, the right fist grasping his yellow leather glove, the mouth small and mean, the piggy eyes direct but inscrutable. The bottom of the tin states 'Henry VIII, School of Holbein, 1537. Fruit Bonbons. No artificial flavours or colours.' Hmm. So what about my portrayal of Henry? Or indeed Shakespeare's? Any artificial flavours or colours?

One day in August 1996 I was in a fitting room at Angels and Bermans, the theatrical costumiers in Camden Town, trying on brown thirties suits for a play in which I was about to appear at Hampstead

17 Paul Jesson as Henry VIII.

Theatre. Robert Jones, our designer, was there and we got chatting, as
you do. 'So what are you doing next Rob?' '*Henry VIII* in the Swan. Greg
Doran's directing. Do you know him?' 'Yes, we've met socially . . .
Who's your Henry?' 'Not cast yet. Why, would you be interested?' Now
I'm not for a moment suggesting that this is how casting is done at
the RSC – it is a famously tortuous and prolonged affair – but it's an
indication of how the part had been creeping up on me. The offer came
through my agent a couple of weeks later – and I'm sure it would have
anyway, even without the Camden Town coincidence.

I *sort of* leapt at it. I felt I could have a good crack at Henry, but I
paused for thought. The part had nearly come my way a few years
earlier, in a production that didn't happen, so I had read the play and
had a few ideas about it, some of them admittedly rather daft. How
about setting it early twentieth-century, Henry as Edward VII? He was
fat and frivolous, went racing, had several mistresses – Katherine as
Queen Alexandra, Anne Bullen as Lillie Langtry. All this really meant
was that I fancied myself in a frock coat, smoking a cigar. Someone will
do it one day. It would at least point up the fact that Shakespeare was
writing about history very recent to his own time.

I was eventually proved right about one thing. The Swan would be the perfect theatre for it. I had thought this ever since I first worked there in 1990: the warmth of what could be Tudor brick, the thrust stage allowing for both pageantry and intimacy, the ambience of a debating chamber. Why in the theatre's ten-year existence had no-one done it? One answer is because *we* were meant to. Another is that people have not thought the play worth doing. Sir Peter Hall has said that he managed to avoid it for twenty years at the RSC and he is part of a long tradition of harsh critics.

It is perhaps not a great read. There is little poetry or psychological depth and the narrative is fractured; one can understand why it is rarely performed. I had seen it once on television, shot entirely on location in various castles, and had been intrigued by it, partly, I suspect, for its novelty value, but also because the cut and thrust of the language came over well. Those who do have a good word for the play usually say 'And of course it has two great virtuoso roles – Queen Katherine and Cardinal Wolsey.' Thanks very much. At one time even Buckingham used to be cast stronger than the King and for a brief while in rehearsal there was talk of calling the play *All is True*. Great. My first eponymous hero at Stratford and they want to change the title – just because that's what it was originally called.

Then there is the question of whether the play is by Shakespeare. Well, even if half of it was written by Fletcher – an issue I'm not going to pursue here so I refer you to the introduction to any good edition – hell's bells, Shakespeare's friends thought it worthy of inclusion in the First Folio and Henry himself was the most significant king England has ever had. Of course I had to do it.

In studying *Henry VIII* one soon gets a sense of its unique documentary quality. The spare, blunt language, sometimes convoluted in the manner of politicians, the realistic characters and the extraordinarily detailed stage directions based on historical record, all contribute to this and gave us licence to go deeply into research – masses of it. Not just research for context or confidence or interest or to ease one's conscience, but for practical application in performance. Some books were confirmatory, others contradictory, but a picture of Henry and his time emerged whose relevance I would categorize under four headings:

1. *Historical accident*: He was not expected to be king because his elder brother, had he not died, would have become Arthur I. As a result Henry received little or no training for the throne.

2. *Historical context*: Although Henry inherited a secure and peaceful kingdom, his father's reign had been troubled by many rebellions and rival claims to the throne. This must have had some effect on the young prince.

3. *Diplomacy and show*: Outward signs of grandeur, power and wealth were not just a matter of vanity. A sovereign's political image depended upon his appearance, particularly when it came to impressing foreign powers.

4. *Henry's character*: This was clearly of most significance to me as I prepared the role, but how to sum him up, particularly as the adjectives were always laid on with a trowel? And in any case it is Shakespeare's portrait that matters, his 'chosen truth' (Prologue 1.18). What struck me most forcibly in the biographies were his extreme nature (he never did anything by halves) and the contradictions. Energetic and lazy, generous and mean-spirited, brutal and tender – he was all these and more. Inconsistent, unpredictable, volatile – these were the qualities I wanted to look out for and emphasize in a perhaps underwritten part. This may suggest that I was drawing the map before making the exploration – well, why not use the knowledge of those who are intimate with the territory, particularly when they were his contemporaries?

He is the handsomest potentate I ever set eyes on: above the usual height, with an extremely fine calf to his leg, his complexion very fair and light, with auburn hair, and a round face so very beautiful that it would become a pretty woman, his throat being rather long and thick.   (Report quoted in Venetian calendar, 1515)

Hard to know why I'd been cast, until I read this:

A pig, an ass, a dunghill, the spawn of an adder, a basilisk, a lying buffoon, a mad fool with a frothy mouth, a lubberly ass, a frantic madman.   (Martin Luther)

Then there is the more balanced view of someone who knew him well:

He is a prince of royal courage and hath a princely heart: and rather than he will miss or want part of his appetite, he will hazard the loss of one half of his kingdom.
(Thomas Wolsey to Sir William Kingston,
Constable of the Tower, November 1530)

That was written after Wolsey's downfall in the year of his death. My favourite, the one that could most usefully be applied to my performance, is by Sir Thomas More in 1518: 'The king has a way of making

18 A page from the Folger Shakespeare Library copy of Cicero's *De Officina*
with the signature of the young Prince Henry.

every man feel that he is enjoying his special favour.' While still under
this heading of 'Character', I should mention that I have had what I
might call personal contact with Henry – and I don't mean anything
supernatural. When, in 1994, I was on tour to Washington DC with the
RSC production of *The Winter's Tale*, we visited the Folger Shakespeare
Library and there in the archive I held in my hands an edition of Cicero's
De Officina that had belonged to the young Henry. It had been published
in 1502 when he was eleven, the year he became heir to the throne, and
was open at a page where, at the bottom, in a bold firm hand, he had
written 'Thys boke is myne Prynce Henry.' There was the man in the
child.

Physically I would have a hard time measuring up to him, in height
anyway. More private matters are anyone's guess, but he was probably
not the sexual athlete of popular myth. He was six feet three inches tall at
a time when the average height of a man was five feet five and he dwarfed
both Katherine and Anne. At least one of the other actors in our company is taller than me, and in spite of the modest lifts in my boots I have
no chance of towering intimidatingly over everyone else as Henry did.
Girth I could, and did, do something about; the rest would have to be
acted. One thing about Henry really surprised me: I discovered that his

voice was, in fact, quite high-pitched. To emulate that, it seemed to me, would be to court ridicule, so I decided to keep to my manly baritone. Perhaps if I were six inches taller I might have dared something a little more shrill.

Fortunately *Henry VIII* was one of the shows opening the Stratford season, which meant several more weeks of rehearsal than usual, more time for us all to share our researches and to bang in the unusually recalcitrant lines. There was one great day in rehearsal when I realized that in Greg Doran we had a Solomon come to direct. Robert Jones was presenting the model of his magnificent set – basically lead doors that opened to reveal Tudor splendour within – and Greg explained his intention to stage a glimpse of the Field of Cloth of Gold after the Prologue. 'So, Paul', he said, 'you will make your first appearance dressed in gold, wearing the crown, sitting on a golden horse.' I could hardly believe my ears. How could anyone get it so *right*? There are times when directors should just be hugged. Or given money. I did neither I'm afraid, but somehow from then on Greg had my complete confidence. (This theatrical coup nearly brought about my downfall, however, as you will hear later.) Rob's costumes took our breath away. Basically Tudor in inspiration, their sumptuousness can only be properly revealed if one bears in mind that deportment was an absolutely essential part of the education of anyone at court, princes especially. I am constantly telling myself to get those shoulders back.

The events of the play from the Field of Cloth of Gold to Elizabeth's christening cover thirteen years, from 1520 to 1533, with Henry ageing from twenty-eight to forty-two. One episode lies outside this time-span – Henry's endorsement of Cranmer, and the incident of the ring. That probably happened in 1545, but it's a detail of no dramatic importance. Much more important is what period it *seems* as if the play covers: I would suggest it's about three years. The historical chronology is both scrambled and compressed and this poses a problem for Henry's credibility. For example, historically about five years went by between Buckingham being committed to trial in Act One, Scene Two, and Henry meeting Anne Bullen in Act One, Scene Four, and yet in performance it seems for all the world like 'later that same night'. There is a danger that this will make any tenderness Henry shows for Katherine (in I.ii) seem like a sham. There is only one possible line of defence against such misrepresentation: complete sincerity on Henry's part. There are occasions when the audience knows that Henry is being two-faced, such

19 Paul Jesson as Henry, with Queen Katherine (Jane Lapotaire) and
Cardinal Wolsey (Ian Hogg) on either side of him, and members of the court,
in the opening tableau of Gregory Doran's production of *Henry VIII*.

as the baiting of Wolsey in Act Three, Scene Two, but Henry is often
completely genuine.

Henry's story is told in eight fairly evenly spaced scenes. (Act Five,
Scene Two is cut in our production.) Because each of his scenes is so
individual and strongly characterized I wanted to treat each one as a
separate entity like a strip cartoon or, more elegantly and colourfully, a
Book of Hours. Not that there isn't a journey, a development – far from
it. But it would be a mistake to think of a connecting through-line as if
one scene necessarily influences the next. Often, as I have said, they take
place years apart, but even when they do not, Henry's actions and moods
are always in contrast to what has gone before. Each scene isolates and
illustrates particular aspects of his personality and they always have to be
played to the hilt. I was determined that what the character lacked in
psychological depth would be made up for in, not inappropriately, the
greatest possible breadth.

So what is Henry's story? It is of a king learning to rule, getting
wisdom, growing in confidence, and by degrees, knowing himself. He

enters in Act One, Scene Two, leaning on Wolsey's shoulder. It is a remarkably specific stage direction: a king in need of support from the most powerful man in the country, the Church upholding the State. Henry is dependent on Wolsey to run the country and only Katherine's humanity can moderate the Cardinal's excesses. Katherine was almost six years Henry's senior and way ahead of him in political acumen. He learned much from her and here we see him still doing so, except when what she has to say is in direct opposition to his will. I have him forcing his personality, bellowing, striding about, pleased with himself when he publicly orders Wolsey to 'send our letters with free pardon' (I.ii.99), but not in control politically, not thinking things through. 'Wherein? and what taxation?' he asks (I.ii.38), bewildered. He must have signed the decree that brought in the taxation, but he is clearly rubber-stamping whatever Wolsey puts in front of him. (According to one biographer he actually ordered a signature machine to be invented.) For all that he wears his kingship with apparent confidence, this is an insecure man who cannot afford to show mercy towards Buckingham – that, to him, would be weakness. Constantly taken by surprise by Katherine, Wolsey, Norfolk, and even by the pathetic Surveyor, he can't wait to dispense with the day's business and go hunting.

And yet there is time for tenderness. This scene presents the only opportunity for Jane Lapotaire and me to show the happiness of Katherine and Henry's twelve years of marriage and their genuine joy in each other. As he raises Katherine to her feet, Henry kisses her with some passion. And the Surveyor's reference to their still-born children – 'if the King / Should without issue die' (I.ii.133–34) – is their closest moment, a moment which pays dividends in the trial, as he takes Katherine's hand comfortingly in his.

In Act One, Scene Four, Henry and his entourage gatecrash Wolsey's party. Greg wanted something more shockingly vital and sexual than the 'masquers habited like shepherds' of the folio. He showed us a video of a Moroccan fertility rite, a frenzied male dancer dressed as a goat. So the masquers became known as the Wild Men and are dressed not so much as shepherds but as rampant members of their flocks. We wear rough costumes with huge horned masks, so that none of us is identifiable, with clogs and gaiters in imitation of hooves. We sport huge phalluses with leather testicles and our behaviour is raucous and threatening. But at least our dance is rooted, so to speak, in Tudor fashion: the galliard, an energetic and complicated sequence of stamping and high kicking, was a dance at which Henry (unfortunately for me) had been expert. The mood is exactly in keeping with the drunken, hell-raising, womanizing side of Henry.

The revellers take partners and Henry chooses Anne Bullen. He is smitten at first sight. Wolsey is fully aware who his uninvited guests are and offers to identify their leader. And here is a curiosity. Shakespeare has Wolsey going straight to the King and bowing to him without hesitation. Contemporary records tell us that Wolsey actually unmasked one of the King's followers at which Henry, roaring with laughter at the success of his deception, revealed himself. How could Wolsey have been mistaken in view of Henry's unique physique and dancing prowess? Wolsey is, of course, humouring Henry's childishness, his love of disguise and dressing up. The production, however, hints at something else: Wolsey mistaking the King, getting him wrong, and Henry again triumphing.

Theatrically the mask is an enormously potent device. It is often thought of merely as a means of concealment and anonymity but its great power is as a liberator – the personality of the wearer can lose all inhibition and become transformed, reckless. And so the masked Henry falls for Anne Bullen, publicly declaring his admiration for her and claiming her with a rough and selfish kiss, the kiss of a man who takes whatever he wants for his own gratification.

We next see Henry in the first of the two scenes (II.ii and V.i) set in his privy chamber, his golden cell. Although Shakespeare has him entering (in II.ii) after the first part of the scene, Greg and I agreed that he should be present throughout. He sits reading the Bible, Leviticus Chapter 18, the mainstay of his case against his marriage to Katherine, and re-reading the letter he is about to send summoning her to the trial at Blackfriars. Here is Henry secret, brooding, solitary, suspicious: Buckingham has just gone to his execution (it took three blows of the axe) and the skull on Henry's table is a constant reminder of his own mortality.

When the Dukes of Norfolk and Suffolk interrupt him he is furious: 'Who am I, ha?' (II.ii.65). At first I took this to mean 'Who the hell do you think you're dealing with here?' – a bullying assertion of status. But perhaps there is something less cock-sure about it, that betrays almost no sense of self. The scene is packed with evidence of his volatility: in the space of sixteen lines (II.ii.63–79) he goes from an explosion of indignation – 'Who's there?', to joyous relief – 'My good lord Cardinal', to emotional confession – 'The quiet of my wounded conscience', to a binding declaration – 'thou art a cure fit for a king', to dignified diplomacy

– 'You're welcome most learned reverend sir, into our kingdom', to urbane hospitality – 'Use us and it', to good-natured self-deprecation – 'My good lord, have great care / I be not found a talker', back to an angry dismissal of the dukes as if they are schoolboys – 'We are busy; go.' Here is a man who may not be sure of himself, but is certainly sure of his position and his ability to terrorize. This is the last time Henry and Wolsey are together on good terms and yet their relationship is at its most intense, quite physical in fact, with Henry dependent on Wolsey for his personal well-being as his confessor. Henry's final lines in the scene are some of his most crucial in the play:

> . . . O, my lord,
> Would it not grieve an able man to leave
> So sweet a bedfellow? But conscience, conscience!
> O, 'tis a tender place, and I must leave her. (II.ii.139–42)

This last line and a half usually gets something of a laugh, not unsurprisingly. At first I found this gratifying and played up to it, feeling rather aggrieved when the laugh was not there. After all, the male heir argument has not yet been heard, and from what the audience has seen, Henry's conscience has been pricked only by the desire to bed Anne. This is compounded by her own first line in the next scene: 'Not for that neither' (II.iii.1), as if to say 'You're not telling the truth'. Thus Shakespeare makes things very difficult for the actor playing Henry. It is a huge struggle for him to assail the moral high ground which Katherine not only occupies in the trial but upon which she builds a fortress. But the attempt must be made and I now see that 'conscience, conscience' must come out of all the integrity that Henry can muster. Conscience is the single most important word in the play, for every character, whether it is to be battled with or obeyed. As Henry himself said, 'The law of every man's conscience be but a private Court, yet it is the highest and supreme Court for judgement or justice.'

The proceedings at Blackfriars, generally known as 'Katherine's Trial', are strictly a trial of the marriage, an annulment hearing, though practically and emotionally it is Katherine who is the defendant. Henry starts the scene (II.iv) in a mood of great impatience. It has taken two years of negotiations to bring his 'Great Matter' to court and the frustration has heightened his hopes of rapidly getting the result he wants. Katherine's refusal to recognize the authority of the court enrages him, but there is nothing he can do or say about it. I am sure he comes to the court intending not to speak at all but to leave all the arguing to his counsel, Wolsey.

Throughout Katherine's appeal to him and the sparring between her and Wolsey, Henry is given absolutely nothing to say. Contemporary records describe him sitting impassively staring straight ahead. The ex-Home Secretary Michael Howard behaved in exactly the same way when under attack by Ann Widdecombe in the House of Commons. (Ms. Widdecombe, incidentally, used the term 'my honourable friend' to a cumulative effect of which Mark Antony would have been proud.) Completely to ignore one's fellow actor rather goes against the grain and it was difficult at first not to respond. This was, perhaps, because Henry's thought process was not clear in my mind. Greg got Jane and me to sit close together face to face for one rehearsal and asked me to attempt replies to Katherine's questions:

> 'Alas, sir, / In what have I offended you?' (II.iv.18–19)
> 'Erm, well, apart from not producing a male heir . . . nothing.'
>
> 'What cause / Hath my behaviour given to your displeasure?'
>   (II.iv.19–20)
> 'None.'

And so on – an uncomfortable but salutary experience. No wonder he had nothing to say.

In arguing on Henry's behalf Wolsey exposes himself to the full force of the Queen's hostility. Henry has never doubted Katherine's integrity and she attacks Wolsey with such conviction that the scales begin to peel from Henry's eyes. The relationship between the two men is never the same again. As Katherine appeals to the Pope and sweeps out of the court and out of Henry's life he does an extraordinary thing. The obvious reaction would be towering fury, but instead he publicly praises her – this is no aside – as the best wife in the world and the queen of queens. Is he being manipulative? Is it a ploy to get the court on his side? I used to think not, because the reaction seemed emotional, not reasoned. I am now inclined to the cynical approach – Henry as the master of public relations. How much has my performance altered in that case? He still has to be convincing, and I discovered in post-performance discussions that people were not inclined to believe him anyway, even when I felt he was being genuine. In playing him *trying* to be sincere rather than *being* sincere I have to ask the question, 'How good an actor was he?', and back comes the answer, 'At least as good as me' – whatever that may mean. But perhaps there is a coolness that was not there before.

There is something of a veiled threat in the way he 'thus far' (II.iv.167) clears Wolsey of Katherine's charges before proceeding to justify his own position. This great speech is the rock on which the character of Henry VIII is based. Several times in rehearsal I thought I had got it and Greg always saw that there was something more to be squeezed out. It's pivotal for Henry, for the play, and, really, for the history of England. It starts in a halting, stumbling, embarrassed way with none of Katherine's eloquence or Wolsey's well-oiled fluency. His argument may be well-rehearsed, but on this occasion it is being dragged up from within, his most private anguish being put on public display – and the audience is recruited willy-nilly to be the 'reverend fathers of the land / And doctors learned' (II.iv.205–206), hearing the case.

It is impossible to overstate the importance to Henry of having a male heir. Even today in many cultures it is hugely disappointing if the first-born is a girl and the Tudors believed it threatened the stability of the country. Whatever hypocrisy Henry may be guilty of, there is no doubting the God-fearing conviction of 'Methought I stood not in the smile of heaven' (II.iv.187). This is a man who went to Mass two or three times a day for fear of dying unshriven. I think it is also borne out by his shocking idea of Katherine's womb as a grave (line 191). Brutal despot he may have been, but I can't believe he was unmoved by the deaths of his infant children. I have a picture in my head of him alone, howling at the news. If Katherine had given birth to even one strong, healthy son Henry would never have needed or wanted to divorce her. There had been mistresses (Anne Bullen's sister for one) and there would be others, but by comparison with many of his contemporaries, including at least one pope, he was discreet and abstemious in this matter.

This heart-felt and exemplary behaviour does not last long, however, and by the end he is lying through his teeth:

> . . . by my life
> And kingly dignity, we are contented
> To wear our mortal state to come with her,
> Katherine our Queen, before the primest creature
> That's paragoned o' th'world. (II.iv.226–30)

Dear oh dear.

The adjournment pulls the rug from under his feet and I have him slamming down the Bible on which he was just perjured himself – it's amazing what conscience can justify when it goes hand in hand with expediency. The break with Rome, the entire English Reformation, is dealt with in one glorious line: 'I abhor / This dilatory sloth and tricks of Rome' (II.iv.237). Longing for the return of Cranmer, the man who will effect what Henry wants, he storms out: 'Break up the court' (II.iv.240). Break up the court, break up my marriage, break up the Church. I alone will hold the country together.

After the events at Blackfriars Henry is far more certain of how he must proceed. He no longer suffers any conflict of conscience and will: he has been thwarted and those responsible must suffer. His handling of Wolsey's fall from office has much less of the shouting and bluster and stamping about that characterized the way he dealt with Buckingham. He is now in complete command of his power and he wields it with economy and ever greater cruelty. Even so he is unable to face Katherine and deals with her at arm's length by sending the cardinals to bully her into submission. Her spirited refusal to comply makes Wolsey desperate and he becomes careless, allowing an incriminating inventory of his possessions to fall into the King's hands. Henry enters briskly at III.ii.106, armed with Wolsey's letters to the Pope asking for a stay of judgement in the annulment, and with the inventory, whose 'proud rate' (III.ii.127) genuinely astonishes him. (Shakespeare has turned the tables on Wolsey: the incident of the inventory was in fact the means by which Wolsey himself brought down the Bishop of Durham.) In the writing you can see that Henry has more authority now; his thinking extends in longer sentences. With 'I presume / That as my hand has opened bounty to you . . .' (III.ii.183ff.) he virtually demolishes Wolsey. But suddenly everything seems all right. Wolsey appears to have passed the test and this man, whom we first saw supporting the king, is now helped to his feet by him. It is at this moment that we see Henry at his most cruel. Richard III never did it better. Henry the sportsman is playing his favourite game – cat and mouse, tormenting for the sake of it – until Wolsey is finally dispatched, almost casually, as Henry hands him the documents.

For a long time in rehearsal I felt that I wasn't bringing Henry to life in this scene. I'd got hold of the idea of authority but was playing it too heavily: he was too forceful. Of course I realized that authority can seem all the stronger by being played lightly, effortlessly, but this was an approach I wanted to reserve for later scenes, particularly for the

Council. I was thinking too much of the pay-off, the destruction of Wolsey; but the setting up was far more important. If that were done properly the rest should take care of itself. Playing the wit a little lighter, making it energetic joshing rather than savage sarcasm, is, I think, just as unnerving for Ian Hogg's Wolsey but allows him more licence to give as good as he gets. The *coup de grâce* delivered, Henry walks out to enjoy a hearty breakfast – something that Wolsey will never do again. It's a moment of great satisfaction for Henry – and for me too, when the scene has gone well.

Henry's next scene (v.i) is the second set in his private apartments. As with the first, Greg wanted Henry present throughout and he is discovered playing primero, a primitive form of poker – gambling while Anne is in labour. The previous scene ends with Katherine at Kimbolton, clearly at death's door. It is documented that when he heard of Katherine's death Henry dressed in yellow and went dancing. Was this a callous celebration demonstrating that he was unaffected or an act of bravado covering up his real feelings? At the start of the scene we have him roaring with forced laughter in response to Katherine's 'I can no more' (IV.ii.173), the laughter equivalent to dressing up in yellow. (Long into the run I learned that yellow was the official mourning dress of the Spanish court!)

Henry is waiting to hear of the birth of his son. Of the fact that it will be a son he tries to have no doubt – but the paranoia lurks just below the surface. News of Anne's suffering distracts him: ' 'Tis true' (oh yes, of course), he says (v.i.82), when he is reminded that Cranmer is waiting to see him. Cranmer is Henry's creature, not with the secular power that made Wolsey almost the King's equal, but nevertheless the King's confidant and confessor. The scene is, I think, the most delicately balanced of all those in which Henry appears. I wanted to show a man who is already indebted to Cranmer for his love and service and yet has to terrorize him because of the heresy charges against the Archbishop. Why doesn't he simply back Cranmer? It's the cruelty of cat and mouse again. A proprietorial arm goes around Cranmer's neck and he is threatened with the Tower.

Henry is approaching the height of his political prowess, using an awkward situation to his own advantage and thereby tightening his control over a fractious and troublesome Council. It is another paradox about Henry that, although he needs people, he is also a secret and solitary operator. He once said, 'If I thought my hat knew my counsel

I would throw it in the fire.' Full of admiration for Cranmer's openness and humility, but contemptuous of his naivety – I have him laughing in derision at Cranmer's notion that his own truth and honesty will save him – he is nevertheless astonished (astonishment again!) to find that he really is true-hearted. As Cranmer leaves, Henry feels in complete control of events, but his self-satisfaction is about to be ambushed by Fate.

The announcement of the birth of the baby is Henry's most fervent moment in the play. In bellowing 'Say "Ay, and of a boy!"' (v.i.163) he is both bullying the Old Lady and sending out a defiant challenge to God. For those few seconds in which he believes he has a son he kisses the Old Lady and dances with Lovell. The truth – that it's a girl – freezes his blood. It is a moral defeat and God's judgement on all that he has been working towards.

There is one particular point in the performance when I have a strong sensation of what it must have been like to be Henry VIII. It happens offstage. Waiting to come on for the Council Scene (v.iii) I stand behind the cloth that conceals the entrance and eavesdrop on the squabbling between Gardiner and Cromwell and the general consternation when Cranmer produces the King's signet ring. It is a delicious moment that informs the nonchalance of the entrance into the scene. In rehearsal we often talked about Stalin as a twentieth-century counterpart to Henry. Both were men who could strike terror in those around them – an appointment with Stalin meant taking along a spare pair of trousers; both had countless thousands of their countrymen executed, and yet both were hugely popular with the ordinary people. To rebuke and reconcile the Council Henry hardly needs to raise his voice. He even has time to admire the stupid courage of Gardiner when he sticks to his guns in denouncing Cranmer.

There was one line that I thought would never get across to an audience: 'Do my lord of Canterbury / A shrewd turn and he's your friend for ever' (v.iii.176–7). It might seem a simple enough line, but I didn't understand it until I discovered that 'shrewd' in this context means 'malicious'. We changed 'shrewd' to 'cruel' which seemed to get the sense across. This was important not just as a matter of comprehension but because, with the humour of both this and 'Come, come, my lord, you'd spare your spoons' (v.iii.166), Henry releases the tension and unifies the Council in laughter. The scene ends with a double declaration of belief:

> . . . I long
> To have this young one made a Christian.
> As I have made ye one, lords, one remain;
> So I grow stronger, you more honour gain.   (v.iii.178–81)

I find the statement of spiritual longing very moving and his temporal desire for increasing power sums up everything we have learned about him. He wants to be acknowledged as the single most dominating influence in world politics, no less.

Since hearing that he has a new daughter Henry seems to have done a *volte-face*: 'With this kiss take my blessing' (v.v.10). It's the unpredictability again; and in any case, as Jasper Ridley puts it in his biography, 'Henry was not the man to be disheartened by a set-back, or to show his disappointment to the world.' And one shouldn't underestimate the effect of the child herself on an emotional man like Henry. The scene we present is not quite the private, albeit crowded, interior originally written. A detail that the dramatist chose to ignore is the fact that Henry was not actually present at the christening. 'What is her name?' (v.v.9) becomes, in our production, no longer a genuine question asked of the Archbishop but part of a ritual presentation to the crowd – and for 'crowd' read 'audience'. The most significant thing about the scene for Henry is his response to Cranmer's vision of the future:

> Thou hast made me now a man; never before
> This happy child did I get anything.   (v.v.64–5)

This is Henry showing amazing openness and humility: until now I have not had the wisdom to know myself; I have never fully achieved anything; never felt fulfilled. Much of what Cranmer has to say is sycophantic, of course, even though he has declared it won't be flattery. But certain aspects of it are quite uncompromising: 'Terror' is sanctioned as an instrument of governance (line 47) and the suggestion that the aristocracy will 'claim their greatness' by the 'perfect ways of honour' and not by accident of birth (lines 37–8) challenges even the King himself to look to his laurels – a thought that is not exactly uncurrent. Cranmer is convincing in what he foresees for Elizabeth (all hindsight for Shakespeare, obviously), but Henry's extraordinary response makes it clear that he believes Cranmer and sees that it's not necessarily such a disaster that he hasn't got a son. It's a new beginning for Henry: Henry as hero – but not without a glance round to see who might be there.

On the morning of the press night I was called to the phone. As I leapt out of bed a sharp pain shot through my right leg and I had to limp to the kitchen to take the call. As the morning progressed, so did the pain, like permanent cramp across my right buttock, down my thigh and the inside of my calf to the sole of my foot. Could it be psychosomatic? If so this was taking first-night nerves to Gothic levels. Perhaps a hot bath would ease it. Not at all, it transpired – worse if anything. There was nothing for it but to telephone Sonja Dosanjh, our Company Manager, and admit my enfeebled state. 'Sonja, I can't walk. I think the sciatic nerve is trapped.' I heard her go pale. So Sonja took me to an osteopath who diagnosed that I had dislocated my pelvis, the right sacroiliac joint to be precise. How could this have happened? Of course! In mounting my beautiful golden horse (now dubbed Clopton after the ancient Stratford-upon-Avon family – also Eric for short) I had been using a low set of steps and had to stretch high and wide to get on and low and wide to get off. I was a victim of repetitive strain syndrome although the strain had been repeated a mere ten times or so. The things we do to ourselves without realizing. An hour with a physiotherapist and an injection of muscle-relaxant from a doctor got me through the show – and even the celebrations afterwards. Not that the effects of the injury cleared up immediately, but they concentrated the mind wonderfully and left no space at all for press night nerves of the conventional kind. I resented my lack of agility and the care with which I had to move, and the critics were deprived of my dancing the galliard, but it did, in a perverse way, bring me closer to Henry. From early middle-age he suffered atrociously with his legs. He had thrombosed varicose veins, ulcers, and osteomyelitis, a condition which could have developed after a jousting injury and which brought on intermittent but excruciating pain. I always knew sport wasn't good for you. A certain stiffness of gait persisted in my perform-ance long after my recovery, particularly in the later scenes – a hint of Henry's advancing years (and of coarse acting). I was promptly provided with a decent step-ladder, by the way.

He who plays the king can, perhaps, be permitted a little *lèse-majesté*. A couple of months into the run HRH the Prince of Wales, who is Pres-ident of the RSC, came to see the production and some of the company were invited to meet him after the performance. During a wide-ranging conversation the Prince said, referring to the play, 'It makes you realize how little things have changed. When one is born into a certain position you have people advising you all the time, whispering in your ear. It's only when you get to my age that you begin to work out who's telling you the truth.'

I don't think I'm being fanciful when I say that I find in Henry echoes of some of Shakespeare's great characters. Richard III and Falstaff are there, Petruccio ('Go thy ways, Kate' (II.iv.133)), and perhaps even Othello's mixture of self-doubt and self-regard. But his strongest precursor is Prospero, which happened to be the last Shakespeare part I had played before Henry. Curious that *The Tempest*, of course, comes immediately before *Henry VIII* in the canon. Both Prospero and Henry have immense power and appear to be confident puppet-masters, their influence felt even when they are absent from the stage; but both have great failings and are greatly vulnerable.

If the portrait that Shakespeare draws of Henry VIII is overall a charitable one, then I think we have to accept it, even if it is the result of the same propaganda machine that paints Richard III as an unmitigated villain. But some credence must also be given to the expressions of deep affection for Henry made by both Katherine of Aragon and Anne Bullen. Perhaps she was hoping for a reprieve, but it must be some indication of life as she had once known it when on the scaffold Anne said: 'I pray God save the King and send him long to reign over you, for a gentler nor a more merciful Prince was there never, and to me he was ever a good, a gentle and sovereign Lord.'

Queen Katherine in
Henry VIII

Jane Lapotaire

JANE LAPOTAIRE is an Honorary Associate Artist of the Royal Shakespeare Company and played Queen Katherine in Gregory Doran's production of *Henry VIII* at the Swan Theatre in 1996–97 and the following
year at the Young Vic Theatre in London and on a tour to the United
States. It was her only role that season. Her long list of earlier work for
the company includes Viola in *Twelfth Night*, Rosaline in *Love's Labour's
Lost*, Gertrude in *Hamlet*, the title role in *Piaf* (for which she won several
major theatre awards), Sonia in *Uncle Vanya*, and Mrs Alving in *Ghosts*.
Shakespeare roles among her wide range of theatre work – for, among
others, Bristol Old Vic, the Young Vic Theatre Company (of which she
was a founder member), the National Theatre, and the Prospect Theatre
Company – include Jessica in *The Merchant of Venice*, Kate in *The Taming
of the Shrew*, Isabella in *Measure for Measure*, and Rosalind in *As You Like
It*, while her one-woman show *Shakespeare As I Knew Her* has been seen
in Bristol, Stratford, Salisbury, France, Cumbria, Cornwall and America.
An extensive range of television and film work includes, among its
Shakespearian roles, those of Cleopatra and Lady Macbeth.

'The role is greater than the sum of the part'

My first reaction when Greg Doran rang to ask if I'd like to play Katherine of Aragon was, 'Do I have to play it in a flak jacket?' As frivolous as
this question might sound, and as inaccurately corroborative as it seems
to be of the assumption that all female actors care about is what they
look like, it contained a fundamental seriousness. We have lately been
subjected to much directorial updating: *Hamlet* in Edwardian tails – so
much for Ophelia's 'with his doublet all unbraced, / . . . his stockings
fouled, / Ungartered, and down-gyvèd to his ankle' (II.i.78–80); *The
Two Gentlemen of Verona* set to Charleston time; and *The Merchant of
Venice* replete with mini-skirts and mobile phones. In spite of how these
comments might be interpreted, I'm not a dyed-in-the-wool purist especially if updating makes the play more accessible to a younger audience

unfamiliar with Shakespeare's work. But I felt that we had recently run the gamut of directorial updating, and that the wave of making Shakespeare fashionable and fashion-full had mercifully run its course, and that it would be a relief to us all as audiences to have that unique experience of seeing a Shakespeare play in the costumes of the time. *Henry VIII* is so essentially Tudor in its mores, its history, its hierarchy, in its treatment of women as male property and heir-bearing machines, that to shift it out of its time zone I felt would be inappropriate and perverse. 'No', said Greg firmly and with great meaning. I breathed out.

My second query (although the play is rarely performed, the last production being at Stratford in 1983, as scholars still dispute how much of it is Fletcher and how much Shakespeare) was to myself: 'Who had played her before?' This is a daunting question that all classical actors have to face when confronted with a role that the late and the great have put their unique mark on, and as a consequence the role has, to a certain extent, become identified with them. The list was awesome. Mrs Siddons, Ellen Terry, Flora Robson, Diana Wynyard, Gwen Frangcon-Davies, Edith Evans and latterly the much loved Peggy Ashcroft. Admiration, fear and flattery mingled. I put the list out of my mind and held my breath. I'm still holding it now, some six months into the playing of her.

We started with three weeks of simply sitting round a vast table reading each speech in order as it became one's turn – much like the dreaded Shakespeare classes at school in my teenage years. Nothing dramatic about it at all, no sense of character, no sense of development, but eventually a thorough understanding of every single syllable of the text, seen more clearly as we were freed from the dread-full obligation every actor feels when confronted with a new role: how am I going to say, inflect, interpret this line? Or this? Or this? Then we progressed to the heady level of being able to read the same character (but not one's own) for a whole scene. So, for example, the actress cast as Patience would be reading the Lord Chamberlain, and the actor cast as Wolsey would be reading Katherine. And, again in turn, each actor, having read a speech, would then have to paraphrase that speech in their own words. This meant that every single member of the company knew exactly what was happening at any given moment of the play, whether they were in that scene or not. This process was hugely useful too, as it often gave one a chance to read one's opponent. I gained great insight into Wolsey, Katherine's arch enemy, by, as luck would have it, having to read him for a whole scene and therefore empathising with his predicament and feelings in a direct way that might otherwise never have been opened up to me.

As always with a Shakespeare history play we did our research faithfully. The walls of the rehearsal room were plastered with family trees – who had married whom and why, what for, and when. Then (as always with a Shakespeare history play) we had to put that out of our minds and play his own particular version and timing of the events, not minding the exclusions – notably Sir Thomas More – and stomaching what seemed initially the fulsome premonition at the end of the play of Elizabeth's glorious reign, written with hindsight and not a small degree of flattery and propaganda for James I's court, populace and benefit. So, separating the real history from the history in the play, but using what was of consequence to both, became for me a way of substantiating Katherine's lines and enriching her character. What were the facts that were true to both regarding this woman?

I've always felt a double obligation when playing a character who actually lived. Every avenue of their life and experience must be opened up, what food they ate, what music they listened to, who they liked and disliked, what they themselves looked like etc., so that no false value judgements are made about them: and by a process of osmosis, all about them is absorbed by the actor, all the pores opened to let the wind of that essence blow right through you. Then you put all that out of your mind too, and simply play the play, hoping that all this will somehow filter through and inform your every move and gesture.

So who was Katherine of Aragon and how is her life relevant to this rarely seen but frequently maligned piece of theatre by Fletcher/Shakespeare? A Spanish princess. The decision to play her with an accent came relatively late in rehearsals (week four or five) and came as a shock when Greg suggested it to me. I had been so caught up in the history of the period of both England and Spain; in all our projects on Tudor London – sewage, streets, crowds, conditions; instruments of torture of the time; our differing personal reactions to Hampton Court. Besides all that there were the difficulties that we all had in dealing with such an irregular text: many twelve-syllable (dreaded Alexandrines!) or eleven-syllable lines, some even with thirteen syllables (heaven help us) and then great wodges of so very regular ten-syllable lines that the words themselves demanded such consciously careful handling and skilful playing in order to avoid a straitjacket monotone of rhythm and delivery. So suddenly to be faced with an accent that was famously difficult on top of all this (Russian, by comparison, is a doddle) – all those 'th's for 'd's, 'j's in place of 'y's, and all those gutteral 'h's: how was I not to sound like the waiter in *Fawlty Towers*? – was, to put it mildly, fairly alarming. In the end, with the invaluable help of Charmian Hoare, the RSC's dialect coach, we dropped the gutteral 'h's and played safe with the rest. The thing with an accent is not to play it once you've learned it; you simply try to do what you normally do in any acting which is to play *the intention of the line*. (In the same way you don't play drunk, you play sober.) Of course Greg was right. It was vital for Katherine to be seen as the outsider, the stranger that she is described as – 'Alas poor lady! / She's a stranger now again' (II.iii.16–17) – and the foreigner that she was. (In the same way that Wolsey's Suffolk accent marks him, in spite of his learning, his ecclesiastical power, and wealth, as a man from rural England – Ipswich, Suffolk.)

She was the youngest of five children born to Isabella of Castile and Ferdinand of Aragon – four daughters and a son who died relatively young; she must therefore have been familiar from an early age (and was to be reminded constantly throughout her marriage to Henry), with the fear that being without a male heir held for a dynasty of kings, especially the one so recently established by her parents, the first Reyes Católicos who, by their marriage, had combined the centre and south of Spain and thus united the country after 880 years of Moorish rule. Not long afterwards, the ships of the Conquistadores were crossing the Atlantic loaded with crosses, missionaries, missals and Christian convictions, and Spain in her heyday saw herself as the champion of Christian orthodoxy whose task was to unite the world in Catholicism. Only in Spain do you hear not only 'Adios' but 'Vaya con Dios' – 'Go with God.'

Catalina, her Spanish name, was born in Granada, and took as her emblem – a more peaceful symbol than the seven arrows in a yoke that formed the crest of Isabella and Ferdinand that she can be seen holding in the Holbein-like painting of her in more mature years – the pomegranate (*la granita*) which can be seen to this day on the colours that are displayed above her very modest grave in the north transept of Peterborough Cathedral. It was to prove, as much in Katherine's life, deeply ironic, for the promegranate was also the symbol of fecundity. Her Catholicism, although a political statement that was born of and strengthened by the early years in which she grew up from the age of six in the palace of the Alhambra where every vestige and emblem of Islam must have been firmly replaced by her parents with a crucifix, was also, as I was to find, a richly vibrant living faith to her personally, and one that was to sustain her through more hardship than most Queens had to undergo. On arriving in England at the age of sixteen, after a tortuous journey that had taken five months, to be married off to Arthur, Henry VII's heir, and speaking only Spanish, her first action on English soil – the land that was to be her home through two marriages, a widowing, a divorce, and five stillbirths or miscarriages – was to give thanks to God in the nearest church. This seemed ample evidence already, and was borne out later by much in the text, to warrant my wearing a rosary and a missal on all my costumes at all times.

It has been a personal foible of mine, developed over the years, to find one line that refers to the character that I'm playing and that seems to hold the quintessential elements of that character. For example, when I played Viola I found Sebastian's line, 'she bore a mind that envy could not but call fair' (II.i.26), replete with everything that Viola is. For Gertrude, Claudius's description, 'The Queen his mother / Lives almost by his [Hamlet's] looks' (IV.vii.11–12), helped me make the decision that faces every Gertrude: whose side to come down on, her husband's or her son's? I was spoilt for choice with references to Katherine. They abound throughout the play and are spoken by every echelon of society:

the good Queen (Second Gentleman; II.i.158)

. . . her
That like a jewel has hung twenty years
About his neck, yet never lost her lustre;
Of her that loves him with that excellence
That angels love good men with . . . of her
That, when the greatest stroke of fortune falls,
Will bless the King. (Duke of Norfolk; II.ii.29–34)

So sweet a bedfellow ironically after he has fallen in love with Anne Boleyn and decided to leave Katherine. (Henry; II.iii.141–)

. . . and she
So good a lady that no tongue could ever
Pronounce dishonour of her . . .
She never knew harm doing. (Anne Boleyn; II.iii.2–5)

Alas, poor lady!
She's a stranger [foreigner] now again. (Old lady; II.iii.16–17)

                                    . . . yourself, who ever yet
Have stood to charity and displayed th'effects
Of disposition gentle and of wisdom
O'er-topping woman's power.   (Wolsey; II.iv.85–8)

That man i' the world who shall report he has
A better wife, let him in naught be trusted
For speaking false in that. Thou art alone –
If thy rare qualities, sweet gentleness,
Thy meekness saint-like, wife-like government,
Obeying in commanding, and thy parts
Sovereign and pious else, could speak thee out –
The queen of earthly queens. She's noble born,
And like her true nobility she has
Carried herself towards me.

           (Henry; II.iv.134–43 – ironically, again, after Katherine has refused to
           acknowledge the divorce court and turned her back on the proceedings)

that honour every good tongue blesses . . . good lady.
                                               (Wolsey; III.i.55–7)

. . . good lady.   (Wolsey; III.i.155)

                           . . . A noble spirit,
As yours was put into you.   (Cardinal Campeius; III.i.169–70)

                           . . . she was divorced,
And the late marriage made of none effect;
Since which she was removed to Kimbolton,
Where she remains now sick.
                     . . . Alas, good lady.
                     (First and Second Gentlemen; IV.i.32–5)

So 'good' seems to be the operative word. But you can't play 'good'.
Good is a value judgement, and all value judgements are made from a
standpoint outside the character, which for me is a very unwise and
unhealthy place to be. If you stand too long outside the character, you
risk putting it 'out there', not letting it 'travel through' you. Also 'good'
often equals boring, and Katherine is anything but boring. Besides I had
already begun to love her. (As she must have loved that greatest icon
of goodness, Jesus Christ. But He also had moments of despair, and
flashes of anger; and later, as the work progressed, I was to find these,
too, in Katherine.) So, I turned to Katherine's own words; her motto
was 'Humble et Loyale' and this too was to be borne out again and again
in the text of the play.

PLAYERS OF SHAKESPEARE 4

20 Jane Lapotaire as Queen Katherine, with Henry VIII (Paul Jesson)
and the dukes of Suffolk and Norfolk (David Beames and John Kane),
Henry VIII, Act I, Scene ii: 'Nay, we must longer kneel:
I am a suitor.'

In her first scene in the play (I.ii) her initial gesture, although a Queen
(and she uses the royal 'we' in her very first line) is to kneel to Henry,
thereby acknowledging his sovereignty and also his embodiment of
the Divine Right of Kings: he is God's representative. Her humility and
devotion to him both as King and husband, and her ability to flatter
him and yet remind him gently of his duty to his position, always keeping within the confines of what is no more than appropriate, is finely
contained and superbly phrased in her first complete speech:

> That you would love yourself, and in that love
> Not unconsidered leave your honour nor
> The dignity of your office, is the point
> Of my petition.   (I.ii.14–17)

The word 'honour' she uses again in 'Whose honour heaven shield
from soil' (I.ii.26), as a request to God for Henry's protection. The word
'loyalty' appears twice –

138

There have been commissions
Sent down among 'em which have flawed the heart
Of all their loyalties . . .   (I.ii.20–2)

Language unmannerly, yea, such which breaks
The sides of loyalty . . .   (I.ii.27–8)

The whole drive of the first half of this scene is indeed her concern that the taxes that Wolsey has imposed upon the weaving trade (using the excuse of the need to finance Henry's wars in France) without Henry's knowledge, are not only causing acute and unnecessary hardship, but are endangering loyalty and obedience to the Crown. She has opted to be a spokeswoman against the exploitation of the poor: 'I would your highness would give it quick consideration, for / There is no primer *business*' – which I pronounce *baseness*, using the useful note in the Arden edition, and experiencing the first of many moments of gratitude for the initially unwelcome Spanish accent. In this relatively short scene for her (she has only eight speeches), she calls Henry 'your Majesty', 'The King our master', 'my sovereign', 'your highness', and prefaces her final explanation of the situation with 'I am much too venturous / In tempting of your patience . . .' (I.ii.54–5). Humble and loyal indeed.

She wins the first round as Henry publicly rebukes Wolsey for instigating a tax that had no precedent, and offers a free pardon to every man that refused to abide by it. But she doesn't fare so well in her second mission for mercy and clemency for the Duke of Buckingham. In spite of her attempt to prevent Wolsey, in his lawyer-like way, from 'blowing the coals' of Henry's anxiety about Buckingham with her gentle reminder to a man of the cloth – 'My learned Lord Cardinal / Deliver all with charity' (I.ii.142–3) – Buckingham receives the death sentence aided and abetted by the put-up evidence of the Surveyor who has been schooled by Wolsey to incite the King's anger and insecurity about Buckingham's threat to Henry's life and crown. I decided to cross myself on hearing this false evidence, and Griffith, who is Katherine's right-hand man, follows suit when the surveyor says 'On my soul, I'll speak but truth' (I.ii.177). Yet even here, faced with a Surveyor who is vengeful as a result of his lost position because the tenants complained against him, Katherine nevertheless pleads for the Surveyor's soul:

                    . . . Take good heed
You charge not in your spleen a noble person
And spoil your nobler soul – I say take heed;
Yea, heartily beseech you.   (I.ii.173–6)

Later, when the surveyor, carried away in our production by his own invention of Buckingham's treachery, lunges at Henry and reports him saying

> . . . I would have played
> The part my father meant to act upon
> Th'usurper Richard . . .
> Have put his knife into him.   (I.ii.194–9)

I cross myself again and utter a quiet 'Madre de Dios'. When Wolsey says of Buckingham (lines 200–201), 'Now madam, may his highness live in freedom / And this man out of prison?', she knows she has lost the battle, and she reverts and refers to that which is her comfort and her strength in moments of crisis, her God: 'God mend all!' She has lost the battle for Buckingham's life, but the war with Wolsey has only just begun.

This first scene held for me all the elements that are essential pointers to the character of Katherine. It also contains what I suppose students of Stanislavski would call super-objectives and objectives, and these have become markers that I remind myself of before each performance. In order of importance Katherine's devotion, loyalty and duty are 1) to her God, 2) to her King, 3) to her husband, and 4) to her people. This is more than just a neat little formula. These four obligations hold water in all of the four scenes that she has in the play – four scenes that Greg and I developed a shorthand for by calling them, albeit loosely, because the analogy doesn't totally hold: Spring; Summer; Autumn; Winter.

In the first scene Henry 'riseth from his state, takes her up, kisses and placeth her by him' (stage direction following I.ii.9). That's evidence of a happy marriage. When I decided to react with sadness to the surveyor's opening words – 'if the King / Should without issue die' (I.ii.133–4) – sad words indeed for a woman in middle age, approaching the menopause, who has had six pregnancies, out of which only one child has survived and that a daughter, a nice little production note of Greg's was to get Henry to touch Katherine's hand in sympathy: more evidence of two people in harmony with each other's moods and needs. Spring is in the air at the start of this scene and the play, but it ends on a dying fall as Henry storms out, enraged by Buckingham's alleged disloyalty: 'By day and night! / He's traitor to the height!' (I.ii.213–14).

'Summer' is full blown, possibly fly-blown and tainted, before we see Katherine next in Act Two, Scene Four, on trial for the continuation of her marriage through no fault of her own, but through Henry's dual voracious needs – for a male heir and for Anne Boleyn. The four reminders I give myself before this scene begins, which are vital if I'm not to become lost and bogged down in one of the longest pieces of rhetoric in the canon – her speech in her own defence – are 1) I refuse to acknowledge this court – it's unfair and unjust and English; 2) I have been a true and humble wife – you can't fault me on that score; 3) Wolsey is my enemy and therefore I refuse to be judged by him; 4) I want time – and help from Spain. But most of all I remind myself that she thinks she is going to win.

As a child she had been made to study rhetoric along with the accepted subjects for women of rank: music, poetry, grammar, embroidery, painting, illuminating, history, Latin and philosophy. She was, according to many historians, a woman of great intellectual ability. Erasmus found her scholarship more impressive than Henry's. She was a shrewd diplomatist and a formidable debater: all this Henry finds to his cost in the trial scene. Having refused to answer to the call of the court that she be present, thereby not acknowledging its legality, and having risen 'out of her chair' to go 'about the court' (stage direction following II.iv.12), she ignores Wolsey and his man from Rome, Cardinal Campeius. We use the auditorium as if it were the Great Hall at Blackfriars (where, ironically, early performances of this play took place) full of the ecclesiastics who only some twenty-six years before (1503) had had to abide by the Pope's dispensation that her marriage with Henry (having been his brother Arthur's wife first) was in fact lawful. What painful thoughts must go through her head as she gives the assembled company such piercing looks – clerics who had debated the most intimate details of whether her marriage to Arthur had in fact been consummated (the indecision about which had necessitated the dispensation); finally she kneels at the feet of her husband and her King and begins her own defence based on the four pointers I remind myself of at the beginning of the scene.

Of course Henry cannot answer. He cannot fault her on her behaviour, her humility as a wife, devotion to such a level that she would suit her every mood to his; she never contradicted him, tried to love his friends even though she knew they were her enemies (this an indirect reference to Wolsey which she picks up in a more direct manner later), gave up her own friends if they angered him; and she sums it all up by reminding him and the court that this devotion, and this marriage, have lasted some astonishing twenty years. The only time I decided that she would falter in this rhetoric would be at the mention of the dead children that she had borne him. The emotional pain at her failure to produce an heir for her beloved husband, and the grief that she must feel for those dead children, plus the unpalatable thought that childbearing is now an unlikely possibility, threaten to overwhelm her. But she's her father's daughter, and drawing on her innate Spanish sense of honour and dignity, she regains her composure and challenges Henry that if she is at fault in any way that he take her life: 'Give me up / To the sharp'st kind of justice' (II:iv.43–4). Again, of course, Henry cannot answer. She then reminds Henry and the court that both Ferdinand of Spain, renowned for his wisdom, and his own father, a prudent and intelligent man, Henry VII, had agreed, along with the assembled clerics of that time, that this marriage is indeed lawful. She is sure of her ground and the justice of this point on which the whole intended divorce rests, and sums up by asking for more time to be advised by her friends in Spain.

That for me became over the weeks of rehearsal quite clearly the end of the speech. She knows she is right and she knows the law is on her side. She knows that Henry cannot fault her. And in the true sense of theatre, drama can only come from the juxtaposition of opposites. She assumes that Henry will be won over; she assumes that Henry will agree. Again, but cataclysmically for her this time, Henry says nothing, and in those few seconds between

> Wherefore I humbly
> Beseech you, sir, to spare me, till I may
> Be by my friends in Spain advised, whose counsel
> I will implore

and

> If not, i'th'name of God,
> Your pleasure be fulfilled
> (II.iv.53–7)

her whole world comes crashing down about her ears. She realizes that Henry does not want her any more. The emotional backwash that this devastating pain causes her is mostly fired thereafter in Wolsey's direction. She turns her tears into anger and turns on him as the reason for her husband having turned against her. She now publicly accuses him of being her enemy and a liar, although her Christianity tempers it into 'not at all a friend to truth' (line 84).

Incidentally there are three examples of rather odd attempts at colloquial speech by Katherine, and interestingly they all take place when

Wolsey is present: in her first scene she describes him as *'putter-on, /* Of these exactions' (I.ii.24–5); in this long trial speech she asks Henry why he should 'proceed to *put me off*' (II.iv.21); and now she describes Wolsey as the person who has *'blown this coal* betwixt my lord and me' (II.iv.79). Similarly Wolsey's attempt to disguise what he wants to say to her in the presence of her ladies in her following scene by talking in Latin, is met with the rejoinder by Katherine: 'I am not such a truant since my coming | As not to know the language I have lived in' (III.i.43–4) – interesting that this battle of words should take place between the two outsiders, by birth, in the court. Here in the trial scene she won't rise to the bait of Wolsey's tortuous legal phrases, but faces them down with a simple and honest, but perhaps overmodest, statement of her weakness as a woman in dealing with his duplicity and word-mongering, and reminds him in true Christian fashion of his personal pride which has overrun his Christian office. The extent of her distress at the whole proceedings, which she is no longer able to hide, is perhaps nowhere more evident than when she snaps at her faithful and beloved manservant Griffith who reminds her quietly, as she attempts to sweep out of the court having appealed to be tried by the Pope, 'Madam, you are called back':

> What need you note it? Pray you keep your way;
> When you are called, return. Now the Lord help!
> They vex me past my patience. Pray you, pass on. (II.iv.128–30)

She finally leaves with 'I will not tarry; no, nor ever more, / Upon this *business*' – I pronounce it *baseness*, as I did in reference to Wolsey's unfair taxations in the first scene – 'my appearance make, / In any of their courts' (lines 131–3). The money-lenders have been scourged in the temple.

The placing of the interval after this scene is very useful for Katherine as it adds to the sense of time passing as she waits for news and help from Spain. I was shocked that Greg wanted Anne Boleyn present in Katherine's next scene (III.i) and for a while found myself very resistant to it. She is indeed 'one of her highness' women' as the Lord Chamberlain says (I.iv.93) and Anne herself confirms to the Old Lady 'The Queen is comfortless, and we forgetful, / In our long absence' (II.iii.105–6), but it was hard to divorce our modern-day notions of the pain that a mistress can cause a wife without having that mistress actually present. Anne isn't in fact listed in the names of the characters that appear in Act Three, Scene One; the opening stage direction simply says, 'Queen Katherine and her women, as at work.' There was, however, a tenuous basis to Anne's presence which I was able later, thankfully, to turn to Katherine's advantage.

It seemed perverse that a Spanish princess, faced with the possibility (that grows more likely every day) of losing her husband, her status, her homes, and her daughter, when asking for a song to cheer her up, should be happy with an English madrigal; odd too that it should be a song about that most faithful of lovers, Orpheus! So the Spanish rendering of 'Orpheus with his Lute' was born. I compounded the felony by suggesting that Katherine and her Spanish maid, whom we named Iñez, should sing several lines of it translated into Spanish; her homesickness is much evident later in the scene and this confirmed the justification for the Spanish element. So Katherine's blue mood is nicely lifting with memories of home and she has been drawn into a dance that she surely must have taught them in her younger days, when Griffith interrupts with the alarming news that the Cardinals have sprung a surprise visit. Obviously the next unwelcome round in the divorce talks is about to begin. Three times in this scene Katherine refers to the frailty of her womanhood (as she did to Wolsey in the trial too) making excuses for herself as a 'poor weak woman' (III.i.20), remarking that 'alas, I am a woman' (III.i.80), and finally claiming 'You know I am a woman, lacking wit, / To make a seemly answer to such persons' (III.i.177–8) – all this from a woman that Thomas Cromwell later described in these terms: 'Nature wronged the Queen in not making her a man. But for her sex she would have surpassed all the heroes of history.' Indeed, in spite of her initial fears ('I do not like their coming' (III.i.21)), she has both the cardinals on the run for a good three quarters of the scene. She refuses (justifiably, given the rout they had in the trial scene when they last met) to acknowledge or kiss Wolsey's Cardinal's ring. She makes a joke about having to earn her living as a housewife if things go from bad to worse. She refuses his suggestion of a private discussion, saying that unlike some women she has nothing to be ashamed of (Anne's presence was very useful here after all!). She won't join in his second ploy to speak in Latin and insists he speak publicly and in English, with a little barb about some of her maids being grateful if he would simply speak the truth. And she makes the saddest attempt at a joke ever: 'The willing'st sin I ever yet committed' (her marriage to Henry, still seen by some as a sin because of the biblical passage in Leviticus objecting to the marriage of a widow to her deceased husband's brother) 'May be absolved in English' (she may be divorced in England).

Wolsey, in his attempt to placate her, uses the most inflammatory word possible to Katherine: 'I am sorry that my integrity should *breed*' (line 51) and inflame her it does. She knows that the situation is very serious indeed when Wolsey starts to pity her. (She says in her next scene of this moment, 'He was never, / But where he meant to *ruin*, pity-full' (IV.ii.39–40).) They are here to castigate her for her behaviour in the trial. Campeius puts his oar in: Wolsey has forgotten 'like a good man' her 'late censure / Both of his truth and him' (III.i.64–5) and offers her a sign of peace and counsel which she reads, in part correctly, as betrayal. But the devastating extent of that ruin and betrayal she is yet to find out. Her anger and fear are now linked to the most deadly irony. She belittles their ability to be honest; she belittles her own ability to be capable of an answer to Wolsey's question:

> to know
> How you stand minded in the weighty difference
> Between the King and you.   (III.i.57–9)

It's a question 'so near mine honour, / More near my life I fear, with my weak wit' (again the self-parody of frail womanhood), and she gets dangerously near to betraying Christian respect for representatives of God by belittling 'such men of gravity and learning' here on 'such business', which I again pronounce as 'baseness' (lines 71–6). A stern look of reprimand at such levity from the devout Griffith puts her back on course, and she addresses the heart of her problem. She knows her position is in jeopardy – 'I feel / The last fit of my greatness' (lines 77–8) – and begs once more for time and counsel as she did in the trial scene. The echo in the words 'friend-less, hope-less' (line 80) adds to our understanding of her forlorn state.

Again Wolsey wrong-foots her by reminding her of 'the King's love' (inappropriate to say the least) and of her 'infinite number of friends' – 'in England', as he says (that is inaccurate at the best). She now gives rein to a fury that until now she has held in check. A spurned wife and a lonely homesick woman is a potent mixture, and by the time Campeius reminds her (line 94) of her 'loving' King, and warns that the divorce may go ahead in spite of her wishes, she has all the ammunition available for a full attack on them both as vacuous representatives of the God they serve, and, in Wolsey's case, a man who has been corrupted by a king – the nearest she ever gets to a criticism of her sovereign and her husband. Having skirted self-pity with 'A woman lost among ye, laughed at, scorned' (line 107), she now gives full vent to that most human of anguishes, a woman rejected because she is old, made all the more potent by the presence of the beautiful and young Anne Boleyn:

> Alas, 'has banished me his bed already,
> His love too, long ago! I am old, my lords,
> And all the fellowship I hold now with him
> Is only my obedience. (III.i.119–22)

Obedience! – it is a Christian duty that hardly describes a matrimonial passion. It is autumn indeed.

This for me is the crux of the scene and the heartbreaking core of Katherine. It makes her the emotional heart of the play. She could finish there. There is really nothing more to be said, but in true Latin temperament and fashion she goes on. She goes on to delineate yet again all her devotions to the King, worst of all being that she has 'Almost forgot my prayers to content him' (line 132): that wifely obligations should have put her duty to her God secondary is unthinkable for her.

I found this 'Have I lived thus long?' speech difficult, in that there is an underlying aura of melodrama and self-dramatization about it, but was hugely grateful for it when I alighted on the idea of spitting out the final three words 'a great patience' in Anne Boleyn's direction, which sends her at last scuttling from the room. This nicely frees up Katherine to be able to make what she assumes is her final and intransigent statement about the divorce:

> My Lord, I dare not make myself so guilty
> To give up willingly that noble title
> Your master wed me to. (III.i.139–41)

Then comes what seems to be yet another unnecessary coda of a speech, until we discovered that whenever Wolsey wanted something very badly he would ingratiate himself by kneeling. This proved the spur to motor yet another emotional, but this time final, outburst. Her anguish over all that she has lost, which again borders dangerously for a Christian on despair and self-pity, is checked by realizing that if she has lost then her maids are lost too: 'Alas, poor wenches, where are now your fortunes?' (line 148). It is apt that she should end her cry of despair with a biblical reference:

Like the lily
That once was mistress of the field and flourished,
I'll hang my head and perish.   (III.i.151–3)

I deliver that line in the direction in which Anne Boleyn has just beaten a hasty retreat, as of course it also applies to her: Anne is 'mistress of the field' indeed. In order to fuel Wolsey's final outburst against the emotional behaviour he has just witnessed, I decided to cross myself in disbelief and self-protection when he describes himself and Cardinal Campeius as being in the business of *curing* sorrows and not *causing* them. The fiery remonstrance that this provokes at her untypical disobedience and wilful stubbornness, coupled with Wolsey's own potent brand of duplicitous praise of her usually gentle and noble temper – the same ploy that he used in the trial ('You speak not like yourself' (II.iv.85)) – topples her. But it is Campeius's 'The King loves you' (line 171) that finally breaks Katherine. She apologizes (line 176) for her 'unmannerly' behaviour (the second time she has used this unusual word: 'language unmannerly' (I.ii.27)) and begs understanding again of her witless state as a woman. And in a formal phrase redolent of the distance that there is already between her and the King and that will tragically increase, she says, as she goes to leave, a broken woman, a forsaken wife, and a ruined Queen: 'Pray do my service to his Majesty' (line 179). But even here, at the height of her loss, like the good Catholic she is, she asks religious counsel of the two men who have been instigatory in her downfall. Having called them 'Cardinal sins' and 'hollow hearts' she now calls them 'reverend fathers'. She remembers all that she has lost since she first set foot on English soil, all that she has had to agree to lose, in order to keep her dignity.

When we next see her, her last and 'Winter' scene, she has precious little other than her dignity, apart from the faithful Griffith and her maid Patience. I asked for my last costume to be changed from the original drawing, although there was a clear progression in what our designer, Robert Jones, had created, a progression downwards from the splendour of the Cloth of Gold dress, to the almost nun-like garb for the trial scene (Katherine, in keeping with her Christian modesty, had, in fact, in her first four-and-a-half years in England only two new dresses). But I still felt that a structured Tudor dress with its corseting and boning was too definite somehow in its silhouette for the frail and ill wraith that she has become. So, with amazing speed and generosity, Rob jettisoned it

21 Jane Lapotaire as Queen Katherine, with Caputius (Rex Obano),
Henry VIII, Act IV, Scene ii: 'Remember me/In all humility unto
his highness.'

and produced a grey shroud-like smock that hung and clung in ageing
folds about my body and accentuated bones and skeleton.

Bereft of everything except her two faithful servants and almost
unable to walk, we wonder what has kept Katherine going. We are surprised to find that it is hatred. Hatred of Wolsey has fed her fires and
fuelled her since we saw her last. And like all creatures who have fed on
poison she has been eaten up by it mentally and physically. She becomes
alert and is intrigued by the manner of Wolsey's death, and makes a
joke of him managing it well as an example for her to follow. I found it
amusing in rehearsal that the great Wolsey, nearing his end, couldn't stay
upright on the mule that he always rode in imitation of Jesus's donkey,
and laughed outright. We decided we would keep it in. The laugh is
wiped off Katherine's face when she learns that he did die in a state of
grace. But she can't resist another defamatory outburst against the man
whom she has blamed all these years for the destruction of her marriage.
(Wolsey *did* want Henry to marry again, but ironically he sought a marriage between his King and the Duchess of Alençon, the French king's
sister; so Katherine's hatred has been partially misplaced. Even a saint
can make mistakes . . .) How often must the poor Patience have been

needful of the quality of her name and the ever loyal Griffith had to hold
on to his 'religious truth and modesty' in the face of frequent outbursts
of this nature against Wolsey? He was a man of an unbounded ambition,
an underhand dealer; he was a law unto himself, one that would even lie
and be duplicitous in the King's presence – her list of his misdeeds is
endless. Worst of all, for Katherine, he was only sympathetic to people
when he was set to destroy them, as he so successfully destroyed her. We
decided to cut the last two lines of this speech as they seemed to be full of
bathos: 'Of his own body he was ill, and gave / The clergy bad example'
(IV.ii.43–4). Stronger to end on:

> His promises were as he then was, mighty,
> But his performance as he now is, nothing.   (IV.ii.41–2)

It also brings us back to the initial subject of Wolsey's death.

Griffith, in the face of this most unchristian outburst, makes a stand
to speak of the transience of good in general and of Wolsey's good in particular, and he does it in such a way that the years of Katherine's hatred
melt away. Her mere admission of the fact that she hated Wolsey is a
giant revelation to her and a huge step towards the truth. She hears that
Wolsey for all his materialism and ambition at the end of his life 'felt
himself / And found the blessedness of being little' (IV.ii.65–6). This
must hit hard as she has never found that blessedness. She has surely
spent her years in exile inwardly bemoaning the wrongful removal of her
divine right as Queen, a right that she had learned at Isabella's knee. But
this huge step of forgiveness, the humbling of her pride and the ultimate
blessing of Wolsey's departed soul, takes its toll on her strength and she
wants to rest, listening to the music that she wishes to hear at her death.
She sleeps and sees a vision.

The vision that she sees caused us much debate. Finally, to my great
relief, the idea of the younger members of the cast tripping round me in
white dresses and cherub wings was scrapped for the simpler (and to my
mind more effective for an audience familiar with the cinematic skills
of Spielberg) pillar of golden light. In this, surely as a reward for her
forgiveness of Wolsey, she sees 'a blessed troop', 'spirits of peace', who
invite her to 'a banquet, whose bright faces / Cast thousand beams' upon
her 'like the sun' (IV.ii.83–9) – what a potent reminder of Spain, even at
this late stage in her life and the play. Their departure leaves her sad-
dened to rediscover the wretchedness of her earthly state. But they have
promised her eternal happiness, the greatest accolade (if that's the right

word for the humbling she has achieved through suffering and Christian endurance): but, as ever, with her truthful mind, she knows that she is not ready for this greatest of tributes yet.

With the same skill that led Shakespeare to introduce the clown with the basket of figs and his jokes just prior to Cleopatra's death scene, Katherine's second reverie is abruptly shattered by a messenger (surely a Kimbolton local) who in the excitement of his errand addresses her with no formality at all: 'An't like your grace' (IV.ii.200). In a flash we see the old Katherine, but one whose years of diminution in status have made her all the more status-conscious. (She would never acknowledge the title that they tried to force on her after the divorce – 'Princess Dowager'.) 'You are a saucy fellow! / Deserve we no more reverence?' (IV.ii.100–1). The saucy fellow has come to tell of a messenger from the King, a messenger that even with the failing of her eyes that grows progressively worse through the scene, is one that she recognizes from Spain – another valuable echo of her homeland, now that she is so near the end of her earthly journey, and the messenger can be a useful tool to carry, at long last, an earlier message she had written to Henry.

Greg asked a very potent question at one point in the rehearsing of this scene, when it seemed to be stuck, not growing or going anywhere: 'What would we lose if the scene ended after the vision?' Quick as a flash we saw what the end of Katherine's role was about. We have to see that she has no grudges against Henry; that she is still concerned for his welfare; that she must remind Henry of his duties towards the child of their 'chaste loves' (especially as another from Anne Boleyn is on the way), and that she must make provision for her faithful servants, albeit that her estimation of how many she has is slightly awry: to the last she is the champion of the poor, although her manservants have grown poor because of their cleaving to her despite her change in fortune. The passion with which I colour 'That they may have their wages duly paid 'em' (IV.ii.150) was based on Katherine having to send messengers home to Spain asking her father to send her money for food when she was pushed out into the paucity of Ludlow Castle in the years between Arthur's death and her eventual marriage to Henry, not dissimilar to the relative poverty in which she must have lived at Kimbolton.

The energy with which she has finally put her earthly house in order so that she may depart in peace costs her dear. She knows that she is near death. With her recently learned humility she tells the messenger to inform the King that 'his long trouble now is passing / Out of this world' (lines 162–3) – what a heartbreaking but nevertheless accurate description of herself! – and adds: 'Tell him in death I blessed him, / For so I will' (lines 163–4). What utter Christian forgiveness and love. This is all the more poignant now, of course, since we have seen her, as frail as she is, claw herself back from the jaws of bitterness and hatred. Again the word 'chaste' appears. How strongly she must have held on to this, through all her years of exile and rejection: 'I was a chaste wife to my grave' (line 170). And she leaves us, having detailed her burial instructions, with a last reminder of who she really is: 'A queen, and daughter to a king' (line 172). Spanish, noble, and dignified to the end, till she 'can no more'. Her actual last words, after she had heard mass at daybreak said by her Spanish chaplain, were in a moving letter to Henry, in which she declared: 'For my part I pardon you everything . . . I commend unto you our daughter Mary, beseeching you to be a good father unto her . . . Lastly I make this vow, that mine eyes desire you above all things.' 'Humble et Loyale' to the very end. The Imperial ambassador Chapuys wrote of her 'that she was the most virtuous woman I have ever known, and the highest hearted.' Me too. It is a privilege and a joy to play her. May she rest in peace.

*

Henry VIII is part pageant, part history play, part the personal downfall of Buckingham, Wolsey, and Katherine, but in keeping with the late, great plays in the canon, *The Tempest* and *The Winter's Tale*, *Henry VIII* is also a play about spiritual rebirth, not just in the symbol of the baby who is to become Elizabeth I, but also through that most difficult of human experiences, the humbling of worldly state that leads to the spiritual state of forgiveness.

Menenius in
Coriolanus

PHILIP VOSS

PHILIP VOSS is an Associate Actor of the Royal Shakespeare Company and played Menenius in David Thacker's production of *Coriolanus* at the Swan Theatre in 1994. In the following season it transferred to the main stage of the Barbican Theatre. His other roles in the 1994 season were Peter Quince in *A Midsummer Night's Dream* and Bassanes in *The Broken Heart*. Earlier parts for the RSC had included Worcester and the Lord Chief Justice in 1 and 2 *Henry IV*, Sir Epicure Mammon in *The Alchemist*, Theseus in *The Thebans*, and Lord Sheffield in *Unfinished Business*. He returned to Stratford in 1996 to play Ulysses in *Troilus and Cressida* and Monticelso in *The White Devil*, and in the 1997–98 season took the roles of Malvolio in *Twelfth Night* and Shylock in *The Merchant of Venice*. A variety of parts for the Royal National Theatre includes Rodin in *The Wandering Jew*, Ferdinando in *Countrymania*, James in *The Strangeness of Others*, and the Troll King in *Peer Gynt*, while for the Shared Experience Company he has played, among other roles, Dr Dorn in *The Seagull* and Chebutykin in *The Three Sisters*. Film and television work includes *Four Weddings and a Funeral*.

Menenius Agrippa, according to my Arden preface, was a legendary figure in *Plutarch's Lives* (Shakespeare's main source for *Coriolanus*) and merely the Senate's persuasive popular spokesman, but given a quasi-paternal relationship with Martius by Shakespeare, becomes the stage voice of an accommodating patrician wisdom. According to Charles Boyce, in his *A-Z Encyclopaedia of Shakespeare*, 'Menenius after Act one, Scene one, is merely a mildly amusing figure, who rejoices girlishly over a letter from his hero and has a moment later on of genuine pathos when he is rejected by Coriolanus'. Harley Granville-Barker, in the best analysis of the play that I have read, refers to him as an 'auxiliary character'.

I had only seen the play once – a stunning production in Victorian dress by Tyrone Guthrie at Nottingham Playhouse in the sixties. I could just recall what I now know to be the famous 'belly speech' from

22 Philip Voss as Menenius, with Toby Stephens as Coriolanus, *Coriolanus*,
Act I, Scene i.

Menenius, and that Dorothy Reynolds was pretty hot stuff as Volumnia,
but the emotional core of that production was the overtly sexual nature
of the Aufidius/Coriolanus relationship played by Ian McKellen and
John Neville: something of a shock in those days.

On reading the play so many years later, I felt that I had been offered
the most wonderful undiscovered role. I realised that Menenius was central to the events that took place, and more than that, he actually helped
to shape them. Throughout the play he has, despite all, the interests of
Rome overwhelmingly at heart. It seemed a great part to me. I worked
on the characterization as I do with every part that I play, which starts
with a systematic analysis of the text. – a process I discovered while
working with Mike Alfreds at Shared Experience and one that I have
followed ever since.

Before rehearsals for *Coriolanus* began, I examined the text four times
in order to make four exploratory lists. First, to set down the textual facts
about Menenius. Second, to find out what Menenius says about himself.
Third, to find out what other people say about Menenius. Lastly, to discover what Menenius says about everybody else. From this information,

I hoped to deduce the governing factors of his character, choose his super-objective which of course could be outside the confines of the particular play, his objective in the play, the main line of action throughout the play, the obstacles against that, and finally, I hoped to discover his 'Laban' category: the type of animal he might be, and the kind of pulse or tempo that governed him.

A word first about Laban: the Laban 'efforts', or 'energies', were developed mainly for dancers and they break down the human psyche into three pairs of elements. The first pair is Light and Heavy. Light is done with ease, it is effortless; Heavy is firm, with an intensity, but not strained. The second pair is Direct and Indirect. Direct is focused with intention to make things happen; Indirect is unfocused when you allow things to happen to you. The third of the combinations is Sustained and Broken. Sustained is flowing and unending, whereas Broken energy has to be constantly renewed and tends to be sudden. Combining these three elements you have eight combinations, covering the whole range of possibilities in the human personality. For instance, a 'Thruster' is heavy/broken/direct as exemplified most prominently by Lady Thatcher and heavy/sustained/indirect would be a Ringer – a typical suicide. Light/sustained/indirect is a Floater. Light/broken/indirect – a Flicker (a fairy perhaps from *A Midsummer Night's Dream*). Light/broken/direct – a Dabber. Light/sustained/direct – a Glider (some rare individual, who finds life completely effortless). Heavy/broken/indirect – a Slasher (a wife-basher maybe). Heavy/sustained/direct – a Presser (whoever that is, he's unpleasant).

All this helps to suggest the character's movement, or give me some early image of what he might be like. I have always (sometimes against the odds) used this method – and for me, it works. So, to start the exploration of Menenius Agrippa:

(1) The facts

Menenius is a Roman.
He loves Rome (passionate about Rome).
He is a patrician, the citizens think he loves them.
The citizens think he's honest.
He calls the citizens his 'countrymen'.
He is a member of the Senate.
He has been aware for a fortnight of the citizens' unrest.

He acknowledges that there is a shortage of food (dearth).

He blames this dearth on the gods, not the patricians.

He is not a Christian – he worships the gods.

He supports the rule of the Senate.

He, in a tale, compares the governing body to the human belly.

He makes his belly smile?

He counters the first citizen's arguments by accusations of impatience.

He calls the first citizen the 'big toe' of the body (or assembly).

He refers to the mob as 'rats'.

He believes in true breeding.

He shuts up when Martius arrives and lets him control the mob.

He is aware that the other side of the city has risen just before he enters.

He delays these citizens, by his tale, from going to the Capitol to join their fellow rioters.

He think Martius a greater human being than all of the plebeians since the Flood, put together.

He refers to himself as 'o' th' right hand file'.

He likes a drink (straight).

He likes a joke.

He is not the most diligent Senator.

He despises the plebeians.

He denigrates the Tribunes.

He throws his cap in the air at the news that Martius is coming home.

He makes up words ('empiricutic'; 'fidiussed'; 'conceptuities').

Coriolanus sends him a letter from Corioles.

He tots up the number of wounds on Coriolanus's body.

He enthuses wildly about Coriolanus's victory.

He presses for Coriolanus to be honoured in the Senate: to be made Consul.

He urges Coriolanus to speak humbly to the citizens.

He attempts to deflect Coriolanus's proud outburst.

He is old.

He is witty.

He is two-faced.

He thwarts the people's intention of killing Coriolanus by use of his mind and tongue.

He urges Coriolanus to be mild in addressing the plebeians.

He weeps when Coriolanus is leaving Rome.

He includes himself in the blame for allowing Coriolanus to be banished from Rome.

He repeats, ironically, 'you have made good work', often to the Tribunes.

He is a passionate man.

He owns armour, but dislikes wearing it.

He allows himself to be persuaded to plead with Coriolanus to spare Rome.

He calls Coriolanus his son.

He calls himself Coriolanus's old father.

He fails to persuade Coriolanus to pardon Rome.

He overvalues his power over Coriolanus.

He describes Coriolanus as merciless and god-like in his behaviour.

He rejoices at Volumnia's success.

He sees himself as a surrogate father to Coriolanus.

He knows that with Coriolanus at the helm, Rome will be safe.

And I wrote in capital letters, at the end:

HE IDOLIZES CORIOLANUS.

And just a selection of lines that helped me towards my eventual conclusions:

(2) What Menenius says of himself

I am known to be a humorous patrician, and one that loves a cup of hot wine with not a drop of allaying Tiber in it. (II.i.44–6)

I'll try whether my old wit be in request
With those that have but little. (III.i.250–1)

He [Coriolanus] called me father. (v.i.3)

. . . when we have stuffed
These pipes and these conveyances of our blood
With wine and feeding, we have suppler souls
Than in our priest-like fasts. (v.i.54–7)

For I have ever varnishèd my friends. –
Of whom he's chief. (v.ii.17–18)

FIRST WATCH: You are a Roman, are you?
MENENIUS: I am as my general is. (v.ii.35–6)

SICINIUS: He loved his mother dearly.
MENENIUS: So did he me. (v.iv.15–16)

(3) What other characters say about Menenius

SECOND CITIZEN: Worthy Menenius Agrippa, one that hath always loved the
   people.

FIRST CITIZEN: He's one honest enough. Would all the rest were so!

                 (I.i.49–52)

BRUTUS: [in a line that was cut in our production] You are well understood to
   be a perfecter giber [joker] for the table than a necessary bencher in the
   Capitol.   (II.i.76–8)

CORIOLANUS: Their latest refuge
   Was to send him; for whose old love I have –
   Though I showed sourly to him – once more offered
   The first conditions, which they did refuse
   And cannot now accept, to grace him only
   That thought he could do more.   (v.iii.11–16)

CORIOLANUS: This last old man,
   Whom with a cracked heart I have sent to Rome,
   Loved me above the measure of a father,
   Nay, godded me indeed.   (v.iii.9–12)

This last was probably the line that most influenced my eventual
performance.

(4) What Menenius says about other characters

(Of the Citizens)
Why, masters, my good friends, mine honest neighbours,
Will you undo yourselves?   (I.i.60–1)

(Of Coriolanus)
it remains,
As the main point of this our after-meeting,
To gratify his noble service that
Hath thus stood for his country.   (II.ii.36–9)

(Of the Mob)
Your multiplying spawn how can he flatter –
That's thousand to one good one.   (II.ii.76–7)

(Of the Tribunes)
You worthy Tribunes.   (III.i.264)

(He says that as they enter. A few lines before that, out of their hearing,
he wishes to have them defeated.)

(Of Coriolanus)
There is no more mercy in him than there is milk in a male tiger.

(v.iv.27–8)

(Of Volumnia)
This Volumnia
Is worth of consuls, senators, patricians
A city full; of tribunes such as you,
A sea and land full.

(v.iv.51–4)

From this information I came to the following conclusions:

His super-objective (which is the most important decision I make) is to safeguard Rome.

At first it would seem that it would be to promote Coriolanus, but I realized from his rejoicing at Volumnia's success that his ambitions went beyond Coriolanus to embrace the safety of Rome. His objective was to see his hero, Coriolanus, as the defender of Rome. His main line of action, to try to make Coriolanus Consul of Rome – I'm sure not only because he loves him, but because he thinks he is the best man for the job. The obstacles against it are: Coriolanus's pride and temper; the two Tribunes manipulating the crowd; the banishment of Coriolanus; and his own miscalculation of Coriolanus's character.

From the choice of Laban energies, I decided that he was a 'thruster', i.e. heavy/direct/broken. His physical centre was split, I felt, between the instincts, the juices and, obviously, the stomach. For an animal I chose an old leopard and his pulse, I decided, was steady. In addition, from real life I took Robert Boothby and William Whitelaw as guides: the first more as a bon vivant and the other as a power manipulating behind the throne.

With all this information under my belt before the first rehearsal I sort of knew where I was going, but not how I was going to get there. David Thacker's process of rehearsal is free enough to allow everyone their own approach to the work, and for the first three weeks we improvised, analyzed each scene and members of the cast read each others' parts. We paraphrased the entire script and there seemed to be no restriction on movement or experimentation. In fact the play was never blocked as such until we first reached the Swan Theatre, eight weeks later.

From Mike Alfreds's work, the most important thing that I learned was to *want* something every time I walked on the stage. That meant finding out what the scene was about, what my objective was in that

23 Philip Voss as Menenius, with Linal Haft as Sicinius Velutus and
Ewan Hooper as Junius Brutus, *Coriolanus*, Act II, Scene i.

particular scene and – come hell or high water – to go on and achieve it,
whatever resistance I was given from the other character or characters.
I want to keep the Mob here and prevent them going to the Capitol; I
want to promote Coriolanus for Consul; I want to stop Coriolanus from
burning Rome.

All very simple, but it gives me a firm track to follow and I can forget
about myself within the demands of the character.

To help give detail, colour and nuance to my performance I improvised, using points of concentration. You can argue that there is no need
to search for a sub-text in Shakespeare. All the information you need
is in the lines and, indeed, Menenius gives a full description of himself
to the Tribunes in Act Two, Scene One, which although it is a defence
against an attack from them, is very near the truth. However, it may
sound too technical but, without ever losing the objective of a scene, I
like to put all the ingredients through a sieve, as it were, and examine
each particular relevant factor. What's good I keep and the rest is
discarded.

The easiest way to explain a point of concentration is through the weather. We behave differently in hot weather than we do, say, in the winter. In a production in 1960 of *The Taming of the Shrew* at Stratford the action was set during the winter with snow everywhere. There were problems, one of them being that we were overlong. Peter Hall took over the production after the second technical rehearsal. We were called together the next morning and told the situation. When rehearsals began again, his first instruction to us was that it was now Spring. The result was that instead of coming on stamping our feet and flapping our arms to get the circulation going, we bounded on with joy and got on with it. The snow came off the roof and twenty minutes came off the running time – all due to changing a point of concentration. When playing Doctor Dorn in *The Seagull*, I used a point of concentration to explore the disgust he felt about other people and I remember snatching the handkerchief from Masha's hand after she had taken snuff and showing her the results of the filth on the white handkerchief. That is something I don't think I would have thought up ordinarily at my desk or in a rehearsal room. In the case of *Coriolanus*, my chief point of concentration is, of course, Coriolanus. Another list, I'm afraid, but here are some of the points I particularly concentrated on at various rehearsals:

Defending him: throughout the play, noticeably in the scene with the Tribunes:

> Yet you must be saying Martius is proud; who, in a cheap estimation, is
> worth all your predecessors since Deucalion.   (II.i.84–6)

Supporting him:

> His nature is too noble for the world.   (III.i.254)

Reprimanding him:

> Come, come, you have been too rough, something too rough.   (III.ii.25)

Taking control of him and the situation after the riot:

> Go, get you to your house! Be gone, away!
> All will be naught else . . .
>   Pray you be gone.
> I'll try whether my old wit be in request
> With those that have but little. This must be patched
> With cloth of any colour.   (III.i.229–30, 249–52)

Touching him:

This was very difficult in the early stages of rehearsal and indeed into performance, as Toby Stephens with all that testosterone would leap into the air the moment anyone touched him. Some examples of different ways of touching him: on 'these are almost thoroughly persuaded' (I.i.199), I linked my arm through his. On 'welcome, warriors' (II.i.182), I grabbed his hand with joy and hugged his arm to mine. During the riot I actually dared to push him off the stage. On 'Nay, temperately! Your promise' (III.iii.67) I gently touched his forearm in an attempt to dilute the violence of the energy inside him.

Cajoling or persuading him:

> Speak fair . . . their hearts were yours.   (III.ii.70, 87)

Finding time to joke with him:

> We have some old crab-trees here at home that will not
> Be grafted to your relish.   (II.i.181–2)

> For though abundantly they lack discretion,
> Yet are they passing cowardly.   (I.i.201–2)

(All this is a means of finding a way to be intimate with him.)

Promoting him: Eagerly pushing through the election –

> Is the Senate possessed of this? (to Volumnia.)   (II.i.127)

In the Senate scene – watching the reaction of the senators to Cominius's praise of Coriolanus, then deflating any attack on him from the Tribunes.

> That's off, that's off!
> I would you rather had been silent.   (II.ii.58–9)

Menenius is a great weeper:

He weeps when Coriolanus returns victoriously; he weeps when Coriolanus is banished from Rome; and in appealing to Coriolanus in Antium, he is weeping. I always kept a handkerchief at the ready.

Loving him:

Believing in his love for me and that I have, through love, a power and hold over him. In performance, to keep things fresh, I would always re-charge this particular point of concentration.

Other points of concentration beyond Coriolanus that I tried:

The Mob:

They are about the smelliest crowd in the whole of Shakespeare, with breaths stinking as 'rotten fens' (III.iii.121), and obviously hungry and filthy. One of the citizens, very kindly, put grease and muck on his palm, which I surreptitiously had to wipe off with my handkerchief after shaking his hand with my typical, seemingly benevolent concern. The mob are a major and vital part of *Coriolanus* and seem to be written in a generalized way, but David Thacker took great care to give each one a specific through-line politically. Their job is particularly difficult: Shakespeare just hasn't given them much to say, and yet they have to maintain a protest at a high energy level throughout the evening and that causes problems for them. It is vital for Menenius to embrace the reactions of the plebians. He must seem to understand them and they must believe, in the main, that he likes them.

Drink:

We considered his life in the club and at one point we were going to play the scene with the Tribunes in a club-like atmosphere, at a table, drinking brandy, chatting, but this seemed to hold up the action. He is obviously a drinker. Was Shakespeare's father a drinker in later life, I wonder? I carried a hip-flask at an early run-through and took a swig at various dramatic high points. This seemed to turn him into an alcoholic, and at the least was overly quirky. I have to say, David Thacker never mentioned it either when I used it, or when I abandoned it.

Food:

I left that to the text. Food is a recurring theme, his belly, corn, wine and feeding. There seemed no need to explore that any further.

His wit:

It is his most vital weapon and he retains it to the very end. Even at his lowest, in the face of mockery from the Watch, he can respond with a bleak and damning humour. 'For you, be that you are, long; and your misery increase with your age!'   (v.ii.101–3)

His clothes:

I had some trouble with my costume. The designer, short of affluent Senators, wanted me in black velvet and gold embroidery. This to me went against my image of him as a man more frequently in the club than in the Senate house. I saw him as a comfortable table-teller, relaxed, glass in hand. The text calls for a hat (we were set in post-Revolutionary France), but the bicorn provided hardly seemed suitable for the scenes amongst the plebeians. It was my aim to look as if I was trying to cross the class barriers and wanted something with far less status attached to it. From a David portrait, the designer found a man wearing a turban, which she then provided in a spotted material with a sash to match, helping the image of my old leopard along.

Eventually, the sash became the means of making the belly 'smile' (I.i.105), by looping it over my stomach as a sort of grin, but that took some time to discover, having experimented, among other things, with belching, as suggested in the footnotes, which helped neither the understanding of the line nor the iambic pentameter. For a while I tried a bit of 'old man acting' and from that retained a walking stick. Virgilia seems to get a raw deal and I found a moment to embrace her just before her husband's return to Rome.

It is to the best advantage, of course, when all the actors are pursuing the same point of concentration, or are, at least, aware of the exercise and part of it. At the RSC this can't be the case. There are so many different ways of working and I have to admit there were one or two clashes with other actors, who couldn't understand what was happening when the intention of the scene seemed to slide absurdly in one specific direction as I followed my point of concentration. I even entered once holding one of the Tribunes' hands (exploring friendliness), which wasn't received at all well.

Coriolanus is the most political of Shakespeare's plays, but it seems to me that Shakespeare didn't want to side either with the right or left. The audience must make up their own minds. Coriolanus, who wishes to 'pluck out / The multitudinous tongue' (III.i.155–6), isn't far short of Hitler, an arrogant monster, but then the Tribunes with their 'Let us seem humbler after it is done. / Than when it was a-doing' (IV.ii.4–5) are manipulative and self-serving. Apart from Virgilia, there doesn't appear to be one nice character in the whole play, and she is dominated by Volumnia. Neither side is wholly good or bad. Certainly playing Coriolanus young it was easier to forgive some of the excesses and easier to identify and understand the power his mother has over him – and Menenius. We are the monsters. We drove him. We brought him up always to do better; to do more. He knows his limitations, but how could he ever feel secure with those two around him?

The text, both verse and prose, is difficult to follow. We cut the script for clarity, though I was able to save my 'made-up words' by claiming them as character traits. Lines break in the middle. Some of the imagery is impossibly dense and complicated. There are few 'beautiful' speeches as in the play's predecessor *Antony and Cleopatra*. But, then again, there are sections that are naturalistic – one-word half-lines, tumbling on one another. It moves. It just gets on with the story, one scene taking over from another.

I am fond of an exercise called 'beats', to help clarify the text. After each separate thought, I say the word 'beat' and make sure that the next thought uses a different tone of voice or colour, even if it is artificially achieved. For example (I.i.53–4): 'BEAT – What work's, my countrymen, in hand? – BEAT – Where go you – BEAT – With bats – BEAT – and clubs? – BEAT – The matter? – BEAT – Speak, – BEAT – I pray you. –' It separates the ideas, and ensures that every word has been examined, and with David Thacker constantly saying 'I don't understand you', or 'What do you mean?', the meaning gradually began to emerge.

And there we have it. It took me a long time to find the 'belly speech', but when I began to talk to the citizens, instead of shouting at them, it fell into place. Trading insults with the Tribunes (II.i.) was the first scene that I truly enjoyed and the character spread from there. Everything is possible for Menenius's dreams to come true until Coriolanus says, 'I banish you' (III.iii.123); then he is desolate. A life's grooming is in ruins – but, of course, there is always young Martius, Coriolanus's son. He has already 'mammocked' that butterfly (I.iii.66). I think Menenius has enough material to work on for the next few years.

For the London run we were transferred from the small stage of the Swan to the much bigger stage of the Barbican. We acquired a brand new, white set, with scaffolding to create the different levels, which dripped with even more blood than at Stratford, while the Delacroix figure of 'Liberty Leading the People' split into two for the upstage entrance. We emerged, as it were, from a womb. The Liberty, Equality, Fraternity banners were abandoned in an attempt to lessen the specific French Revolution parallels. We lost all entrances through the auditorium and some of the production's chamber quality of intimacy had to be sacrificed.

Three unhappy plebians were allowed to leave the cast and were replaced by six (very enthusiastic) drama students. There was a highly successful poster campaign across the town, of Toby, drenched in blood and advertised as a 'Natural Born Killer'. For Menenius, I had a new coat for the scene in the Senate – black velvet, richly embossed with gold filigree at last, which increased my status considerably as I engineered his election as Consul. I returned to my comfortable old coat for the rest of the play.

We had a very short run of twenty-five performances and we were happily a sell-out with long queues for returns. Pretty good.

Friar Lawrence in
Romeo and Juliet

Julian Glover

JULIAN GLOVER is an Associate Actor of the Royal Shakespeare
Company and played Friar Lawrence in Adrian Noble's production
of *Romeo and Juliet* at the Royal Shakespeare Theatre in 1995 and the
following year at the Barbican Theatre. His other role that season was
Cassius in *Julius Caesar*. Earlier Shakespeare work for the RSC had
included Warwick in 1, 2, and 3 *Henry VI*, Aufidius in *Coriolanus*, and
the title role in 1 and 2 *Henry IV*, for which he won an Olivier Award.
Other RSC performances have been in *The Man of Mode*, *Cousin
Vladimir*, *The Changeling*, and *The Oz Trial*. A very wide range of work
in London and provincial theatre, on film, on television, and on radio,
includes a great deal more Shakespeare, including performances with
the Prospect Theatre Company (*Much Ado about Nothing*), the Old Vic
world tour (*Hamlet*), Actors in Residence, US (*King Lear*), the Royal
Court (*Twelfth Night*), and, on television, *An Age of Kings*, *Henry V*,
Henry VIII, and *King Lear*. He has recently directed *Hamlet*, with his son
in the title role.

'Absolutely *not*, Adrian' – this to the Artistic Director of the Royal
Shakespeare Company. 'You know how I feel about that part; look, I've
already said I'll do Cassius for Peter Hall, please don't make me feel
guilty about this. Anyway, the only reason I'd even *think* about doing
anything else in the season would be to work with you again.' 'Well, I'm
directing *Romeo and Juliet*', he replied.

Ouch! And that's how it came about. Well, a bit more thought went
on, but the end result was that I said yes. Why actors accept parts is not
usually very interesting, or relevant to the outcome, but I mention it in
this case because my initial reluctance was most influential upon my
approach.

I'd also had a rather unpleasant brush with the Friar during a previous
season with the RSC. I was playing the title role in the *Henry IV* plays,
and threw in Chorus and the Duke in *Romeo and Juliet* to be a GCM

(Good Company Member). The actor who was to play Friar Lawrence understudied my Henry IV, and judging from his performance of the part in the understudy run-through that I witnessed, quite obviously held my interpretation in deep contempt. We were only a few weeks into rehearsal for *Romeo* when it was decided that this actor was not acceptable to the director, and I was asked to take over Friar Lawrence. With the best GCM will in the world, I could not, of course, do that to the actor, and he was eventually replaced from outside the company. The incident left a very bad taste in my mouth, and a further prejudice against the good Franciscan.

But my attitude towards him was already pretty firmly entrenched. I'd only seen one performance that I thought worked at all, that of Milo O'Shea in the Zefferelli film, and I certainly couldn't think of playing it in his gentle, wise, Irish way. But even Milo couldn't persuade me that the character was anything but a bumbling, boring old twerp who gets it all wrong and screws up everybody's lives. (When I told the actor Richard Johnson, a fine Romeo in his day, that I was to take on the part, he was vehement – 'He's an old bastard, I hate him!') He enters the play after a full fifty minutes when everything is going along fine, thank you, and we are learning about all the people concerned, and frankly the last thing we want is a vicar with a very long speech about 'nature'. He also has a dreadfully tiresome speech at the end, when all the audience wants is to go home, in which he tells us in lugubrious detail the story we already know. The man is a complete waste of time, a bland, ineffectual fool who merely exists as a catalyst. He hasn't even got any jokes!

Great start! But I was saddled with a task, and had to attempt to disprove all this if I was to endure as a rational human being for the eighteen months I would be performing the play; and I must do this, of course, within the parameters of the text, not with a gimmicky imposition. Ian McKellan once said while playing Richard III and Kent in tandem, that the latter was his 'evening off'. It showed, to be honest, and I was determined that this should not happen with my Cassius/Friar Lawrence double.

When in doubt with Shakespeare I go to the First Folio. This version is not the Bible, but can be a great source of inspiration if you know the sort of clues to watch out for. I visited Patrick Tucker, founder and director of the Original Shakespeare Company, and we tackled the first scene of the part (II.3). I began to read the long opening speech, but had spoken only a few lines when Patrick stopped me: 'Watch the punctuation', he advised. I did so, and soon realized that there are no full stops

24 Julian Glover as Friar Lawrence, in the costume so criticized by his wife and never worn after the first preview, with Romeo (Zubin Varla), *Romeo and Juliet*, Act II, Scene iii: 'Holy Saint Francis! What a change is here.'

for the first *fourteen lines!* – commas, colons, semi-colons a-plenty, but no full stops. Those lines were obviously intended to be delivered all in one lump, the various ideas they express all contributing to the final conclusion. They start with a description of the morning weather, the rising of the sun, the collecting of plants and herbs, the association between birth and death and that nothing that is made is the same as anything else:

> Many for many virtues excellent,
> None but for some, and yet all different. (II.iii.9–10)

What a glorious span of information, how extraordinarily energetic! No humming and hawing here; not a trace of bumble. What next? He wonders at the diversity of creation, and (so often Shakespeare's way) illustrates the grand theme: yin and yang, the entirely opposite qualities inherent in everything so that balance is maintained, with a tiny example, that of both the poison and medicine contained in a single 'infant' flower, comparing this with the condition of mankind:

> Two such opposèd kings encamp them still
> In man as well as herbs – grace and rude will. (II.iii.23–4)

167

And such language! 'Chequering the eastern clouds with streaks of light'; 'darkness fleckled like a drunkard, reels'; 'baleful weeds and precious-juicèd flowers'. This man is not the ruminating bore we've always thought him: he operates on the front foot! (I failed to persuade Adrian, by the way, that there might be useful resonances in following the Folio in having both Romeo (at the end of II.ii) and Friar Lawrence (at the start of II.iii) repeat those four lines about the coming of dawn 'chequering the eastern clouds . . .': we gave the lines to Friar Lawrence.) Far from being a bore, indeed, the Friar, when Romeo comes to find him, makes a risqué joke: 'God pardon sin! Wast thou with Rosaline?' (II.ii.40), he asks, when told that the boy has not been to bed all night. He then ticks him off roundly for his fickle attitude to women before quickly realizing that the Romeo/Juliet union is not the impossible objective one might suppose, but a way to bridge the rift between the feuding Montagues and Capulets. So much has happened in ninety-four lines, the story kicked from romance to pragmatism.

I am now totally hooked, and look forward to applying the new attitude to rehearsal.

One of Adrian Noble's greatest strengths is in not only permitting but encouraging an actor's ideas. If they are found, after a reasonable period of work, to be wanting, he will put a stop to them of course. But if they seem to be developing well, he feeds and nurtures them. I soon came to look on the Friar as that singular maverick priest, so often featured in the films of Fellini and Antonioni, one trained in a particular discipline, yet free to think and act on his feet; a thoroughly good man, a thinker and dedicated scientist with a nimble mind, one used to solving, or at least dealing with, problems both medical and moral, brought to him privately, outside the confessional. Adrian could not have been more supportive of this approach. So I visited a Franciscan monastery in South London to find out whether such a creature as I wished to impersonate could possibly come out of this brotherhood. And I found that indeed he could and that it is fairly common for monks to break away from the parent order to work as a solitary, that they often wear 'civvies' when out on pastoral duties, that they do a lot of gardening, and have the power to marry and bury in the name of God – most important these last three, being specified functions in Shakespeare's play (well, I suppose he did his homework too!). I also noticed that they were a bit grubby – that could be useful.

My first disagreement with Adrian came at once – the proposed setting of my first scene (II.iii). He'd not considered it much, I suspect, and thought a sort of front-cloth 'outside the cell' would be OK. I was determined that it should be *in* Lawrence's cell, and that maybe the interview with Romeo should be in the form of a confession. I lost, because the set was already being built, and did not include a cell. (Why not? Four crucial scenes take place in it!) But a wonderful solution presented itself. The centre of the play was being rehearsed around the café society of any given Italian town – it was perfectly natural for the lone Friar to be discovered there at 5.15 in the morning, having coffee before going about his herbal business, where Romeo, who's been up all night, finds him. Clever Adrian – and out went the confessional!

The second and last disagreement with Adrian – and it hardly amounted to that – concerned my wish to change out of my civvies (a rather natty brown suit) into cassock, etc. *during* the wedding scene (II.vi). I wanted a locker for this – such a one as is to be found in any vestry. Again no deal, as such an addition to the set would not be possible at this stage. (A whole essay needs to be devoted to this pre-planning of design before rehearsals take place – but not here.) But, once more, my loss was my gain. It being no longer appropriate to change on stage, plus the fact that no-one in the play seems to have gone home since the marriage idea was mooted in Act Two, Scene Six, I threw out the suit idea for use later, and merely added a scapular for the wedding, tidying up my unbuttoning and general scruffiness as we talked. This decision was greatly influenced too, I have to say, by my wife's very unfavourable reaction to the suit ('Far too smart – rough yourself up!').

The above considerations must seem superficial. But they were greatly influential in my search for the man himself to put into the clothes and the settings. I had to discover where he came from, what is his function in Verona. Astonishingly, he would appear to be the most important cleric in town – even the great, rich Capulets consult him, and use him for their necessary religious ceremonies. And Paris, the Prince of Verona's nephew, the best catch in Veronese society, is happy for him to officiate at his own wedding, even allowing an argument with him as to its appropriate timing. Why not the Bishop, or at the very least the parish priest? No, it must be Friar Lawrence.

> . . . this reverend holy Friar,
> All our whole city is much bound to him,   (IV.ii.31–2)

cries Capulet when he believes Juliet has been persuaded by the Friar to marry Paris.

It occurred to me that his position is not unlike that of a guru-figure – though one intensely practical – he who will unblock your drains as soon as your morals; a sort of touchstone of goodness and emotional responsibility, accessible to people of every age, class or political persuasion. Such figures seem invariably to come from outside the community in which we find them. The maharishi's influence on the Beatles would have been far less, I suggest, had he been born in Toxteth. Even Jesus Christ, when he made his fatal entrance, hadn't been to Jerusalem for perhaps eighteen years since his twelve-year-old precocity in the temple, by which time he'd achieved an almost God-like status outside the city.

I therefore resolved that my man comes from well outside Verona, probably from a very far province indeed, and one associated with the recluse, meditative, self-supporting religions. Well, I don't know about places like that in Italy, but in any case Shakespeare's language is English, so a provincial Italian accent would be unacceptable (*any* Italian accent would be unacceptable!). So where, in the group of islands in which the author wrote, would be a suitable starting point for the novice Lawrence, a young man determined to learn of God and His creation from the bottom, before, he hopes, going out into the world to teach His Glory? Well, he must be a Celt, so it has to be Ireland, doesn't it? But alas, Milo O'Shea had trodden that path so honourably, and, now I come to think of it, it's *so* obvious as to be a cliché – the upright Irish priest with all the answers.

But Celtic is good – those strong, flinty seascapes, those harsh mountains, the hard, hard life in which to face and conquer the temptations sent to test us. Lindisfarne? No, not far enough away somehow, and to make it clear I'd have to do a Northumbrian dialect which would make an audience wonder why the Good Friar came from Newcastle! All of which is why I gratefully settled on the North-East of Scotland, which has precisely the right terrain and a muscular, tough language, musical but not fey, and also *comprehensible*.

It was a very cheeky idea, and I broached it very tentatively to Adrian. However, he was terrific, said to give it a whirl, and has never referred to it since except in an affectionate teasing way: the accent, which I specified with the estimable dialect coach, Joan Washington, immediately took to the text:

> O mickle is the powerful grace that lies
> In plants, herbs, stones, and their true qualities. (II.iii.11–12)

> Romeo, come forth. Come forth, thou fearful man.
> Affliction is enamoured of thy parts,
> And thou art wedded to calamity . . .   (III.iii.1–3)

and with a little prayer to William Shakespeare, I changed 'Our Romeo hath not been in bed tonight' (II.iii.38) to 'Our Romeo hath not been in bed *the* night'. I don't think he'd have minded – he was an actor too.

Every phrase seemed easier, each idea more clearly expressed, because, of course, it wasn't just the accent but all the aforementioned luggage that went with it. I started really to motor from now on and problems, before impenetrable, began to open themselves up for treatment.

We left our hero at the end of his talk with Romeo, resolved to marry the young couple – once wed, he reasons, it will be possible to mediate between the parents and perhaps sort out their squabbles. Interestingly, the Friar has no scene with Juliet to confirm *her* intentions. Shakespeare would have written it very prettily, but we don't need it; she confirms them so clearly in other scenes after all. So the marriage takes place, and so do the deaths of Mercutio and Tybalt and the banishment of Romeo, none of which events is even remotely to do with Friar Lawrence except in their consequence; how could he possibly have foreseen such a catalogue of disaster? Which means, of course, that the marriage cannot be spoken of, the likelihood of reconciliation between the families being totally out of the question.

In Act Three, Scene Three the Friar is naturally relieved about the banishment, but at the same time very angry indeed with the impetuous young man – a fight is one thing, murder another. He is understanding but furious at Romeo's lack of gratitude to the Duke for his clemency: 'This is dear mercy, and thou seest it not' (III.iii.28), and when the nurse comes to tell of Juliet's similar reaction, which makes Romeo even more maudlin, really slams into him, peremptorily ordering him out of town. But he instructs him to consummate the marriage first:

> Go, get thee to thy love, as was decreed.
> Ascend her chamber. Hence and comfort her.   (III.iii.146–7)

What young man could resist this advice?

Practical again, facing the alternatives, finding and promoting the only possible solution. Contact will be maintained via Romeo's servant, Balthazar, and an interim observed to give time for the dust to settle and, with luck, forgiveness to be bestowed. Then the marriage can be admitted with a good chance of reconciling the families.

But he hasn't reckoned on Paris's matrimonial hopes. This persistent suitor sees Juliet and her parents at a very low ebb, and grabs his chance. Capulet is now keen on the idea, and the Friar's plans are again knocked awry. And when Juliet comes despairingly for help, there really is nothing for it but to give some.

I sincerely doubt that many of my readers have ever experienced a passion such as that between Romeo and Juliet, one so powerful that they truly intend to kill themselves if they cannot be together. Already Romeo has had to be physically restrained from suicide:

ROMEO: In what vile part of this anatomy
         Doth my name lodge? Tell me, that I may sack
         The hateful mansion.
FRIAR: Hold thy desperate hand.
                                                    (III.iii.106–8)

And now Juliet proposes to do likewise:

> . . . ere this hand, by thee to Romeo's sealed . . .
> Turn to another, this [knife] shall slay them both.   (IV.i.56, 59)

No chance for Paris at all.

At this point (IV.i) in my performance I do something Shakespeare has not instructed me to, but I'm *sure* he would approve. I see on my workbench the flower to which I referred in my first scene, the one which contains both poison and medicine, and make a connection between it and Juliet's needs. If a potion could be made from this flower, one that will temporarily kill and later revive, a message could be taken to Romeo to come back and collect her from her tomb, and whisk her off to Mantua. In a burst of inspiration I remember such a recipe, find it at the back of an old book, and make it up before your very eyes, mixing this and that clear liquid and adding chopped flower – the mixture becomes translucent red at one point – which enchants Juliet and I hope engages the audience. I instruct Juliet as I work.

This all came about because of a concern with the bald text:

> Take thou this vial, being then in bed,
> And this distilling liquor drink thou off.   (IV.i.93–4)

I simply couldn't imagine that such a bottle containing such a fluid would come easily to hand. Herbalist he may be – there would be palliatives for

25 Julian Glover as Friar Lawrence, with Juliet (Lucy Whybrow), *Romeo and Juliet*, Act IV, Scene i: 'Tomorrow night look that thou lie alone.'

coughs and headaches and sore feet, balm for bruises and cuts, sleeping draughts even – but what would he *ever* want with a drug that kills someone for a day and a night:

> . . . For no pulse . . .
> No warmth, no breath, shall testify thou livest   (IV.i.96, 98)

then wakes them with no after-effects: 'and then awake as from a pleasant sleep' (line 106). Yes, fiction it may be, but fiction should sound true, and this didn't. And here, once more, Adrian was perfect. Having denied me a cell he suggested a table covered in tubes and pipettes and books and rabbits' feet and bottles and a bowl of flowers, etc., and thus I began to design the most elaborate prop I've ever had – with, naturally, the co-operation of the designer, Kendra Ullyart, and the brilliant prop department at Stratford. Once built, we also put it into the previous scene (III.iii) as set dressing, so we could, at last, describe my area as 'Friar Lawrence's cell'.

And, lo, it all turns out as foretold; Juliet goes to sleep, is buried, and left to moulder:

> ... and as the custom is,
> And in her best array, bear her to church   (iv.v.80–1)

commands the Friar (I preferred the Folio reading here), so pleased with the success of his plan that he takes the opportunity roundly to rebuke the parents, implying that it's their fault that God is dealing them so many bad hands:

> The heavens do lour upon you for some ill,
> Move them no more by crossing their high will.   (iv.v.94–5)

It is not long, though, before the bubble bursts. Having carried out the burial (off stage – Shakespeare doesn't need to bother with it, even if Elizabethan law hadn't forbidden him from putting a church sacrament on stage, for all the lamentations in Act Four, Scene Five provide a perfectly adequate alternative), Friar Lawrence is woken in the middle of the night (v.ii) with the news that plague has prevented delivery of the message to Romeo. And this is where I use my unpriestly clothes, wearing only trousers, hastily putting on a shirt, hair disarranged and sweaty from anxious sleep.

At this point the oak is felled with one blow; the Friar undergoes the most significant emotional upheaval of his life. To discover the nature of this fall I had to go to the last scene of the play – the famous 'tomb scene'. In this he 'trembles, sighs, and weeps' (v.iii.184), has the long speech of explanation mentioned earlier, and offers up his life as penitence. What brings this about? He could so easily have said nothing at all. Both witnesses to his deeds are dead, nothing useful can come of a confession, certainly the audience doesn't need it, so it seems somewhat superfluous.

For the first few weeks of rehearsal I floundered about doing as instructed by the author, generalised sighing and weeping and repentant confession, but without my heart in it. I could not grasp why such a strong, practical, intelligent and pragmatic man should go so completely to pieces – particularly considering that the plague was not his fault and that up till now everything had been going hunkydory.

I wish to stress here, in parentheses, that contrary to widely held opinion, and mine, previously, Friar Lawrence does *not* screw up; circumstances, as so often in life, screw up, but he does not. 'The best laid plans . . .' So, why?

Well, I was blessed – almost literally. A couple of weeks before the production was due to open, His Holiness the Pope issued another of his encyclicals. This took the form of dire warnings against interfering with the mechanics of the female body. If I remember correctly, the essential differences between medical and surgical treatments which were approved of, and the matter in hand which wasn't, were not very clearly expounded. But the core of the message was that artificial insemination, and fertilization of eggs outside the body, and all recent advances in reproducing *homo sapiens* apart from the natural one of sexual intercourse, were a question of mortal wrong-doing. The message I received, as an actor trying to justify Friar Lawrence's behaviour in Act Five, Scene Three of *Romeo and Juliet*, was that *any* re-arrangement of the natural sequences in human life, if not concerned with healing processes, must be considered by a deeply spiritual man to be essentially sinful. And it is not until the forward impetus of his plans is thwarted by that wretched plague that Lawrence suddenly perceives the enormity of what he's done. If I could take this concept into my actor's brain and heart, it would, surely, enable me to deal with the apparent inconsistencies to come.

The Friar's entrance to the tomb is tentative to say the least:

> . . . How oft tonight
> Have my old feet stumbled at graves! (v.iii.121–2)

And he's scared: 'O much I fear some ill, unlucky thing' (v.iii.136 – again I preferred the Folio reading).

And he immediately encounters the double disaster of Paris and Romeo dead and lying all over the sleeping Juliet. He has only three lines in which to take this in before Juliet awakens. His bottle completely goes. He recognizes the impossibility of the situation, and the realization of his own guilt overwhelms him to such an extent that his intelligence deserts him along with his nerve and he runs away, leaving Juliet to kill herself – as he must have known she would. When he is discovered snivelling in the graveyard and brought back to the tomb, there indeed is a very dead Juliet. The Duke asks for information and the Friar gives it. And I at last knew why that speech is there. Surely not to tell the audience what it already knows, surely not to fill in the Duke – that could be done later, off stage. Shakespeare is cleverer than that, and any long explanation he writes must have a purpose (see Benvolio's account to the Duke of the fatal brawl, which is truthful in so far as it favours Romeo and omits any mention of provocation by the Duke's nephew, Mercutio – wonderfully subtle writing).

The purpose is now so clear that I don't know how I missed it. The speech is there for Friar Lawrence. It is there to give him the chance to explode all those emotions he's been bottling up for three days, and to belch out the misery and despair of his guilt, ending with the plea for capital punishment.

> . . . let my old life
> Be sacrificed, some hour before the time,
> Unto the rigour of severest law.
>
> (v.iii.267–9; and again I prefer the Folio reading)

This the Duke tacitly refuses to do – 'We still have known thee for a holy man' (line 270) – which means the Friar will have to live out his days with the weight of moral responsibility for the demise of three people on his conscience.

The man is dead inside – but not so dead as to fail to register the reconciliation between the Montagues and Capulets he'd hoped for in Act Two, Scene Three. My Friar ironically crosses himself here, knowing he will never be able to bless anyone again.

I personally think the play should be re-named something like 'The Tragedy of the Good Brother'. The children have passed over to a better place – he has to stay and suffer in this one.

Brutus in
Julius Caesar

JOHN NETTLES

JOHN NETTLES played Brutus in Sir Peter Hall's production of *Julius Caesar* at the Royal Shakespeare Theatre in 1995. His other roles that season were Buckingham in *Richard III* and Merecraft in Jonson's *The Devil is an Ass*. Earlier work for the RSC had included Thersites in *Troilus and Cressida*, Lucio in *Measure for Measure*, Bassanio in *The Merchant of Venice*, Albany in *King Lear*, Page in *The Merry Wives of Windsor*, Leontes in *The Winter's Tale*, and Octavius Caesar in *Antony and Cleopatra*. His wide range of theatre work in London and the provinces includes seasons at Bristol, Exeter, Manchester, and Edinburgh, as well as tours to the USA with ACTER. He has also worked extensively on radio and on television, particularly with his long-running series *Bergerac*.

THE BRUTE PART

'What character does Shakespeare mean his Brutus to be?'
(Coleridge)

We may share the bewilderment of Coleridge. The answer to his question is as difficult to find in the rehearsal room as it is in the study. But Brutus has to be found and found within the eight weeks rehearsal time allowed. Where to begin? Brutus will be found, if at all, in what he says of himself, what others say of him, and his actions and reactions during the course of this remarkable play. To begin at the beginning.

The Brutus we discover for the first time in Act One, Scene Two is depressed and withdrawn, far removed, it seems, from his normal gentleness and affability. He will not go to the games. His initial replies to Cassius are curt, their brusqueness emphasized by large gaps in the verse lines:

26 John Nettles as Brutus, with Cassius (Julian Glover), *Julius Caesar*, Act I,
Scene ii: 'I love/The name of honour more than I fear death.'

CASSIUS: Will you go see the order of the course?
BRUTUS: Not I.
CASSIUS: I pray you, do.
BRUTUS: I am not gamesome: I do lack some part of that quick spirit that is in
           Antony. Let me not hinder, Cassius, your desires; I'll leave you.
CASSIUS: Brutus, I do observe you now of late . . .   (I.ii.25–32)

There are certainly two, probably three, awkward pauses in that exchange,
and given their full value in the playing, they become an excellent index
of Brutus's disquiet.

It is plain he is deeply troubled, but he will not be explicit about what
precisely it is that is troubling him beyond saying, for reasons to be discovered later, that the thoughts which assail him are of a conflicting and
contradictory nature, difficult to resolve, difficult to bear with equanimity. He then listens to Cassius for a hundred lines or so in near silence.
That silence is eloquent. What Cassius says moves Brutus, he says so
himself (lines 166–7). There is a thunderous pause after Cassius's great
speech beginning 'Why, man, he doth bestride the narrow world' (line
154) and climaxing with the jeering accusation that Brutus is a coward, a

man of nothing and a betrayer of his noble heritage. Given the deeply wounding nature of the charge, Brutus stays remarkably calm, outwardly, but we are aware that a nerve has been touched. How raw that nerve, how deeply touched, we are to learn. Brutus promises further discussion at some unspecified time in the future. After the scene with Casca in which Caesar's alleged ambition to be king is again talked of in even more biting terms Brutus becomes more precise. 'Tomorrow', says he to Cassius, 'if you please to speak with me, / I will come home to you; or if you will, / Come home to me, and I will wait for you' (I.ii.301–3). The matter, in Brutus's mind, has become more urgent, those 'high things' are to be addressed and that right quickly.

What are these 'high things'? What exactly is troubling the noble Brutus? The answers, nearly all of them, come to us in the orchard scene in which Brutus, on his own, addresses the audience directly. As with Hamlet, I take Brutus to be telling the truth about himself and about his thinking in his monologue, but that truth, so revealed, is a strange truth, difficult to understand, lacking coherence, problematic and highly disconcerting to the actor playing him. Far from making the character clear to an audience, and to the actor, it seems at first blush to do the exact opposite. The picture of Brutus which emerges seems very far removed from that of a man noble of mind, philosophically admirable and gentle of spirit. It is very much worthwhile to look in detail at the opening long speech of Brutus beginning 'It must be by his death' (II.i.10) because this speech above all would seem to subvert the notion of Brutus the noble thinker, Brutus the man who sits high in every Roman heart. Caesar has to be killed, must be killed. Why is Brutus so certain that this is the only course open to him? Because, he answers himself, Caesar is likely to become king. This will make him into a vicious tyrant who will enslave the Roman people and destroy everything that Brutus holds dear. Brutus, in the great tradition of his family, who 'did from the streets of Rome / The Tarquin drive, when he was called a king' (II.i.53–4), will therefore kill him. Not, note, for any personal grievance against Caesar, but for the general good. Brutus would have us believe, as he believes, that he is advancing a straightforward and justified argument for tyrannicide. But I think it is clear, even to a casual observer, that it is nowhere near such an open and shut case as he wishes to believe it is. If it were true that Caesar were the man bound to become an oppressive tyrant when once made king, then Brutus's position would be tenable. But Brutus himself states twice in the course of this opening speech that the facts do not support his case; indeed more, that all the known facts directly contradict the case:

> Th' abuse of greatness is when it disjoins
> Remorse from power; and, to speak truth of Caesar,
> I have not known when his affections swayed
> More than his reason. (II.i.18–21)

Simply, tyrannical behaviour for which Brutus is going to kill Caesar, is defined as self-interested rule, exercised without compassion or scruple; but Brutus himself says absolutely clearly that to date no example, not one, exists of Caesar so behaving. There is no ground for Brutus's believing that Caesar will become a tyrant. Where, then, can Brutus turn? He has recourse to a metaphor, but in a typically dubious intellectual fashion uses it as a self-evidently true universal premiss to further his argument. This species of sophistry happens twice in this opening speech:

> . . . But 'tis a common proof,
> That lowliness is young ambition's ladder,
> Whereto the climber-upward turns his face;
> But when he once attains the upmost round,
> He then unto the ladder turns his back,
> Looks in the clouds, scorning the base degrees
> By which he did ascend. (II.i.21–7)

The implication is clear. Caesar, despite all appearances to the contrary, has, for years and years and years, been hiding a vicious political ambition beneath a cloak of reasonable, proper, and honourable conduct. There is not, and cannot be, an iota of proof that this is true, but it has to be true if Brutus is to embark upon his course of principled assassination. Brutus admits to himself and to us that there is this difficulty when he says:

> . . . since the quarrel
> Will bear no colour for the thing he is . . . (II.i.28–9)

Well, yes indeed, and then what does he say?

> Fashion it thus: that what he is, augmented,
> Would run to these and these extremities;
> And therefore think him as a serpent's egg
> Which, hatched, would, as his kind, grow mischievous,
> And kill him in the shell. (II.i.50–4)

'Fashion it thus', means, in this context, 'assume it to be the case without bothering to prove it'. As an example of shoddy thinking it takes some beating. Yes, it is true that if Caesar were a serpent's egg then he would hatch, necessarily, in the nature of things, into something mischievous (tyrannical). The question of whether Caesar himself is in fact a serpent's egg is mightily begged. Brutus himself says there is not the slightest evidence that he is so and yet – and yet – he chooses to ignore, or just does not see, the problem and drives through, a prisoner, it seems, of his controlling metaphor to the conclusion that Caesar must be killed. We are talking of killing a man: killing a man for no other reason than that he might become something there is no evidence for saying he will become. Admit this as sufficient ground for killing and everything is permitted. If we are free to assume that all appearances are false then we might have crucified Mother Theresa in the certain knowledge that she would have turned into Antichrist. It is a form of thinking which amounts to a licence for mayhem, a road to bloody anarchy. It scarcely needs Mark Antony to point this out. It is obvious. It is clear. Dare one speculate that the playwright intended the audience to be aware of the weakness of Brutus's position?

The arguments he advances are not by any measure sufficient to justify the killing of his best beloved Caesar, but there are others which he admits as being crucial. What are they? They are those of Cassius. It is Cassius who has pushed Brutus from melancholic but passive observation of the political scene towards action of an extreme kind. Brutus admits that the ultimate persuasion has come from Cassius. What is the content of that persuasion? Cassius wants Caesar dead because, quite simply, he envies him his glory with a rancorous and passionate vehemence. It has all to do with hate and little to do with reason. It is hardly a sophisticated piece of political thought to suggest that a man is unfit to exercise great political authority because he cannot swim (Mao Tse Tung aside). Nor is it axiomatic in any philosophy I know that a man cannot achieve greatness because he suffered at one time a severe attack of influenza. Cassius's arguments are nasty arguments. They are generated by jealousy, unalloyed and deadly. He then goes on to rouse that same emotion in Brutus:

> Since Cassius first did whet me against Caesar,
> I have not slept.
> Between the acting of a dreadful thing
> And the first motion, all the interim is
> Like a phantasma or a hideous dream.   (ii.i. 61–5)

That 'first motion' is begun because of Cassius's poison. It is reasonable to suppose that Brutus is sincere in his belief that he is killing Caesar for the good of Rome as he proudly proclaims to the people, but there is another motive as well and it is the same as Cassius's motive. He too is jealous of Caesar's greatness. Brutus does not proudly publish that motive, ever, but it might be that an awareness of this ignoble and therefore unspeakable emotion within him explains the anguish he endures as he communes with himself. It seems that Brutus's motives are a queasy mix of bad logic and corrupting envy dressed up in the clothes of a spotless political idealism.

Interestingly enough, when Brutus talks to the conspirators he seems a changed man from that of the earlier monologues. His arguments have an unexpected force and certainty. Far from there being no evidence at all for presuming Caesar will become a tyrant when once a king, as he himself has said, suddenly there is a mass of it:

> . . . the face of men,
> The sufferance of our souls, the time's abuse
> If these be motives weak, break off betimes,
> And every man hence to his idle bed. (II.i. 104–7)

(This to men suddenly changed from a monstrous conspiracy into noble Romans.) If indeed 'the time's abuse' were so obvious and of such an order as to justify absolutely Caesar's assassination, why did Brutus spend so long previously agonizing over the fact that no such justification existed? He seems to be giving a spurious force to his argument by inventing facts. It is called lying, but perhaps not straightforward lying; more like some strange species of self-deception. This is a major example of how Brutus behaves in the play. Time and again Brutus invents circumstances which do not exist in the real world to justify his thoughts and his actions at any given moment. But he seems blissfully unaware that he is distorting reality in this fashion. When he speaks he is always persuaded of the truth of what he says at the time he says it, even if it contradicts what he has said a moment before or what he will say a moment later. Brutus, in short, seems always at some distance from reality and makes mistake after mistake about its nature. He misconstrues everything to the very end, to the point of destroying himself, and seems to learn nothing along the way. There appears very little development in Brutus's character from the orchard to Philippi.

In the orchard, talking to the conspirators, Brutus is seen most clearly in all his paradoxical glory. He is mistaken in his assessment of the wrongs visited upon the Roman people by Caesar, mistaken in the belief that Caesar can be carved as a dish fit for the gods, not butchered as a carcass fit for hounds, mistaken in the belief that the populace will understand what the conspirators are doing and applaud them as purgers of the body politic, and, lastly and fatally, mistaken in assuming that Mark Antony poses no threat and need not be killed along with Caesar. The stage is set for tragedy, a tragedy born of Brutus's inability to understand anything of the world in which he finds himself. Far from creating a wonderful commonwealth by sacrificing Caesar he lets loose the dogs of war and in the conflict Brutus loses everything he ever owned or loved. That is the price he pays for his mistakes.

The killing of Caesar is a bloody mess. Desperately seeking to give the murder some resonant ritual quality, he has to resort, above all things, to the hunters' practice of daubing their hands with the blood of the butchered quarry. Then Brutus commands his fellow conspirators to walk 'to the market place' and 'waving our red weapons o'er our heads / Let's all cry, "Peace, freedom, and liberty"' (III.i.108–10). The sight must have been astonishing in its presumption.

Brutus is surprised at the adverse reaction of the people and senators who, instead of rejoicing at Caesar's death, fly away and barricade themselves in their houses as if Doomsday were come. But Brutus thinks he has only to address them and apprise them of the true nature of his actions for them to applaud him as the saviour of Rome. It is a peculiar speech in many ways, not least in that there is no reasoned justification for the killing of Caesar, just the bald statement that Caesar was ambitious and that if he had been allowed to live the Roman citizens would all have become slaves. Brutus, because he loved Rome more than Caesar, therefore took upon himself the job of rescuing Romans from such a fate. No public reasons, nor any other kind of reasons, are rendered for Caesar's death. The people are asked to believe Brutus for his honour and have respect to his honour that they may believe. That is as far as the reasoning goes. The assumption he is asking them to make must be that Brutus is an honourable man and as such would be incapable of dishonourable actions carried out for dishonourable reasons. What reasons he actually did have for killing Caesar, honourable or otherwise, are not clearly stated. Caesar is killed for his ambition, says Brutus. How, or if, that ambition, if it existed, would lead to tyranny which would justify assassination is never explained.

In the playing of it the speech seems too short, even perfunctory, really to fulfil its purpose, and, particularly when contrasted with Mark Antony's much longer oration, it appears not a little arrogant in its brevity and lack of substance. Brutus has laid himself wide open to the piercing oratory of Mark Antony who deals very specifically and clearly with facts about the real world, not politically expedient suppositions. The very weakness in Brutus's position (which Brutus himself has seen in the orchard monologues) is taken up and mercilessly exposed to the public gaze. Mark Antony is a considerable orator but he is helped enormously in his attack on the conspirators by the grotesque shortcomings of Brutus's thinking. As a target they do not come any bigger than Marcus Brutus.

Brutus's characteristic inability to think straight is evident throughout the course of the drama. He shouts at Cassius for not passing on some of that money to pay his legions, seemingly unaware of the paradox involved in accepting tainted money at two removes which he would refuse on principle to collect himself directly:

> ... What, shall one of us,
> That struck the foremost man of all this world
> But for supporting robbers, shall we now
> Contaminate our fingers with base bribes? (IV.iii. 21–4)

In so far as he is willing to accept the money so vilely raised, the answer has to be 'yes'. (Incidentally, I think that the phrase 'But for supporting robbers' is descriptive, not of Caesar, but of Cassius and Brutus, the sense of the lines being 'shall we who heroically killed great Caesar soil our heroic hands with criminally obtained money for no better reason than to support robbers?')

So far, so inexplicable; but perhaps there is another reason for Brutus's passion and contradictory behaviour in the tent scene which does seem on the face of it to be a mighty storm in a very small teacup. I think the scene has more to do with Brutus's grief for the death of his wife than with base bribes. Brutus may be a blunderer in the world of public affairs, but all the indications are that his private life with Portia is very rich indeed. The loveliest words Brutus speaks describe his feelings for her:

> You are my true and honourable wife,
> As dear to me as are the ruddy drops
> That visit my sad heart (II.i.288–90)

The words sing in the air; they are unforced and flow with a beautiful necessity indicative of great feeling. When she dies, Brutus cannot howl with grief; a Roman does not do that. But he can shout at Cassius, the other love in his life, and shout he does. Cassius has never seen him so angry, but the anger is not quite what it appears to be. It is, I think, Brutus expressing his sorrow for Portia's death. Once he has done that, he can then play the charade with Titinius and Messala of pretending that he has not heard of Portia's death before their arrival. Now he can play for their benefit, and for his own, the noble Roman who can bear great loss with patience and equanimity:

> Why, farewell, Portia. We must die, Messala.
> With meditating that she must die once,
> I have the patience to endure it now. (IV.iii.188–90)

And he can play this role so well because he has spent the previous half hour letting his feelings out with rare passion.

The endgame for Brutus begins with his characteristically mistaking what is going on. He is no better a military strategist than he is a political philosopher, and against the advice of Cassius, he marches to Philippi to face Mark Antony and Octavius Caesar there. Before the battle Cassius asks him what he will do if they are defeated; Brutus answers that he will place his trust in a benign providence which will see him safely through the worst ordeals. His belief in this 'providence' is so absolute that he despises those men, like Cato, who commit suicide for fear of what might be. Cassius then asks Brutus if he will not contemplate suicide in the event of defeat: will he be prepared to be led in triumph through the streets of Rome? No, says Brutus, because he bears 'too great a mind' (V.i.112). Hasn't he contradicted himself? In any event, at the end of the play he commits suicide.

What character, then, have we discovered Brutus to be? He is a man who thinks much, but none too well; a man whose assumptions about the world he lives in are almost all mistaken; a man who, acting on these assumptions, achieves the exact opposite of what he intended. He is a political disaster – and yet he is not without a certain nobility. There is sense in Mark Antony's praise of him as the noblest Roman of them all. Brutus believes what he believes with passionate intensity. He honestly believes that he is acting altruistically for the good of Rome. He honestly believes the reasons are sufficient for the purpose of justifying his actions. That those reasons are palpably not sufficient is a judgement we make of them – Brutus himself sincerely thinks otherwise. The confidence he has in his powers of thought borders on arrogance. 'Brutus thinks it, therefore it must be right', he seems to be saying. He is a dangerous man; a man who acts on the directions of a defective judgement. He believes passionately in what he does. He acts according to high principles, sincerely, for the good of Rome. If he has nobility, then it consists of that; but it is an odd kind of nobility. One may sincerely believe almost anything but it is not believing sincerely that, of itself, makes a man noble. Whether or not a man is noble must have something to do with the quality of reasoning that leads to that belief. After all, Hitler sincerely believed that Jews should be killed. We would not call him noble because of his sincerity: we would call him the reverse because of the nature of his belief.

Here is the main problem with playing the character Brutus. The reputation, and the expectations we have of the man, are destroyed in the course of the play. Whatever he was before the play begins, during the play he is shown over and over again to be a man over-impressed with his own judgement, a man totally unsuited to political action, a man of endless opinion and no knowledge, a man who destroys the very things he wants to preserve. And at the end of the two hours traffic of the stage it seems he still has no knowledge of the enormity of his mistakes or the extent of his responsibility for them:

> My heart doth joy that yet in all my life
> I found no man but he was true to me.
> I shall have glory by this losing day
> More than Octavius and Mark Antony
> By this vile conquest shall attain unto.   (v.v.34–8)

It sounds noble, but it seems dreamlike in its distance from reality; he is again, it seems, inventing a world in which he can play the hero rather than recognizing a real world in which he is, arguably, the greatest villain. But we, the audience, can see what he is doing – and I the actor can see it.

Brutus began the play mistaking the world he was in and he ends the drama, and his life, in the same fashion. The contradictions in his character remain unresolved; there is no getting of wisdom for Brutus. Hamlet goes on an extraordinary voyage of discovery, he is hurt to the quick by his experiences, he is changed by them, he learns from them, his wisdom grows because of them: and this being so, the Hamlet at the end of the play is a very, very different character from that at the beginning. Brutus, it appears, goes through no such transformation. His suffering is not rewarded with spiritual catharsis. Brutus remains the same at the end as he was at the beginning, only increasingly bewildered by his situation, unable to understand or change it.

The problem remains of how to play him. This is a big problem. Actors always want, and rightly so, to make their creations understandable, sympathetic, accessible and attractive. The problem with Brutus, I suspect, is that if you play what is written Brutus is not understandable, becomes unsympathetic, is certainly inaccessible, and for all this remains strangely unattractive behind the noble appearance. The solution, at least the solution we have gone for in this, Sir Peter Hall's production of 1995–6, is to play the contradictions and shortcomings of Brutus for all that they are worth and not to gloss over them, hide them, or in some way lessen them. The point of Brutus is precisely the contradiction he embodies, the contradiction between appearance and reality. Brutus appears a noble Roman stuffed with high principles and lofty thought, an ideal man to lead his fellows. The reality is that Brutus is that most dangerous of men, a misconstruer of events and men, who is given power to demonstrate how mortal that can be.

From the practical point of view of putting Brutus on the stage decisions have of course to be made as how precisely to present the man properly and fairly as a rounded human being. True, the intellectual weakness of his thinking must be shown clearly; true his heroic affectation must not be underplayed. But equally the gentler, more ordinarily emotional aspect of his character must be portrayed for the no better, but still very good, reason that it will bring Brutus closer to the audience, make him appear less removed and Olympian, and more accessible. Brutus may sometimes appear beyond the reach of normal understanding, but still we must try to make him a human being and not a one-dimensional caricature of bad political thinking.

We are on fertile ground. There are a number of exchanges which happily demonstrate this finer behaviour. True, some of them might appear of little account, but they all show Brutus in a kinder light than when he is inveighing against Caesar or plunging unknowingly into the chaos of civil war. This first conversation with Cassius illustrates perfectly what I wish to say and to play. Cassius chides Brutus for not being as loving and gentle towards him as he has been before. Brutus's apology is immediate, admirably sincere and comprehensive: it is not haughty or distant but direct and deeply felt. It has simplicity and honesty.

Great advantages accrue from playing the attractiveness of Brutus's honesty here for many reasons, but chiefly because it gives an inkling of what Brutus was before the opening of the play, and more because it can provide Brutus with an extraordinary journey as he walks, half unknowingly, from the moral uplands of honour, love, and gentleness into the dark pit of murder, terror, and civil war. Brutus must appear downcast at first sight, yes, but nonetheless noble, honest, loving and decent. In pursuit of this effect we have chosen what I believe to be the better option of making Brutus's remark about Antony

> . . . I do lack some part
> Of that quick spirit that is in Antony   (I.ii.28–9)

less bitter and contemptuous than some commentators would have it. This serves an important double purpose. Firstly, it presents Brutus initially in a gentle, perhaps even a wittily wistful, fashion and secondly points up dramatically how much Brutus misunderstands and underestimates Mark Antony, a man who at this stage does not figure large in Brutus's thoughts at all, certainly not to the point of exciting any deep emotion of envy, fear, or contempt. No, Brutus must appear at first as he would like to think himself: upright, grave, honest, noble, and above all, honourable. The playing, I think, should be straightforward and unadorned – time for histrionics later.

The orchard scene has been analyzed at length for its political content. There is difficult verse from an increasingly complex man, but there is also a small, simple, but effective counterpoint to all the anguish running through the scene which resurfaces in Act Four, Scene Three, and I think that Brutus takes great delight in it. Perhaps an audience should too. That counterpoint is Lucius, the young and innocent boy-servant who is having a very hard time chez Brutus. If it is not his master demanding attention deep in the night, it is his mistress hearing strange voices and sending him off on pointless errands. Lucius can provide a lovely, near-comic relief in the orchard scene and certainly we play for this to happen. The comedy lies in the fact that Lucius is not very good at being the servant boy, willing though he may be. At the beginning of the scene Brutus calls, not once but several times, for Lucius. Lucius is asleep. Brutus asks Lucius if tomorrow is the ides of March; Lucius does not know. Someone knocks at the gate; Lucius has to be told to go and answer it (at least in our production he has, for he has fallen asleep again). The conspirators finally leave and Brutus calls for Lucius once

more – and once more, predictably, Lucius is asleep. It is a sweet and
human moment and Brutus responds, perhaps more wisely than he
knows, when he contrasts his state to that of Lucius:

> Thou hast no figures nor no fantasies,
> Which busy care draws in the brains of men;
> Therefore thou sleep'st so sound.   (II.i.231–3)

Later in the play, towards the end of the tent scene, Lucius is once more
called upon by Brutus, this time to sing and play. Again the gentle youth
falls asleep, innocently asleep. Brutus was not kind and loving to Caesar,
but he is touchingly kind and loving to Lucius:

> If thou dost nod, thou break'st thy instrument;
> I'll take it from thee; and, good boy, good night   (IV.iii.269–70)

says he, remembering perhaps his own long-lost innocence which allowed
him, too, such peaceful slumber. In any event it is a moment of blessed
calm and sensitivity in a play of such noise and cruelty and as such we
have sought to play it as feelingly as possible in order to show, among
other things, how Brutus achieves a certain nobility in his domestic life
which he signally fails to do in his public life.

This is achingly clear in his confrontation with his wife Portia. Cassius
and the conspirators have left. There follows a beautiful scene about two
people who love each other very much. Brutus loved Caesar too, but he
loves Portia better. They both die because of him, but one death Brutus
willed the other he did not, and how very much he did not is evidenced
by this scene. The language is the language of deep devotion and affection, not of a new love, hot and untried, but of a deep, mature, considered
and abiding love – and all the more touching for that. If nothing else, the
scene will show how much Brutus has changed, for we may see through
Portia's eyes the lovely man Brutus must once have been. Again, as in
the opening scene, I try to make the playing as deeply felt and unaffected
as possible; no place here for Brutus to go into rhetorical overdrive as he
has done with the conspirators a few minutes earlier. All that is needed is
honest playing and the point will have been made.

There is, of course, a problem. There always is with Brutus. He promises faithfully to tell his wife everything he is thinking and doing. Caius
Ligarius appears, Brutus seemingly instantaneously forgets Portia and
rushes off to kill Caesar. That is the way he is. Sir Peter Hall thinks this to
be yet another example, albeit a poignant one, of Brutus's feverish state

27 The death of Brutus (John Nettles as Brutus, Paul Bettany as Strato),
Julius Caesar, Act V, Scene V: 'Caesar, now be still; / I killed not thee with half
so good a will.'

of mind: he is in a phantasma, or a hideous dream, and sometimes knows not what he does. Yes he is, and I believe that the language he uses, standing with dripping knife over the body of Caesar, reinforces that view. He says that he is very regretfully going to kill Caesar. He is not going to like doing it much, for the man is his friend, but he has to do it for the good of Rome; but when he actually does the deed his language is the language of delight, of exultation, of blood lust. I think and I play that Brutus liked it very much, this killing of Caesar. Ambition's debt may be paid, but my goodness how Brutus enjoyed collecting! No use in underplaying this or trying to gloss over it. From the gallows humour of:

> So are we Caesar's friends, that have abridged
> His time of fearing death (III.i.104–5)

to the exuberant exultation of:

> Stoop, Romans, stoop,
> And let us bathe our hands in Caesar's blood
> Up to the elbows, and besmear our swords;
> Then walk we forth, even to the market-place,
> And waving our red weapons o'er our heads,
> Let's all cry, 'Peace, freedom, and liberty!' (III.i.105–10)

Brutus's repressed motives seem to be evident, and I believe the actor must play the scene so that the audience is aware of this, that is to say with an overweening joy. There is nothing noble about this killing. Brutus, with bloodied hands, stands shoulder to shoulder with those other conspirators who killed out of personal hatred, malice and envy. He is no better than they.

It is an unattractive prospect to play Brutus at this point in the drama as a vicious killer, but that is what he has become and this is what must be played despite his speech to the people in which he reiterates yet again that he killed Caesar not because he loved him less but because he loved Rome more. Typically, there is no glimmer of a hint in Brutus's oration that he is being insincere. True, he uses many a rhetorical trick; true, he is good with form but short of substance, but he believes what he is saying while he is saying it. We may say, as an audience, that he is self-deceived, but the actor must, I think, play him as if he were what he thinks he is, with all the oratorical ability at his command. There is no good point in the actor nudging the audience into an understanding that Brutus cannot truly believe in what he is saying, because Brutus does believe it; the self-deception is absolute, it seems, and because of this his own bloody end is guaranteed.

As I have said before, the curious feature of Brutus's journey towards that end is that there is no development of insight or understanding in him. He fails to acquire wisdom. He continues to make awful mistakes; he continues to change his mind from moment to moment; he continues to contradict himself despite his 'great mind'! A man who understands so little of himself and the world will soon be destroyed by that world. So it is with Brutus, but even in this extremity the speech just before his death that I quoted earlier ('My heart doth joy' (v.v.34ff.)) betrays no awareness of his own personal failure unless one can so colour the line 'my bones would rest, / That have but laboured to attain this hour' that it means 'All the great things I strove for are turned to dust and ashes'. I have tried in performance to gloss this line to show, however late in the day, some degree of self-awareness in Brutus, some knowledge of the enormity of what he has brought about, but I do not think it works because it flies in the face of everything we have learned of Brutus. I believe the better option is to present him at the end as in the orchard, a man who does not know himself, a man who deceives himself and cannot develop or grow because of these flaws in his nature. This is not to say that the man is essentially evil. By all accounts, before the events of the play,

> His life was gentle, and the elements
> So mixed in him, that Nature might stand up
> And say to all the world, 'This was a man!'   (v.v.73–5)

But during the drama he casts himself in the role of noble hero and the saviour of Rome and thereby is o'erparted to a tragic degree.

Macbeth

Derek Jacobi

SIR DEREK JACOBI is an Associate Actor of the Royal Shakespeare Company and played the title role in Adrian Noble's production of *Macbeth* at the Barbican Theatre in 1993 and the following year at the Royal Shakespeare Theatre and on a national tour. It was an independent production, not part of a normal RSC repertory season. Derek Jacobi's only previous Stratford season had been in 1982 when he played Benedick in *Much Ado about Nothing* (a production that toured the United States after its London season), Prospero in *The Tempest*, and the title role in *Peer Gynt*, adding to these in their London year the title role in *Cyrano de Bergerac*. His Shakespeare work with Birmingham Repertory Theatre, with the Royal National Theatre (where he did nine years), with the Prospect Theatre Company, at the Phoenix Theatre, and elsewhere, has been wide-ranging, including, among much else, Octavius Caesar in *Antony and Cleopatra*, Sir Andrew Aguecheek in *Twelfth Night*, and the title roles in *Pericles*, *Hamlet*, *Richard II*, and *Richard III*. He directed the Renaissance Theatre Company's production of *Hamlet* and has, more recently, been artistic director of the Chichester Festival Theatre. Films include *Henry V* and *Hamlet* and on television he has played Hamlet and Richard II, and, among many other parts, the title roles in *I, Claudius* and the *Cadfael* series.

Macbeth was the first Shakespeare play I was ever in at school, doubling Fleance and Lady Macbeth, but the offer from Adrian Noble to play the title role came as something of a surprise. I had never really thought of myself for the part, which had always seemed to me a bass role – and I'm a tenor. Physically, too, I'm light to look at, which isn't normal casting for the part. However, Adrian must have felt I had the right potential – just as Terry Hands, the last time I worked for the RSC, had found the anger in me to play Cyrano de Bergerac. Macbeth would have to be found, searched for and projected: and I would have to think hard about the way I would put it together physically, and facially, too. The colour, as it were, had to change. Those who had never seen the play before, I thought, would find it easier to accept me as Macbeth than those who came to it with a great deal of watching Shakespeare behind them.

As always with major productions, there was inadequate opportunity for the actors to be involved with the preliminary concepts and ideas. Discussion before we started rehearsals was not in great depth, really; nor was there much time. I saw the mock-up of the set, but it didn't make a great deal of impact on me: it was basically a big black box, which seemed acceptable. The costumes were to be very eclectic, coming from past, present, and future. Costumes are a strange area for me: as long as they're comfortable, feel like clothing, and leave me free to get on with it, I tend not to worry. They were made of a variety of materials, but with quite a lot of suede, which does not like sweat – and actors sweat. During the run, therefore, the costumes came to look muddy and dirty, which was no bad thing.

I learned the part before rehearsals began. This is becoming rather more frequent for me and comes of not wanting to waste precious rehearsal time, especially on such a big play. I learn it just simply: no decisions, no inflexions, just the words. During the course of rehearsal I want to find out what those words mean, how I'm feeling and saying them, what I'm doing; but the words are already there. This was very important to me for Macbeth: it's a big part, with a great big fight at the end, and we weren't going to be playing it in the normal RSC repertoire situation but in a single run, for quite a lot of which we would be doing eight performances a week. When we came to work on Macbeth's big set pieces, the soliloquies for example, knowing the words was a great help. I didn't know how to say them, how to think them, but with the words already there, the long hard work we did on them in rehearsal became extraordinarily exciting and stimulating. Looking back I think ultimately I did some of the soliloquies too quickly. My sense as we worked on them was that Macbeth's mind is working with enormous speed and I wanted to reflect that in the speaking; he is thinking very rapidly, all the time, and thought and speech come simultaneously. 'I'm not going to do it'; the thought simply hits him, just like that, until Lady Macbeth comes in; and he's like that all the time, the thoughts coming so fast. Perhaps I made the mistake of trying to reflect this a little too much in the speaking, getting myself into a state of anxiety, as Macbeth does; but my approach to all the speeches was to make them as true as possible, and as light as possible too, so as not to impede the thought. When an audience knows lines well (and in this play a lot of them know what you're going to say before you've said it) it's harder to make them listen to what you are saying, and how you are saying it. I wanted very much to make people listen with new ears to, 'If it were done' and 'Tomorrow'.

I found in rehearsal that the first section of the play, the establishing of who Macbeth was before the start of the deterioration, came quite easily. The ending, trying to show him still aware of what he had lost, realizing where he now was, was wonderful to do but took more searching for. Macbeth didn't seem to me, at the start, to know more of evil than any other soldier of his time who is used to killing people. What caught my imagination was the effect of evil on him, the changes it brings about. We spent a certain amount of time in rehearsal thinking about what is frightening, what is palpably evil, what is out *there*; the forces that seem to lurk malevolently around the world of the play. This was an area we tried to work hard on, with as much psychological depth as possible.

Macbeth is given a tremendous build-up for his first entrance; everyone talks about him in such glowing terms. I wanted to show a man arriving on stage at a pitch of exhilaration at what he's just done: the fighting, the blood-lust, the victory have put him on a high, which he shares with Banquo. They are together in this moment – together in companionship, in victory, in blood – as the Third Witch says:

> A drum! a drum!
> Macbeth doth come.   (I.iii.29–30)

I suppose we might have had a cohort of men coming; but we didn't have lots of extras, so I thought I would provide the drum myself, picked up, perhaps, from a corpse on the battlefield. He's banging it, banging it, unaware of his surroundings, drunk with it all. In he comes on this great big wonderful high, this man you've been hearing so much about, this great victor, winner of ten gold medals at the Olympics: in he comes, at the height of his power. I didn't want to show a man in the least exhausted by the battle, but revelling in it; a man in his glory, a great powerhouse. 'So foul and fair a day' (I.iii.37) does not, it seems to me, refer to the weather: 'foul' is about those heads he's cut off and bowels he's ripped out; 'fair' is because it was all worth it, for this great victory. That is the state of mind he is in, as, just by chance, he repeats the phrase that the witches have used.

Macbeth is mesmerized by the witches and, to an extent, excited by what they have to say, but instinctively he's afraid of them, though he doesn't know why. Because of his mood of elation, however, he's perfectly ready to try to find out why he fears them, by asking them questions and trying to persuade them to stay. He is startled by their greeting 'that shalt be king hereafter' (line 49) primarily because he's thought about it already – oh, yes, he's certainly thought about it. Why not? It's perfectly natural for a man so near the top as Macbeth to have thought about being king: every member of every cabinet must at some time think about being Prime Minister. When the Third Witch says it, therefore, she is echoing Macbeth's own thoughts, perhaps not particularly present at that moment – though, in his present state of mind, aware that a triumphal entry (at the very least) awaits him, perhaps the idea does occur to him that he could become king because of the victory he has just won. Whatever the reason, the greeting gives him pause, makes him reflect – and that is what Banquo picks up on.

The sudden awareness that Banquo is deeply intrigued and looking at him very searchingly is something I tried to use to whip Macbeth out of his reverie and bring him back into focus. He listens to what the witches prophesy for Banquo and tries to detain them, to hear more, as they begin to leave. I tried to suggest at this point that he attempts to wipe these things from his mind, to make a joke of them with Banquo, their little exchange finishing with them both laughing. But there is an odd edge to it, because they are not exactly sure what they are laughing at; the end of the conversation is strained and awkward. This is a significant moment, for it marks the beginning of their divergence, of their ceasing to trust each other. It must be plotted, because their relationship is so important, but it must not be overdone. They have been shown as pals (there's just a few seconds to do that), but if you show the distrust here too big and too soon you've got nowhere to go. It is merely a thought at this point. At the end of the scene, after the news of Macbeth's elevation has come from Ross and Angus, Macbeth says to Banquo 'Think upon what hath chanced' (line 153) and it seems as though they are about to talk to each other again in the old way. Then Macbeth says 'Till then, enough', and I tried to suggest that he was about to say something serious and confidential, then paused and instead said 'enough', implying uncertainty about sharing his thoughts with him: the process of separation has gone a little further. Even the final 'Come, friends' seemed to have a double edge: 'Come, . . .' – and what am I to call them? Are they friends? Yes, everyone is a friend at the moment. What *am* I worrying about?

Macbeth's response to the witches' greeting is hesitant and interrogative. He considers the idea, the pause I used on the word *king* in 'to be king / Stands not within the prospect of belief' (I.iii.72–3) seeming to hold it up for momentary examination. To the news from Ross and Angus, on the other hand, his reaction is much more fearful. The very thought of it makes his heart beat and his hair stand on end. This was very important to me, one of the through-lines for Macbeth. I went through the play marking the times he speaks of fear, particularly in relation to himself. He does so in every scene: it is paramount for him; the man is constantly fearful. He says so to himself, he says so to his wife: it never changes. When the witches said he was going to be king, I had dropped the dagger which I'd been using to beat the drum and bent to pick it up and put it away. I took it out again in the middle of Macbeth's long aside (I.iii.126ff.) and was very conscious of it on 'Present fears / Are less than horrible imaginings' (lines 136–7) because those imaginings are already of killing the king. It was only a momentary thing, but still the dagger came out when he thought of being king. The dagger was a constant emblem for me: the physical dagger, one of his essential accoutrements for battle, was from the beginning connected with the idea of his kingship, leading inevitably to 'Is this a dagger that I see before me?' (II.i.33) and to the drawing of the dagger in earnest to commit the terrible murder. Obviously this is just an actor's finessing: it doesn't have to be there for this aside, but it seemed to me to create a link with the next stage of the play – and it was no doubt useful for the other actors, biding my soliloquizing, to look across at Macbeth and see that he has a dagger in his hand that he is twisting and looking at and yet not really seeing.

Macbeth, then, before the end of his first scene, has faced the thought of killing the king. 'Why do I yield to that suggestion', he asks (line 133), and the word is *yield*. The thought could have been repulsed immediately, but it's not repulsed, it's accepted. And the thought terrifies him. He is in an extraordinary mood; the adrenalin is coursing through him and he's not thinking totally straight. Because of the victory he is in a state of high excitement and of emotional exhaustion. He has been killing all day: he is covered with blood. In this state he gets the news: in this state he must react to it. The speed with which things happen in the next phase of the play is to a large extent conditioned by Macbeth's physical and mental state when he receives the witches' greeting.

In his next scene Macbeth meets Duncan. I don't think they are in any sense bosom pals. 'Duncan comes here tonight' (I.v.58) sounds to me surprised: I don't believe Duncan has stayed in Macbeth's house before. There has always been a certain distance between them: the lack of prowess on the battlefield shown by Duncan's sons would have been noted by Macbeth. He would see it, of course, as his absolute duty to uphold Duncan's power, his tenure of the throne. Macbeth is, I think, in awe of the whole concept of kingship, but attracted to it too, and fascinated by it. He is now, obviously, the man of the hour, being publicly honoured by Duncan for the first time; and he revels in the situation. Before he was one of the many; now he's the top man, a Field-Marshall. There they all are, applauding him, and he's acknowledging the applause, loving it, hugely enjoying being on the winner's podium. At the same time, however, and because of the scene before, he notices that Duncan actually touches Banquo: 'let me enfold thee / And hold thee to my heart' (I.iv.32–3). He didn't do that to Macbeth: he was much more formal with him. I was aware that Banquo was getting the hug, and the kiss, and that I wasn't.

Moments later Duncan has declared Malcolm heir to the throne as Prince of Cumberland. Banquo and I had a glance at each other at this point, and a little grin: 'I know what you're thinking; you know what I'm thinking; we're both thinking the same thing.' But there is as yet no serious rift between them. At the beginning of my Prince of Cumberland soliloquy I went over to Malcolm and did what Duncan had just done to Banquo – gave him a big manly hug and patted him on the face: 'Great that you're around, Prince of Cumberland, absolutely great . . . You little bastard'. That got a laugh at most performances, which I loved. There aren't many laughs for Macbeth, and I meant this one here, and the bathos of it. All that it means to be a king is here visible to Macbeth, and to the audience. It is no accident that the play moves him directly from that first soliloquy of thoughts of kingship into the royal presence, to being touched by the king's hand, irradiated by the king's electric field. By the end of the scene his thoughts are racing: perhaps there is a possibility, perhaps there is; I must tell my wife; I must write; where is the messenger to take the letter. And then he gets on his horse and tears off to her. By the time he gets to her she is in a state that he was not expecting: the letter has had an effect way beyond what he had supposed. He had, of course, imagined that she would be glad at what has happened to him, but he never realized that the idea of his becoming king would affect her as it has.

I'm sure the play's time-scheme is here very fast and that only hours have elapsed before we see the Macbeths together. We wanted to present a couple much in love and comfortable with each other. We also wanted to show the contrast between Macbeth the warrior, whose duty is killing and maiming, and Macbeth the husband, the lover, the domestic, cultured man who dances and listens to music. Off the battlefield he isn't in the least gruff or brutal in his behaviour. There is quite another side to him, a much gentler side: the fact that he fights well does not imply that he is a hoodlum, a yob. He is a man of enormous imagination, who has a life going on all the time in his head. He doesn't say very much in the letter scene. His first words are 'My dearest love' (I.v.56), a very romantic phrase, which he doesn't use again – his language to his wife becomes, indeed, progressively less endearing. To her question (line 57) 'And when goes hence?' his reply ('Tomorrow, as he purposes') can be understood in any way one likes. I took it to mean that he was surprised by the question, and by her asking it; then, realizing why she had asked it, I saw that she was thinking what I wanted her to think and that we knew each other better, perhaps, than we had thought. And then, as he wonders tentatively what they may be thinking and saying, very suddenly, she lets him know with astonishing directness: 'O, never / Shall sun that morrow see' (lines 58–9). The phrase a little later in her speech (line 63) about his looking 'like the innocent flower' always seemed to me to tie in with my worries about whether or not I looked right for the part. I felt that she was describing what she saw when she looked at him. She has been going on about his abilities and his talents, about his desire to be great but his lack of the 'illness should attend it' (I.v.18), about his deficiency in that little streak of nastiness that allows you to get to the top. And now she looks at him again, and sees the 'innocent flower' and knows that he will get nowhere without 'the serpent under it'. He *needs* all this if he is to rise higher; and again his reaction is not to say 'forget it', but rather 'We will speak further' (I.v.69).

Time for such further thought is hardly available, however: if Duncan is to be killed, it must be done that night. The swiftness of the time-scheme is reflected in the swiftness of the language. Sometimes it is almost telegrammatic. The actor will wish to get his point across, his interpretation of a particular line, but it's not always easy because it's all so densely written. There may well be six images in a line and you have to choose only one or two – you can't do them all, you can't play

28 Derek Jacobi as Macbeth, with Lady Macbeth (Cheryl Campbell),
Macbeth, Act I, Scene vii: 'Was the hope drunk/Wherein you dressed yourself?'

everything. (One is frequently criticized for not playing one of the possibilities as though one hadn't been aware of it; the fact that one didn't
play something does not, however, mean that it wasn't considered, but
rather that on this occasion the other road was chosen; it would be nice
if critics were more often willing to recognize this.) The density of the
language is all part of Macbeth's thought-process: he is thinking at the
speed of light as he begins his soliloquy, 'If it were done when 'tis done'
(I.vii.1ff.). He is the host; he is providing for the king and his retinue; and
yet he has left the banqueting room. It's all going on back there, but
somehow he has extricated himself. How has he got out of that room?
Presumably he's been sitting next to the king with the knowledge that
if it's to happen, if he's actually going to do it, it's got to be very soon:
'How many hours have I got before I must do it? It's got to be now.'
He's been sitting there thinking like that and his head's coming off with
the thought; he's been boiling and sweating, and he's absented himself
because he's just got to get out to breathe, to be on his own. Perhaps he
excuses himself because he's had a hard couple of days, with all the fighting. However he achieves it, he leaves; and now, alone, he talks himself,

quite rapidly, out of the idea. What has been spurring him on, he wonders: only 'vaulting ambition' (i.vii.27) is prompting him, and that implies landing on your arse on the other side. He reaches his decision – and then Lady Macbeth comes in. If she had not come in at this point I do not believe he would have gone through with it. She uses all the predictable arguments – 'When you durst do it, then you were a man' (line 49) – and if you presuppose, as we did, that they are in love, then of course it's very difficult for him to take. Without her arrival at that moment, he would never have done it.

The soliloquy is full of extraordinary images – 'pity, like a naked newborn babe', and so on – all occurring to him on the instant. He is a highly intelligent, imaginative, articulate man, quite unlike the brutal, nonthinking slasher of the battlefield, the tried, and honed, killing machine. Here we are in contact with that other side of him, the great contrast with his life as a soldier; in his own head he lives in an astonishing imaginative world which he is able to express sensationally and beautifully. His head is full of the mixture of good and evil. At this moment the evil side of him, which we all possess, is getting the upper hand and in order to balance it he brings up the best, the purest, the most innocent of images, of angels, and new-born babies, and the sky. They are all pure, unsullied, wonderful images; goodness pours out of them; they're shining. And on the other side are the dark, blood-driven, evil, dank thoughts. Eventually in this soliloquy he chooses good; the good images win – until Lady Macbeth comes in and taunts his manliness. It is her intimation that he's a coward, that he has no balls, that turns him. She goes for the jugular. She has always been his inspiration. Before a battle I'm sure that his thoughts were always with her. She makes him the man he is, encourages him, stirs up his testosterone. Without her he would never be so rampant. He needs her. And in this very short scene she quickly forces him back onto the path.

We had decided that somewhere in the past of their relationship they had lost a child. There are many other possible interpretations, but you have to decide for one. It's something that really needs a programme note: you can't act it, really, though you can think it. When she mentions having 'given suck' (line 54) I immediately went towards her, to stop her talking about it, as if to say 'Don't talk about it; you know what it does to us.' And she does know, of course, which is why she brings it up here. It's a vulnerable point for him. The moment the subject is mentioned he's automatically on the defensive and she uses all that. She is very

29 Derek Jacobi as Macbeth, *Macbeth*, Act II, Scene i: 'Come, let me
clutch thee.'

clever, brilliantly manipulative, as she is in their first scene – and no doubt always has been with him. The appalling image of the braining of the child comes from the hardness that is within her, the hardness that she wishes him to share, that soon he will more than share.

Then she comes very close to making a mistake. 'When Duncan is asleep', she says, and if Macbeth is the man I think he is trying to be he must feel 'O, no, I've got to kill him with his eyes open. I've got to give him a bit of a chance. An old man, the king, a guest in my house, unguarded, and asleep: that is pure cowardice, murder of the innocents.' And the extraordinary thing about this image of Duncan asleep is that from this moment on it is going to be Macbeth who cannot sleep and Lady Macbeth who is unable to wake up. That becomes the symbol of their partnership.

On his way to Duncan's chamber Macbeth meets Banquo. Banquo is no fool and is keeping his eye on Macbeth. I enjoyed this scene: I enjoyed its surprises, and Banquo's obvious relish of the moment when he gives Macbeth the king's gift. Lady Macbeth has made great efforts to screw his courage to the sticking place; he's on his way to do the deed; everybody is supposed to be in bed; and of all people he meets Banquo. He shows his surprise at the meeting, and at the king's present, and with his surprise he shows his tension, just an inkling of it. And Banquo senses it, straightaway, because he's got to suspect him – got to, otherwise the part doesn't make sense. In this moment Macbeth gives himself away and Banquo makes it clear that he knows what is happening and that he wants no part of it: 'I . . . keep / My bosom franchised and allegiance clear' (II.i.26–8).

'Is this a dagger' (II.i.33), like 'To be or not to be', is the line they're all waiting for. Once again it's a question of choice. Is he surprised to see the dagger or did he expect it to be there? Has he seen it before? Is he frightened of it? Do his eyes attract him to it? Does his choice of the word 'clutch' mean that the dagger is pulling him forward, or is it repelling him as he tries to grasp it? (I think I tried for both – a bit of repel, a bit of attract.) Does 'let me clutch thee' mean 'dare I clutch thee'? And so on – all choices. Again I tried to give him a last-minute reprieve: right at the end of the soliloquy there's a moment when he speaks of taking 'the present horror from the time' (line 59). I paused here as I had him going towards the door but still not being able to go through it. 'Whiles I threat, he *lives*', he says, and adds 'Words to the heat of deeds too cold breath gives' (lines 60–1) – 'while I'm still talking about it I'm putting off doing it'. And at that moment Lady Macbeth appears: 'appears' in the ringing of the bell. The bell is her; she is ringing it. It's not the bell he hears; he hears her ringing the bell. That's what propels him through the door.

He comes out of it a changed man. Never can he be the same man again. There is not a single moment that he enjoys the thought of killing. It torments him, though it also impels him. And never does he enjoy the fruit of his killing. He comes out of that room demented. He went into it terrified, as he says all the time; he comes out of it crazy. Lady Macbeth has never before seen the man who comes out of that door; he is a stranger to her. They have stopped communicating and there is no way that they will ever communicate again. She had no idea that that was going to happen. He did it only to please her, to prove himself to her. Had she been other than she was he would not have done it. The thought may have been present, but so was the fear of the thought: the first time we see him think it his hair stands on end. Always the thought strikes fear into him. The moment before he does the murder he is afraid – the dagger speech is a fearful speech, the utterance of a terrified man. He does the murder for her, and it destroys them both.

He has no idea what he has done with the daggers. They are simply there; he's not conscious of them at all. It's only when she asks 'Why did you bring these daggers from the place?' (II.ii.48) that he realizes that they are on the ends of his hands. I tried to throw them away, but they wouldn't go; he can't physically get rid of them because the blood on them is sticking to his hands. Again he talks of fear: 'I am afraid to think what I have done' (line 51). I wanted to emphasize that, because I think it's an answer to her rather than a statement of his own feelings. She goes on and on about him being fearful and he says 'Yes, I *am* afraid. You're absolutely right. I'm quaking to think what I've done. I *am* afraid. Look what a state I'm in now.' Up to this point he has spoken of being afraid only to himself; to her he has wanted to appear always the man. But here he confesses his fear to her, the first indication of the new state of their relationship.

Macbeth then has a short time off stage, during which the actor is doing precisely what the character himself would be doing: trying to wash all the blood off, and changing his costume. He comes back on again into the public scene of the discovery of Duncan's murder. Intelligent and imaginative man that he is, and having had his hysterical, terrified scene after the murder, he now has to think quickly, and rationally, if he is going to survive. This is going to be a very tricky moment for both him and Lady Macbeth, but from the audience's point of view he seems fine at the start, totally calm. He shows Macduff the door to Duncan's chamber: he doesn't offer to take him in himself. Then he's left with Lennox, though of course his mind isn't on the conversation at all: it's on what Macduff is about to see. He spent all that time with the dagger, terrified, before going into that room. In the preceding scene he refused to return there – 'Look on't again I dare not' (II.ii.52). Now he has to face it; he plucks up his courage and follows Lennox into the room.

When he comes out he is absolutely riven by it. What he says is real, and genuine: 'Had I died an hour before this chance, / I had lived a blessèd time' (II.iii.88–9). He means it; it is the simple truth. Then he makes the mistake of saying that he killed the grooms. He has to cover up and he starts to get hysterical again, as he was over the daggers. The silver skin and the golden blood and the gashes all come into his imagination, and then the crucial image: 'their daggers / Unmannerly breeched with gore' (lines 112–13). He is working himself up again, just as he did after the murder; it's all tumbling out and she thinks 'O, Christ, what is he going to say?' One passage of the speech seems to me specifically directed at her:

> . . . Who could refrain,
> That had a heart to love, and in that heart
> Courage to make's love known.   (lines 113–15)

I don't think he's saying that he loved the king so much that he had to murder his grooms. I think he is saying to Lady Macbeth, eye to eye: 'I proved my love to you by killing the king. O, yes, my heart loved you, and in that heart was courage. You said I hadn't got courage, but I had courage to make my love known to you. In fact I killed him to show you how courageous I was.' She knows what he means: he's looking directly at her, and she's terrified at what he might say next. And so, manipulative and resourceful as ever, she faints. It's the only thing she can do. He's getting himself into a terrible state: he can't speak (he's silent, in fact, for nearly twenty lines): he's hyperventilating. The rest might take it as grief for the king, but she knows it's something else and creates a diversion to get him out of it.

The next time we see them together they are king and queen. Time has elapsed – time enough (we learn from Macduff) for them to have been to Scone to be crowned. How much time was a question we ultimately decided we couldn't bother about. It's stage time, which is continuous (unless you deliberately pause to indicate the passage of time), and the speed with which this play moves – and we did it without an interval – is remarkable. But clearly there has been time for a further change in their relationship: he is now dismissing her from his company. The moment is preceded by the last meeting with Banquo. Both Macbeth and Banquo know what has happened; neither is saying, but both know. That, any-way, is how we played it: he knows; I know that he knows. As he left, Banquo turned to look at me and suddenly Macbeth wants everybody else out: he wants to get rid of them all, to be alone. He's also arranged his meeting with the murderers. I went up to Lady Macbeth and when I reached her said 'We will keep ourself till supper-time alone' (III.i.43), with *alone* said straight to her: 'that includes you'. As she stood her ground I looked at her and called Seyton behind me. She tried to stay, but for the first time the boot is on the other foot and she has to go. For the first time she has to do what he tells her.

After his scene with the murderers she comes back and more or less has to ask Seyton's permission to speak to him. She can't understand the new situation: 'Why do you keep alone?' (III.ii.8). After a while he gives in a little: 'O full of scorpions is my mind, *dear* wife' (line 36). I wanted to show the pull of that other side, that the forces which are dragging him in one direction are still meeting with some resistance. This is the last relic of 'my dearest love' earlier. For one moment he's gentle with her; he clasps her and they're cheek to cheek and there is love between them again. But immediately the fact that Banquo knows the truth about him comes back into his mind – and he's off again. She tries to be reassuring: 'nature's copy's not eterne' in Banquo (III.ii.38), but it's not enough for him, though the moment when they were together again has had its import-ance. At the end of the scene, as he hints at the murder of Banquo, he says to her 'prithee go with me'. I'm sure this doesn't just mean 'Go with me from this room'. It's much more of an appeal: 'Go along with me, support me in what I'm doing. I'm terrified: don't desert me and leave me to do this on my own.' But she does desert him, of course. He deals with the murder of Banquo alone and he's alone from then on.

The banquet scene marks the next stage in the decline of their rela-tionship. Such lines as 'Our hostess keeps her state; but in best time / We will require her welcome' (III.iv.5–6) are said directly to her, with the implication: 'You're making me do all the work, love. Isn't it time you did a bit of queenly acting – I'm doing all the kingly acting up my end of the table?' It has ceased to be a nice relationship: in our production he tried to kiss her and she turned her face away. After the murderer had reported the death of Banquo (and the escape of Fleance) I spoke the lines 'Here had we now our country's honour roofed, / Were the graced person of our Banquo present' (III.iv.39–40) directly to her rather than to the table generally, with the meaning 'I told you I'd kill him, didn't I – and I have, haven't I?' He's trying to get her to react; it will mean so much more if she shares it. Meanwhile he's desperately trying to be one of the party, one of the boys. I went round the table filling the glasses, trying to get the evening to go with a swing, and she not helping at all.

I think the audience is cheated if they don't see the ghost of Banquo – the chase round the table and all. We always intended that he should be there. And when the ghost has gone, and she's done her best to excuse him (and she's only just able to keep herself together), and the end of the scene has been reached and the awful realization that

> . . . I am in blood
> Stepped in so far, that, should I wade no more,
> Returning were as tedious as go o'er   (III.iv.135–7)

there is a kind of terrible regret in them both. The man still has that extraordinary imagination; it's never deserted him, right through the killing. He knows where he's reached, he knows what he's lost, and he knows what it entails. What I called on God, and on the images of the naked new-born babes, to stop me doing, what I desperately tried to persuade myself not to do, I have done. I have given in to the evil that I fought not to give in to and it has grown like a cancer within me. It is now terminal and in order to survive at all I have got to be wholly taken over by it, and quickly. I thought more than twice about the shedding of innocent blood, but now I must be constant about it, do it again and again, if I am going to survive. 'We are yet but young in deed' (line 143): it is awful, awful, coming from that man. He is not someone who enjoys what he has to do, but he knows what now has to be done. If Macbeth is a monster, the out-and-out black-hearted monster that they all say he is later on, then much of the heart of the play is missing. We were trying in our production to show the audience the other side of this man. The people who are the victims of his monstrosities will, of course, call him a monster, but it was the other side that I wanted to show – and particularly with me playing Macbeth, for that is a side that is part of me anyway. I wanted him to appear as a man driven, sent mad by what he experiences, but still with the imagination to see clearly where he has come from, where he is now, where he has to go to, but, above all, what he has lost. 'Honour, love, obedience, troops of friends' (v.iii.25), these are not to be his any more, he now knows that. But they *could* have been: at the beginning he had them all, all of them, and, wilfully, he has got rid of them, cast them away. His wife's death makes him again aware of these things, and of his great love for her, but by then he has become more or less catatonic, living only inside his own head, thinking neither very long, nor very far.

Before then, however, he has a journey to travel, and the next stage on it is his second visit to the witches. They were very up-front with what they had to say to him last time, but on this second occasion they're rather more cagey. He is no longer afraid of them – not at all afraid to go back. He says later (v.iv.9) that he has 'almost forgot the taste of fears', a line I tried to do as a kind of revelation: 'I always used to be afraid; I've been frightened for so long, but now I seem not to be. What's happening?' The route to that is through the ossifying of the mind and emotions, and we see that in this second encounter with the witches. He is truculent with them, and ready to believe in their obviously riddling prophecies – as he has to, as justification for it all. At the end of the scene he can say quite dispassionately that he is going to have Macduff's wife and babes put to the sword – and in our production go and carefully check that it's been done. He gives the order with no sense of the before and after, with no emotion. That is the true monstrousness; it is that appalling lack of emotion that he has to come to terms with at the end.

Shakespeare gives Macbeth a short rest while the English scene is in progress. I had a costume and wig change during it but I tried to use the time to think myself into the sort of stillness and quietness that is needed on Macbeth's return. Perhaps I erred a little too much on the side of loudness earlier, but I certainly wanted to show him a very different figure at the end. He has aged in the interim and returns an older and a physically different man. There is a slowness about him, as though everything has collapsed. The hands are still, the speech is quieter and slower. It's as though his blood has been let, as though the leeches have been at him. Great swathes of time have passed for Macbeth, if not for everyone else. This seemed very important to me, though I think some people who saw the production were puzzled by it. I wanted a huge contrast with his behaviour at the beginning, leaping onto the stage, banging his drum, his blood coursing through his veins; now he comes on with seemingly no blood flowing at all. I played with the dagger again; it never left my hands throughout this final sequence as I turned it obsessively in my gloved fingers – the gloves concealing the fact that his hands are as blood-covered as Lady Macbeth's. Two acts earlier he had gone off washing his hands as she had taken the daggers; now here he is with gloves on, constantly playing with a dagger, his figure bloodless.

I took 'I have lived long enough' (v.iii.22ff.) as a momentary considera-tion of the possibility of suicide. I had the dagger in my hand and the idea occurred of simply ending it all – 'I wonder why I don't just kill myself' – until the thought was interrupted by Seyton's entrance and a little of the old blood starts coursing around again. Macbeth knows he is defending a lost cause, in spite of the witches' prophecies – for I suspect that, deep down, he has never really believed in them, however desper-ately he hoped they were true. At the end, when their falsity is revealed, he speaks of the 'juggling fiends' that 'palter with us', and of their break-ing 'the word of promise to our . . . hope' (v.vi.58–61): he hoped, but he didn't ever fully believe; Macbeth is too intelligent really to have believed. There is a kind of pathos about the way he has almost know-ingly deluded himself. He knows about what Hamlet calls his 'god-like reason . . . looking before and after', but because of his enthralment to Lady Macbeth he chooses to ignore it. And he *is* in thrall to her: she has played continuously on his status as a man and that has made him go the way he has. 'Honour, love, obedience, troops of friends' were his as the successful general of the beginning of the play; in 'Tomorrow and tomorrow' he faces the fact that they will never be his again.

I do not think Macbeth is mad at the end of the play, though he encountered madness during the banquet scene. The horrors of that experience for him were palpable; he could not understand why no-one else perceived them and he lost his reason completely. He lives partly in this terrifying world of the imagination, but he lives also in a world of the senses, and at the end of the banquet scene his reason starts to take over again. There is no escape into madness for him at the end. His solilo-quies before he dies record with grim sanity the emotionless state at which he has arrived.

The hint at the idea of suicide on 'I have lived long enough' was in part preparation for Macbeth's death. Suicide is clearly in his mind: 'I 'gin to be aweary of the sun' (v.v.49); 'Why should I play the Roman fool' (v.vi.40) – he keeps using phrases that incorporate it. I wanted to show this at the end. Adrian Noble had made an early decision (with which

I was perfectly content) that I should die on stage, not go off and have my head chopped off and have it brought back on again. So, with the co-operation of Michael Siberry as Macduff, we worked out a death sequence in which Macbeth and Macduff fight (and fight, and fight), and then he disarms me and I pull his sword into myself. Macbeth's last words – 'And damned be he that first cries "Hold, enough"' (v.vi.73) – seem to me to be about damnation. Whether the line can bear this interpretation I don't know, but in my own head I was saying 'damned be he' (pointing upwards – 'damned be He') 'who first says to you "Hold"'. And then 'Now, now'; and I pulled the sword into me, so that there was a degree, in his last moments, just a degree, of the old magnificence that he had had at the beginning. Some of that old strength came back and he spoke here of his *own* damnation, aware of the powers that had caused it, and, with something of his old dignity, accepting it.

Macbeth is an exhausting role – psychologically, mentally, emotionally and physically. I tried to play him, not as monster but as hero, as flawed hero. I think the man's journey is much more interesting than that of unchanging monster from start to finish. I wanted my Macbeth to be very different at the end from the man we had encountered at the beginning, though with recollections of what he has been that inform so much of what he says in the final stages. I tried to plot his journey from the golden boy of the opening to the burnt-out loser accepting his own damnation of the conclusion.

Production credits

Productions are listed in the order of essays in this volume. Dates are those of the first preview performance, with the press performance approximately a week later. With the exception of *As You Like It*, *Henry VIII*, and *Macbeth* all productions played in repertoire at Stratford through the season in which they opened and then, during the following year, in Newcastle-upon-Tyne and at the Barbican Theatre in London. *As You Like It* (like other plays from the 1996 season) went directly from Stratford to the Barbican without the sojourn in Newcastle, and *Henry VIII* played in both Newcastle and Plymouth before a London season at the Young Vic and a tour to the United States. *Macbeth* opened at the Barbican and played a solo run there from December 1993 before moving to Stratford in March 1994 (again for a solo run, not in repertoire) and a British provincial tour. In addition, *The Winter's Tale* followed its London season with a British provincial tour and a tour of several European countries and the United States, New Zealand and Tokyo, and *Love's Labour's Lost* was revived in 1995 in the year after its first London season, for a further run at the Barbican, a British provincial tour, and a short season in Tokyo.

The Merchant of Venice
RST, 27 May 1993
Director: David Thacker
Design and costumes: Shelagh Keegan
Music: Gary Yershon
Lighting: Clive Morris
Movement: Lesley Hutchison

Love's Labour's Lost
RST, 21 October 1993
Director: Ian Judge
Designer: John Gunter
Costumes: Deirdre Clancy
Music: Nigel Hess
Lighting: Alan Burrett
Choreography: Lindsay Dolan

As You Like It
RST, 18 April 1996
Director: Steven Pimlott
Design and costumes: Ashley
    Martin-Davis
Music: Jason Carr
Lighting: Mimi Jordan Sherin
Movement: Liz Ranken
Fights: Terry King

The Taming of the Shrew
RST, 15 April 1995
Director: Gale Edwards
Designer: Russell Craig
Costumes: Marie-Jeanne Lecca
Music: Stephen Warbeck

Lighting: Hugh Vanstone
Movement: Emma Rice

The Winter's Tale
RST, 25 June 1992
Director: Adrian Noble
Design and costumes: Anthony Ward
Music: Shaun Davey
Lighting: Chris Parry
Movement: Sue Lefton

Richard III
RST, 31 August 1995
Director: Steven Pimlott
Design and costumes: Tobias Hoheisel
Music: Jason Carr
Lighting: Hugh Vanstone
Movement: Liz Ranken
Fights: Malcolm Ranson

Henry VIII
The Swan Theatre, 20 November 1996
Director: Gregory Doran
Design and costumes: Robert Jones
Music: Jason Carr
Lighting: Howard Harrison
Movement: Terry John Bates

Coriolanus
The Swan Theatre, 18 May 1994
Director: David Thacker

Design and costumes: Fran Thompson
Music: Adrian Johnston
Lighting: Alan Burrett
Movement: Lesley Hutchison
Fights: Terry King

Romeo and Juliet
RST, 30 March 1995
Director: Adrian Noble
Design and costumes: Kendra Ullyart
Music: Shaun Davey
Lighting: Hugh Vanstone
Movement: Sue Lefton
Fights: Terry King

Julius Caesar
RST, 30 June 1995
Director: Sir Peter Hall
Designer: John Gunter
Costumes: Deirdre Clancy
Music: Guy Woolfenden
Lighting: Jean Kalman
Fights: Malcolm Ranson

Macbeth
Barbican Theatre, 10 December 1993
Director: Adrian Noble
Design and costumes: Ian MacNeil
Music: David Bedford
Lighting: Alan Burrett
Fights: Malcolm Ranson